Human Ecology of the Canadian Prairie Ecozone

Library and Archives Canada Cataloguing in Publication

Human ecology of the Canadian prairie ecozone / edited by B.A. Nicholson.

(Canadian plains studies, ISSN 0317-6290 ; 61)
Includes bibliographical references and index.
Issued also in electronic format.
ISBN 978-0-88977-254-0

    1. Human ecology--Prairie Provinces. 2. Environmental archaeology—Prairie Provinces. 3. Ecological zones—Prairie Provinces. 4. Indians of North America—Prairie Provinces—Antiquities. 5. Prairie Provinces—Antiquities. 6. Prairie Ecozone. I. Nicholson, B. A II. University of Regina. Canadian Plains Research Center III. Series: Canadian plains studies ; 61

GF512.P7H86 2011   304.209712   C2011-906561-4

Library and Archives Canada Cataloguing in Publication

Human ecology of the Canadian prairie ecozone [electronic resource] / edited by B.A. Nicholson.

(Canadian plains studies, ISSN 0317-6290 ; 61)
Includes bibliographical references and index.
Electronic monograph in PDF format.
Issued also in print format.
ISBN 978-0-88977-255-7

    1. Human ecology—Prairie Provinces. 2. Environmental archaeology—Prairie Provinces. 3. Ecological zones—Prairie Provinces. 4. Indians of North America—Prairie Provinces—Antiquities. 5. Prairie Provinces—Antiquities. 6. Prairie Ecozone. I. Nicholson, B. A II. University of Regina. Canadian Plains Research Center III. Series: Canadian plains studies (Online) ; 61

GF512.P7H86 2011a   304.209712   C2011-906562-2

Human Ecology of the Canadian Prairie Ecozone

edited by

B.A. Nicholson

Copyright © 2011 Canadian Plains Research Center Press
Copyright Notice
All rights reserved. No part of this work covered by the copyrights hereon may be reproduced or used in any form or by any means—graphic, electronic, or mechanical—without the prior written permission of the publisher. Any request for photocopying, recording, taping or placement in information storage and retrieval systems of any sort shall be directed in writing to Access Copyright.

Index prepared by Adrian Mather, AMindexing, Edmonton, AB.

We acknowledge the financial support of the Government of Canada through the Canada Book Fund for our publishing activities.

This book has been published with the help of a grant from the Canadian Federation for the Humanities and Social Sciences, through the Aid to Scholarly Publications Program, using funds provided by the Social Sciences and Humanities Research Council of Canada.

We acknowledge the Government of Saskatchewan, through the Grants to Publishers Fund, for its financial support.

Printed in Canada

Contents

Introduction to Human Ecology of the Canadian Prairie Ecozone

    B.A. Nicholson 1

Chapter 1
Human Ecology of the Canadian Prairie Ecozone ca. 9000 BP:
The Paleo-Indian Period

    David Meyer, Alwynne B. Beaudoin and Leslie J. Amundson.....................5

Chapter 2
Human Ecology of the Canadian Prairie Ecozone ca. 6000 BP:
Hypsithermal Adaptations to the Canadian Prairie Ecozone?

    Gerald A. Oetelaar...55

Chapter 3
Human Ecology of the Canadian Prairie Ecozone ca. 3000 BP:
Post Hypsithermal Adaptations to the Canadian Prairie Ecozone

    B.A. Nicholson and Sean Webster..81

Chapter 4
Human Ecology of the Canadian Prairie Ecozone ca. 1500 BP:
Diffusion, Migration and Technological Innovation

    Scott Hamilton, Jill Taylor-Hollings, and David Norris............................99

Chapter 5
Human Ecology of the Canadian Prairie Ecozone ca. 500 BP:
Plains Woodland Influences and Horticultural Practice

    B.A. Nicholson, David Meyer, Gerry Oetelaar and Scott Hamilton.......153

Index..181

Contributors 189

Introduction to Human Ecology of the Canadian Prairie Ecozone
B.A. Nicholson

The Canadian Prairie Ecozone (CPE) is spatially defined by the foothills of Alberta on the west and the boreal forest/parkland interface on the north and the east (Fig. 0.1). This natural boundary will have moved over time, in response to climatic variables such as the onset of the progressive Hypsithermal desiccation between ca. 8000 to 4000 BP (years before present) and to more *localized* cultural practices such as the use of fire ecology to control game resources. The southern boundary is a political boundary, the 49th parallel of

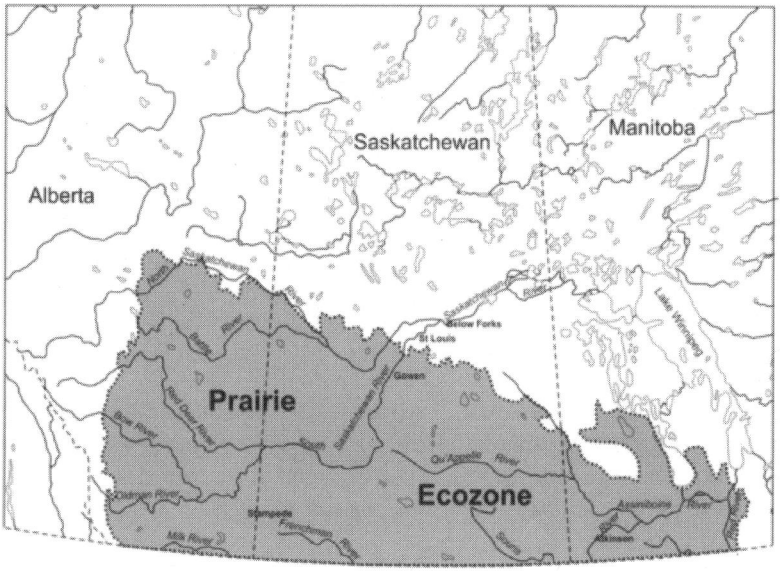

Figure 0.1. Canadian Prairie Ecozone

latitude. This arbitrary demarcation would have had no influence on events prior to European intervention, but necessarily impacts the scope of contemporary primary archaeological research on either side. This being said, we have relied on published works of researchers in the United States when appropriate.

The SCAPE Project research focused on areas of high biodiversity within the CPE. These included glacial moraine uplands such as the Tiger Hills, sand dune areas such as the Lauder Sandhills, riverine complexes such as the Forks of the North and South Saskatchewan rivers, and remnant uplands such as the Cypress Hills. It was found that these areas were less severely impacted by drought, and were characterized by a more broad range of plant and animal resources than the surrounding prairies. Boyd (2006: 232) has noted that "[a] multidisciplinary approach to the reconstruction of detailed landscape histories indicates that certain habitats and local environments maintained a high degree of stability during these vicissitudes and offered hunter-gatherers a measure of security in times of stress." These results have been integrated into our narratives.

This is the third edited volume from the SCAPE (Study of Cultural Adaptations in the Canadian Prairie Ecozone) Project. Volume 1, *Changing Opportunities and Challenges: Human-Environmental Interaction in the Canadian Prairies Ecozone* (Nicholson et al. 2006) presented early results of regional analyses and ethnohistoric aspects of the SCAPE research. Volume 2, *Building a Contextual Milieu: Interdisciplinary Modeling and Theoretical Perspectives from the SCAPE Project* (Nicholson and Wiseman 2007) presented a theoretical and methodological perspective on the building of a Contextual Milieu, followed by an examination of the learning experiences of team members as we entered into the exercise of developing an interdisciplinary approach to the collection and interpretation of data in this large project (Nicholson and Wiseman 2007: 3).

In this volume, *Human Ecology of the Canadian Prairie Ecozone*, we examine the human ecology of groups living in the CPE over the past 11,000 years, with an emphasis on the Precontact utilization of areas of high biodiversity (Fig. 0.1). In our initial grant application to the Major Collaborative Research Initiatives Program (SSHRC) we decided to divide this long time interval into five focal periods. These were 9,000 years ago, 6,000 years ago, 3,000 years ago, 1,500 years ago and 500 years ago. We were successful in identifying archaeological sites for excavation within the framework of this proposal. SCAPE team members that had excavated sites from these time slots were asked to write individual chapters for this volume and to engage other researchers in their work. In this volume we have expanded the time frame of these focal dates to present a continuous narrative over the 11,000 years of human occupation in the CPE.

It is our intent, in this volume, to synthesize our SCAPE derived data with other published materials for the region and to present a comprehensive overview of the successive groups that lived in the CPE. This overview is presented in the context of the changing physical, biological and cultural milieus that were present in their lifetimes.

In Chapter 1, Meyer et al. present an overview of human occupation in the CPE beginning ca. 11,200 BP as the Pleistocene glaciers retreated and the more moderate Holocene epoch emerged. As the climate ameliorated, the glaciers retreated and ice-front lakes formed and then drained. The early Llano people were replaced by the succeeding Plano tradition that responded to changes in the flora and fauna over the next 3,500 years. The authors reconstruct the changes in the physical and biological environment that occurred, and the cultural adaptations that were developed to meet the mix of challenges and opportunities that these shifts presented to them. These changes involved the development of new tools and technologies, and careful modifications to settlement patterns, including an increased use of areas characterized by high biodiversity, within the CPE.

In Chapter 2, Oetelaar focuses on the human response to the Hypsithermal desiccation and the inherent variability in the intensity and duration of dry episodes across the expanse of the CPE, during this climatic episode. This warming period had a widespread effect upon the availability of potable water, plant cover and distribution of subsistence resources. Human settlement distribution was affected by these events and resident people developed coping strategies, including an increased use of areas of high biodiversity or *refugia*, which usually included permanent water sources. Bison remained the dominant food source although other species and plants increased in importance in this time period. Changes in social organization, food preparation and storage, are also indicated as a part of the human response.

In Chapter 3, Nicholson and Webster examine the post-Hypsithermal Oxbow, McKean and Pelican Lake complexes that followed the Mummy Cave/Gowen occupations in the CPE. The origins and lifeways of these successor groups within the region are examined in the context of changing physical and biological environments and their cultural responses to these changes. Across the CPE, there is evidence for a diversity of subsistence strategies followed by these groups, largely conditioned by the local resources available to them. The bison remains as the principle food resource, although broad spectrum foraging also played a significant role for these groups. Areas characterized by high levels of biodiversity continue to play a major role in the subsistence and settlement patterns of these groups. There is relatively little evidence for interaction between these groups, although the radiocarbon dates indicate some degree of overlap.

In Chapter 4, Hamilton et al. open their discussion with a brief examination of technologies and migration derived from the Eastern Woodlands that appeared in the CPE. This is followed with an overview of variation and change in climatic and biological parameters over time, across the wide expanse of the CPE and more particularly within the eastern sections. These variables, coupled with the cultural practice of these immigrants, shaped their subsistence strategies, and their overall lifeways, throughout the period under study. The succession of archaeological cultural groups that utilized the CPE in the time between ca. 2000 BP and 1000 BP and their distinctive technologies and sociocultural patterns are examined in an environmental context, as they appear in the archaeological record.

In Chapter 5, Nicholson et al. begin with a discussion of the cultural landscape in the CPE ca. AD 1000, and note the succeeding population shifts that took place over the next 700 years. They have also offered some possible ethnic assignments (cautiously) for some of the late period inhabitants of the region and relationships between these groups based upon early protohistoric accounts and relationships between late archaeological assemblages. The dominant cultures in the region are discussed within a contextual milieu that includes discussion of the physical, biological and cultural context of their lifeways. They conclude with a brief overview of these archaeological components of the CPE by province.

Acknowledgements

The authors gratefully acknowledge the support of the Social Sciences and Humanities Council through a Major Collaborative Research Initiatives grant (grant #412-1999-1000) and for additional support through provincial granting agencies and the home universities of the authors of this volume. We also gratefully acknowledge the dedicated work of the many undergraduate and graduate students (over 300) who participated in the fieldwork and lab analysis accompanying this project.

References

Nicholson, B.A. and Dion Wiseman. 2006. "Introduction" in "Changing Opportunities and Challenges: Human-Environmental Interaction in the Canadian Prairie Ecozone," *Memoir 38 Plains Anthropologist* 51: 199, 231–34.

——— (eds.). 2006. "Changing Opportunities and Challenges: Human-Environmental Interaction in the Canadian Prairie Ecozone," *Memoir 38 Plains Anthropologist* 51: 199.

———. 2007. "Building a Contextual Milieu: Interdisciplinary Modeling and Theoretical Perspectives from the SCAPE Project," *Canadian Journal of Archaeology Special Edition* 31, no. 3.

Chapter 1
Human Ecology of the Canadian Prairie Ecozone ca. 9000 BP: The Paleo-Indian Period

David Meyer, Alwynne B. Beaudoin and Leslie J. Amundson

KEYWORDS: Clovis, Folsom, Paleo-Indian, Canadian Plains, archaeology, points

This chapter presents an overview of the Paleo-Indian lifeways of the whole of the Canadian Prairie Ecozone (CPE), with particular attention to the Greater Forks region, an area broadly encompassing the confluence of the North and South Saskatchewan rivers in central Saskatchewan. We highlight lithic collections and sites from central Saskatchewan, several of which were investigated as part of the SCAPE project, most notably the Fenton Ferry and St. Louis Bridge sites. In general, the Paleo-Indian occupation of the CPE was a northward extension of that present on the adjacent American Plains.

Almost all of the Greater Forks region was inundated by an early stage of Glacial Lake Saskatchewan and therefore, was not occupied during Clovis times. However, after 11,000 years before present (BP), the latter proglacial lake fell to a lower level and the western and southern parts of the Greater Forks region became available for occupation by people who made a basally-thinned triangular point form that developed out of Clovis. The Goshen point is also present in this region.

The following Plano Tradition is well represented in the Greater Forks study area, beginning with the Agate Basin complex. By this time, ca. 10,500 BP, Glacial Lake Saskatchewan had coalesced with Glacial Lake Agassiz and most of the Greater Forks region now became habitable. Spruce parkland now dominated Saskatchewan and Manitoba, with grassland in Alberta, and clearly this environment supported substantial game populations. The Fenton Ferry site, with a number of broken Agate Basin points, endscrapers and drills, provides evidence for a home base occupied by a whole social group. It appears, therefore, that the population was somewhat larger and this increase continued into the following Alberta and Cody complex times, beginning around 10,000 BP.

Diagnostic points and knives of these cultural complexes are well represented in the study area. It is noteworthy that southern ties were maintained, as evidenced by the presence of a number of tools of brown chalcedony and fused shale. Evidently, well-established and well-adapted social groups were present throughout the grassland and deciduous parkland that dominated the CPE by this time.

The late Plano occupation of the CPE appears to reflect the in-movement of peoples—apparently from the west and northwest. By this time, ca. 8500 BP, the climate was becoming drier and milder, encouraging the expansion of open grassland. Lanceolate points of this period are common finds and since they are mainly made of local materials (sometimes relatively low quality), it appears that these people were more regionally based, with fewer external ties. In the Greater Forks region a late Plano component has been excavated at the St. Louis site, and dated to ca. 8000 BP.

Around 9000 BP was the earliest time slice chosen for the purposes of the SCAPE project. Due to the imprecision of dating control across much of the record, we envision the 9000 BP slice as an interval rather than a precise point in time. Therefore our concept of this slice is a span of about a thousand years centred on 9000 BP. The 9000 BP date falls at the beginning of Cody complex times. While the latter complex is discussed in this chapter, to provide a broader context there is also discussion of the complete sweep of the early occupation of the CPE, ca. 11,200–7800 BP. Conventionally referred to as the Paleo-Indian or Early Prehistoric period, two cultural traditions (or patterns) may be recognized through this lengthy time period: Llano (c. 11,200–10,200 BP) and Plano (c. 10,500–7800 BP) (Dixon 1999: 213–14; Stanford 1999: 326; Wright 1995: 3). On the northwestern American plains, the Llano tradition begins with the Clovis complex and is followed by the Goshen and Folsom complexes (Frison 1999; Stanford 1999). The subsequent Plano tradition begins with the Agate Basin complex and is followed by the Hell Gap, Alberta, Cody, Frederick and Lusk complexes (Hofman and Graham 1998). In general, it appears that this cultural sequence can also be recognized in the CPE.

Paleo-Indian Cultures in the Canadian Prairie Ecozone
The 9000 BP time slice falls after the Pleistocene-Holocene transition. It follows an interval of rapid and substantial climate and landscape change at the end of the last major glacial episode. The SCAPE study area lies within the envelope of the Laurentide ice-sheet. By 9000 BP, much of the area would have been ice-free, though still under the waning influence of the ice mass to the north and east, while large areas of southwest Manitoba through central Saskatchewan were inundated by a progressive sequence of proglacial lakes. Under these altering conditions, environmental change was substantial and continuous as the landscape adjusted to the postglacial situation. This resulted in landscapes that often looked very different to present across the region,

CHAPTER 1: Human Ecology of the Canadian Prairie Ecozone ca. 9000 BP

complicating the search for and interpretation of sites of this interval. Palaeoenvironmental sites spanning this interval are scarce across the prairies. Fortunately, several records from southern Alberta and central Saskatchewan extend to the 9000 BP time slice. Of these, the most critical for this study are the records from the Harris Lake site on the north slope of the Cypress Hills (Sauchyn and Sauchyn 1991), Lake A and Lake B in central Saskatchewan (Mott 1973), and Flintstone Hill in southwest Manitoba (Boyd 2003) (Figure 1.1). Other "snapshot" records, yielding information for short time spans rather than continuous intervals, are obtained from sites in the prairie pothole region, hummocky terrain that is widespread across southern Saskatchewan and Alberta, as well as adjacent areas of the northern USA (see sites discussed in Beaudoin and Oetelaar 2003, and Yansa 2006, 2007).

This chapter also includes a more detailed consideration of the Paleo-Indian occupation of the Greater Forks region (Figure 1.1). This region was one of three nodes in the CPE chosen for concentrated work by the SCAPE project. Our work there has uncovered new data and consolidated pre-existing information on human occupation in this critical time slice. The Greater Forks region encompasses the lower North and South Saskatchewan river valleys, as well as the confluence (The Forks) of these rivers, the upper Saskatchewan River valley and the adjacent Carrot River valley to the south. In terms of the topography, much of this region has very little relief because it was once the bed of

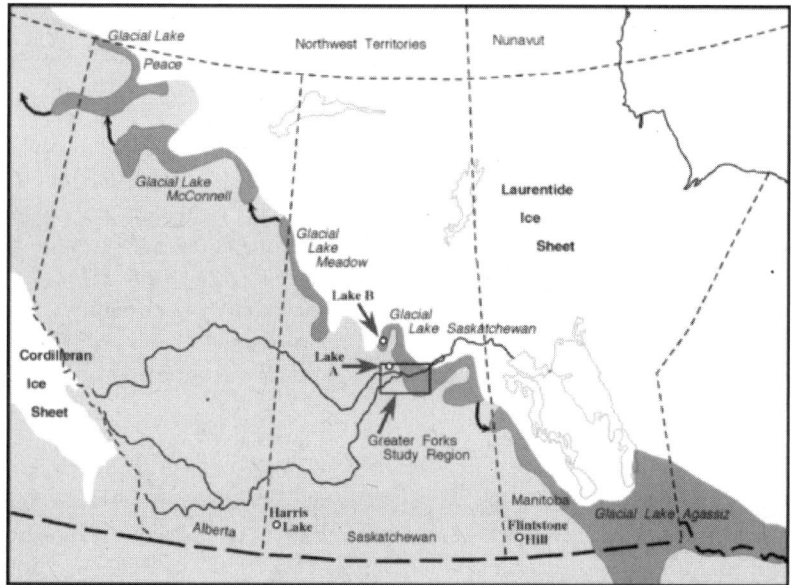

Figure 1.1. Ice sheet positions and proglacial lakes, ca. 11,000 BP (after Dyke et al. 2003), with the locations of paleoenvironmental sites and the Greater Forks study region.

Glacial Lake Saskatchewan. The only significant changes in elevation are those of the Lake Lenore upland (Richards 1969: 40–41), which extends into the south side of the Greater Forks area, and the deeply incised valleys of the North and South Saskatchewan and Saskatchewan rivers. At present the Greater Forks area encompasses the transition from the aspen parklands on the south to the boreal forest on the north. Much of the area to the south of the Saskatchewan River lies within the aspen parkland zone, with the boreal forest on the north side of the latter river.

The majority of the Paleo-Indian tools considered in this article were collected from the surfaces of cultivated fields in the Greater Forks region by knowledgeable avocational archaeologists who resided or worked in the Greater Forks region. Several collections have been particularly important in this regard: (1) that from the vicinity of the town of Birch Hills which was amassed by Lawrence and Lenore Hanson, with their son Russell; (2) the collection from the Melfort region which was made by Victor Vigrass and his son-in-law, Frank McConnell; (3) the collection from the Pathlow area made by Thomas Smith; (4) the material obtained by Thomas Phenix in the course of his work-related travels through central and east-central Saskatchewan; and (5) the specimens that Douglas Frey has recovered from fields to the northeast and east of the city of Prince Albert.

One early research project, the Glacial Lake Agassiz survey, 1965–68, has also contributed information to this study. The project was directed by Dr. Zenon Pohorecky, who was assisted by his student and field supervisor, Dennis Anderson. While this project was focused in the Red Deer River valley of east-central Saskatchewan, some work was also done in the eastern part of the Greater Forks region (Pohorecky and Anderson 1968: 49).

Cultural resource management (CRM) studies have also provided information. In particular, some Plano specimens were found in the course of the Nipawin Reservoir Heritage Study, 1981–85. As well, in more recent years large-scale archaeological surveys have been conducted in the Fort à la Corne provincial forest by Golder Associates Ltd. and by Western Heritage Services Inc., and have resulted in the recovery of a Cody knife. Particularly important was the reconnaissance by Stantec Consulting Ltd. of a bridge right-of-way near the village of St. Louis. This led to the discovery of a late Plano occupation, which is reported on in this chapter.

Our archaeological dataset, therefore, is formed from the integration of previously reported material with less well-known collections from avocational archaeologists and CRM studies. In particular, the SCAPE project provided an opportunity for detailed examination of several sites and collections—notably the Fenton Ferry and St. Louis Bridge sites and the Phenix collection—which have not hitherto been reported in detail.

CHAPTER 1: Human Ecology of the Canadian Prairie Ecozone ca. 9000 BP

Llano Tradition
The Llano tradition comprises three complexes: Clovis, Folsom and Goshen. By 11,200 BP, it is apparent that, south of the continental glaciations, there was widespread human occupation of North America. Not surprisingly, it is also apparent that as the continental glaciers retreated some of these early peoples moved north into the CPE to occupy the newly exposed lands. At this time (c. 11,200 BP), glacial ice still covered much of Manitoba and, given the presence of an early stage of Glacial Lake Agassiz (Dyke et al. 2003), only the extreme southwestern corner of the province was available for occupation (Figure 1.1). In Saskatchewan, the southern half of the province was ice-free although two large glacial lakes, Meadow and Saskatchewan, occupied much of the ice front. A larger section of Alberta was ice-free although, again, large proglacial lakes, notably Glacial Lake Peace and Glacial Lake McConnell, fronted the ice (Dyke et al. 2003).

Although ice-free land was available for human colonization, it was not necessarily hospitable. As Wilson and Burns (1999) have pointed out, a broad zone bordering the ice front would have consisted of an unstable landscape of eroding slopes, collapsing permafrost and buried blocks of melting ice. Given this chaotic terrain and the cooling effect of the remaining Laurentide ice, tundra vegetation can be expected in this band (Mandryk 1992; Strong and Hills 2005: 1055; Turner et al. 1999; Yansa 2006: 270). Beyond this zone, there is evidence that the initial vegetation was an open steppe, predominantly grasses and herbaceous plants such as sage (Mandryk 1992, in Gillespie 2002: 35; MacDonald and McLeod 1996). It is quite likely that some shrubs, such as willows, were also present in more sheltered or stable areas. The resulting vegetation mosaic has been characterized as "herb/shrub tundra" (Gillespie 2002: 37). Across much of the Prairie Provinces, glacial deposits would have been potentially nutrient-rich, although some leaching and weathering would have been needed to lower the pH and make nutrients available for plant use. Hence many of the early plant colonizers would have been adapted to rapid dispersal and also capable of nitrogen fixation. By 12,000 BP this herb/shrub steppe had come to dominate much of southern and central Alberta (Beaudoin and Oetelaar 2003: 196), and it appears that it was also present throughout Saskatchewan and Manitoba south of the Laurentide ice sheet (and the proglacial lakes fronting it) (Ritchie 1987; MacDonald and McLeod 1996). This open steppe vegetation was present in southern Saskatchewan until about 10,300 BP (Yansa 2006: 273).

In terms of fauna, a typical Late Pleistocene species suite was present on the Alberta plains at this time. This assemblage included woolly and Columbian mammoths, the Niobrara horse, the Mexican half-ass, yesterday's camel, as well as elk and bison (Burns 1996; Wilson 1983; Kooyman et al. 2006). Caribou and muskoxen were also present, presumably most abundant in the Arctic-like environment closer to the ice front (Mandryk 1992), although finds of these taxa are rare in Alberta (Jass et al. 2009). All of these species would also have been present across Saskatchewan and into Manitoba and could have formed the basis of early hunter-gatherer subsistence economies—such as those of the peoples of Clovis culture.

Clovis Complex

Clovis is the first widely recognized archaeological complex of North America south of the Laurentide ice sheet, including the northern plains, and has been dated to ca. 11,300–10,900 BP (Holliday 2000: 265). Using AMS dates on highly purified materials, Waters and Stafford (2007) propose that Clovis spans a much shorter interval, ca. 11,050 to 10,800 BP. (but see Haynes et al. 2007: 320). Clovis across North America is distinguished by well-crafted fluted or basally-thinned projectile points. This technology is also known for the presence of bone or ivory rods (Lahren and Bonnichsen 1974; Stanford 1990, 1996). These rods are believed to have formed part of the foreshafts of spears or, more likely, atlatl darts (Hutchings 1997; Dixon 1999: 153). In some parts of North America, people of Clovis culture also produced blades, which were struck from prepared cylindrical cores (Beck and Jones 2010: 88–93; Green 1963; LeBlanc and Wright 1990). A number of tools were made on these blades. On the American plains it is now known that these people "had a generalized foraging economy that utilized a wide variety of resources" (Stanford 1999: 326), including large, late Pleistocene fauna (see also, Grayson and Meltzer 2002: 349). Presumably, the same subsistence economy was present in the CPE.

It is apparent that by 11,200 BP the newly established plant and animal communities of the CPE had become sufficiently productive to support human hunters and gatherers–peoples of Clovis culture (see also Beaudoin and Oetelaar 2003: 199). Several surface-collected Clovis points have been found in Alberta (e.g. Gillespie 2002; Gryba 1985, 1988, 2001; Ives 2006), Saskatchewan (e.g. Kehoe 1966; Dyck 1983; Hall 2009; Pendree 1981; Pettipas 1975), and Manitoba (e.g. Pettipas 1969, 1970; Buchner and Pettipas 1990: 54). As well, a bone rod similar to those known from Clovis assemblages has been found near Grenfell, in southeastern Saskatchewan (Wilmeth 1968).

In situ Clovis occupations have not been encountered on the Canadian Plains (but see Kooyman et al. 2001, 2006). This is probably because of a sparse population, which produced a limited archaeological signature, and because the landscape was still in flux, given the lingering presence of buried ice blocks and slowly thawing permafrost (Mandryk 1996; Yansa 2006). This likely led to the disturbance of many Clovis occupations and, in some cases, deep burial (Ives 2006: 25; Wilson and Burns 1999: 234, in Gillespie 2002: 158). Given the very different landscape configuration at that time, we can expect Clovis (and other Llano) sites to have a different landscape signature and distribution to those of the Middle and Late Prehistoric, further reducing the likelihood of site discovery.

Anderson and Gillam (2000) have argued that Clovis populations were involved in a rapid expansion across the continent, leapfrogging over some regions. Given Anderson and Gillam's (2000) model, Ives (2006: 19, 27) has suggested that the Clovis occupants of Alberta may have "leapfrogged" into this part of North America and become relatively isolated from people to the south— considering the few Clovis points found in adjacent Montana and the fact that the points in Alberta tend to be made of local materials. The Saskatchewan population may well have been part of this relatively isolated northern group.

During Clovis times, most of the Greater Forks region was inundated by an early stage of Glacial Lake Saskatchewan and the North and South Saskatchewan Rivers formed a large delta that extended into the western end of the lake (Christiansen et al. 1995: 346). For over half a century, the possibility of Clovis occupation in the lands bordering the southern shore of Glacial Lake Saskatchewan has been of intense interest to Thomas Smith (1964, 1967, 1972), an accomplished avocational archaeologist and resident of this region. However, with two possible exceptions (Wilson and Smith sites, see below), Clovis points have not been found in the Greater Forks region.

Presumably, the landscape was still in the early stages of recovery following deglaciation, and animal populations were not large enough to attract much human attention. Indeed, given the proximity of a large, cold glacial lake and cold katabatic winds blowing off the ice sheet immediately to the north, the environment may have been challenging for human occupation. The larger fauna would have been dominated by caribou, with some muskoxen—perhaps not of great interest to hunters accustomed to hunting the Late Pleistocene species of the more productive steppe lands to the immediate south.

At the end of Clovis times, about 10,800 BP, a major climatic shift took place in the northern hemisphere. The climate abruptly cooled, by at least 6°C mean annual temperature, and this continued for over 1,000 years—the Younger Dryas episode (Berger 1990). The cause of this event has variously been attributed to a major outburst of Glacial Lake Agassiz (Broecker 2006) or, more recently, a cometary explosion over the Laurentide ice sheet (Firestone et al. 2007: 16016–21). Indeed, this hypothetical event has been posited as the factor that led to the extinction in North America, at ca. 10,900 BP, of many of the late Pleistocene large mammals, including the mammoths, horses and camels (Anderson and Gillan 2000). It has also been argued that this event decimated the Clovis population and resulted in significant cultural change— the end of Clovis culture (Firestone et al. 2007: 16021). However, the geological data adduced for this event have been questioned (Holliday and Meltzer 2010; Paquay et al. 2009; Pinter and Ishman 2008; Surovell et al. 2009), corroborative evidence from other studies is lacking (e.g. Gill et al. 2009; Marlon et al. 2009) and recent analysis of radiocarbon dates (Buchanan et al. 2008) shows no support for a Clovis population "bottleneck" at this time (see also Meltzer and Holliday 2010: 26,30). Currently, meltwater routing remains the most plausible explanation for the Younger Dryas event.

Basally-Thinned Triangular
It is possible that, during the Younger Dryas episode, life became more difficult for the occupants of the CPE, although Yansa (2006: 277) has observed that there "is no evidence of Younger Dryas cooling in the fossil records of the northern great plains." The occupants of the CPE during the Younger Dryas climatic interval were evidently descendants of the Clovis culture colonists. Their points were similar to the Clovis type, clearly a development out of that style. These have been referred to as "atypical fluted" (Kehoe 1966: 534–35), "generalized fluted" (Meyer and Walker 1999), "basally-thinned triangular" (Gillespie 2002), "northern fluted" (Clark 1991) or "Northwestern Fluted" (Hall 2009: 16) and are often shorter than classic Clovis points, with multiple, elongated flakes removed from the base. As noted above, Ives (2006: 27–28) has argued that a discrete Clovis population took up occupation of the Canadian plains (Alberta, in particular) and maintained little contact with people to the south. In this situation, cultural drift appears to have occurred, resulting in the development of the basally-thinned triangular point style. It appears that carriers of this technology expanded north as the ice retreated, as evidenced by the occupation at Charlie Lake Cave in northeastern British Columbia (Fladmark et al. 1988), dating to ca. 10,500 BP (Driver et al. 1996). Fluted points have also been found scattered to the north, through Yukon and into Alaska (Clark and MacFadyen 1983; Clark1984), although their dates and cultural affiliations remain unclear.

Unlike Clovis, *in situ* basally-thinned triangular points have been excavated in Alberta (Peck 2011: 49–53), although outside the prairie ecozone, as strictly defined, being located in the uplands to the west of our main SCAPE study area. Two basally-thinned triangular points have been recovered in excavation at the Sibbald Creek site (EgPr-2) in the foothills west of Calgary. These were found less than half a metre below the surface in deposits that also contained Plano tradition points (Gryba 1983). Unfortunately, there was not a discrete occupation by makers of basally-thinned triangular points. Such a separate occupation appears, however, to be present in the deepest component (Occupation 9) at the Vermilion Lakes site (EhPv-8) at Banff (Fedje 1986). Although diagnostic fluted points were not recovered, several radiocarbon dates were obtained and these indicate an occupation between 10,000 and 11,000 BP, probably close to 10,400 BP (Fedje 1986: 36; Fedje et al. 1995). This, therefore, was very likely a component produced by makers of basally-thinned triangular points (Ives 2006: 10–11).

The basal section of a basally-thinned triangular point was recovered *in situ* at the Twin Pines (EkPu-8) site, located in the eastern slopes of the Canadian Rockies some 100 km northwest of Calgary (Beaudoin et al. 1996: 121; Peck 2011: 52). Here, in James Pass, an intact component was encountered about 0.5 m below the surface (Ronaghan 1993). The recoveries included several lithic tools and some bone fragments, one of which was dated to 9750 ± 80 BP (TO-2999) (Beaudoin et al. 1996: 121).

CHAPTER 1: Human Ecology of the Canadian Prairie Ecozone ca. 9000 BP

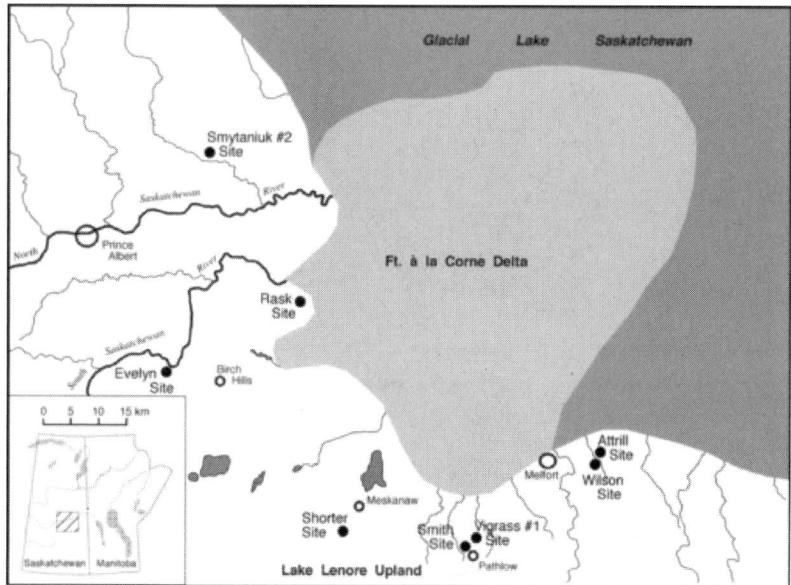

Figure 1.2. The Greater Forks study area showing the Fort à la Corne delta of Glacial Lake Saskatchewan, ca. 11,000 BP, and the sites of basally-thinned triangular points and a Folsom point (Shorter site).

In situ components with basally-thinned triangular points have not been excavated on the Saskatchewan and Manitoba plains, although a number of the points have been found (e.g. Kehoe 1966: 534). In the Greater Forks region, seven such specimens have been identified. All were found in fields a few kilometres from the shores of Glacial Lake Saskatchewan (Figure 1.2), at the level (460 m above sea level [asl]) it occupied ca. 11,000–10,200 BP (Christiansen et al. 1995: 346). At this time the Fort à la Corne delta was actively in formation as the North and South Saskatchewan rivers emptied large volumes of glacial meltwater into the western end of Glacial Lake Saskatchewan. These rivers deposited enormous amounts of sand, forming a huge delta stretching some 68 km east-west and 71 km north-south.

One of these points (Figure 1.3a) appears to be a preform, considering that it lacks basal thinning and grinding of the edges; however, the shape and flaking style is characteristic of basally-thinned points. This point, from the Smytaniuk #2 site (FhNi-85),[1] is composed of poor quality Swan River chert. This latter chert often has vugs, and in this case one of these has produced an

---

1. Borden designations are included whenever they are available. However, many of the artifacts that are considered here are from private collections and the sites at which they were found have not yet been assigned Borden designations.

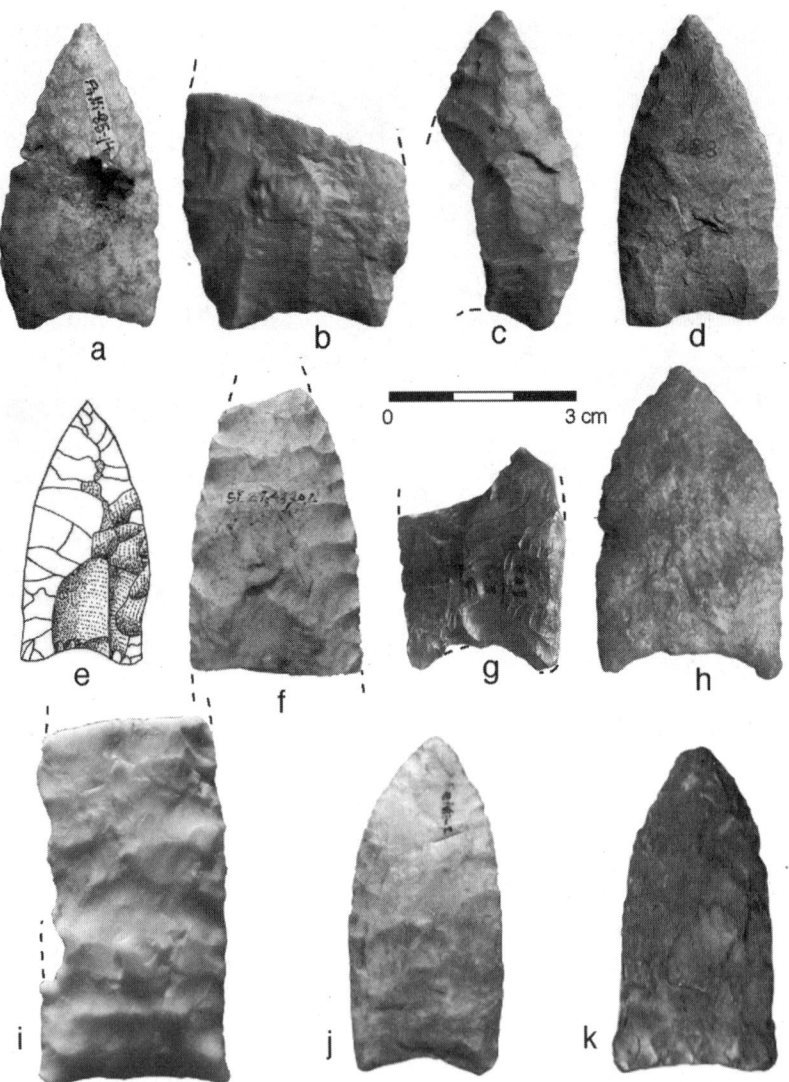

Figure 1.3. Paleo-Indian points from the Greater Forks study area: a-f, basally-thinned triangular; g, Folsom; h-k, Goshen. (The drawing of "e" is by Dennis Anderson.)

opening through the central part of the point (Frey 1993). This specimen was found on a field surface about a kilometre north of a local stream, the Garden River, just over 20 km northeast of the city of Prince Albert (Figure 1.2).

To the southeast, some 27 km, the proximal half of a basally-thinned point has been found at the Rask site (Figure 1.2). Two large basal thinning flakes have been removed from each surface of this Swan River chert specimen

(Figure 1.3b). Since the basal concavity and the lower edges are not ground, this point may be unfinished. Some kilometres to the southwest, a second basally-thinned point has been recovered from the Evelyn site which overlooks the valley of the South Saskatchewan River (Figure 1.2). This point—of glassy, heat-treated Swan River chert—has had multiple flute-like flakes removed from the concave base (Figure 1.3c). This piece does not bear grinding on the base or lower edges, and like the point from the Rask site may have been broken before completion. While the Smytaniuk #2 and Evelyn sites are many kilometres west of the Glacial Lake Saskatchewan delta, the Rask site is much closer to the delta, at an elevation of about 457 m.

In the southern part of the Greater Forks region, a basally-thinned triangular point, previously identified as a Clovis point, was found at the Wilson site, located on cultivated land about 8 km east of the town of Melfort (Figure 1.1) (Dyck 1983: 72). Made of a gray lithic material, probably a siltstone, multiple flakes have been removed from the basal indentation on both surfaces of this point (Figure 1.3d). As well, there is grinding on the lower margins and the base. Also from the immediate vicinity of Melfort, is a point from the Attrill site (Figure 1.1) (Pohorecky and Anderson 1968: 61). This specimen is made from off-white chert and has been basally thinned on one face (Figure 1.3e). The lower margins of this point are slightly indented and lightly ground.

Another early point has been found at the Smith site, which is located in the Pathlow area, some 20 km southwest of Melfort (Figure 1.1). This fragmentary piece lacks both its tip and its base; however, the distal end of a flute is present on each face (Figure 1.3f). Made of fine-grained, off-white chert, it is very likely that this is the remnant of a basally-thinned triangular point or a Clovis point (Smith 1972). Also in the Pathlow area (Vigrass #1 site) is a nearly complete point of Swan River chert with three long flakes removed from the base on one side (Campbell and Meyer 1970: 19, 21).[2] The asymmetrically concave base and the lower margins of this point have been lightly ground.

The makers of the two Melfort area points stood on land that, at 480 m asl, was well above Glacial Lake Saskatchewan and its delta, at 460 m asl; however, they were only a few kilometres from the shore of the lake. Therefore, looking north these hunters would have viewed the imposing, 110 km wide expanse of Glacial Lake Saskatchewan and its delta (Christiansen et al. 1995: 346). The Pathlow points were found at an even higher elevation, 490 m, on the Lake Lenore upland, a well elevated expanse of rolling hills (Richards 1969: 40–41). The shore of Glacial Lake Saskatchewan lay some 4 km to the north.

Shrubby steppe vegetation likely occupied much of the CPE at this time, extending north into the Greater Forks study region. The Fort à la Corne delta was in active formation as well, and while parts of it were certainly sub-aerial,

---

2. In Meyer and Campbell (1970), this specimen was incorrectly assigned to the Cumberland Reserve site (FgNe-3).

these were being reworked into sand dunes by the prevailing westerly winds (Wolfe et al. 2006). The Lake Lenore upland, at the northern limit of the shrubby steppe, was probably more attractive for human occupation, with ponds in the hollows between the grassy hills. Fringes of shrubs would have surrounded the ponds. These uplands would have supported some bison—presumably the large, late Pleistocene species, *Bison antiquus*—and likely supported higher biodiversity and hence more varied resources than the delta areas. However, the glacial front was only 120 km to the north and would have chilled the local environment, particularly since nearly constant cold dry winds blew off the ice-sheet (Yansa 2006: 271). Therefore, adjacent to Glacial Lake Saskatchewan and the ice front next to it, Arctic-adapted fauna, including caribou and muskoxen, can be expected to have been prominent.

In any case, makers of basally-thinned triangular points clearly occupied, albeit lightly, that portion of the Greater Forks area outside the shores and delta of Glacial Lake Saskatchewan. With the exception of the siltstone point from the Wilson site, these points are all of Swan River chert. This chert originates in bedrock outcrops (mainly Devonian) in west-central Manitoba (Grasby et al. 2002), from where it was eroded by the Laurentide glacier as it moved southwest. As a result, this chert has been glacially transported across the plains of central and southern Saskatchewan and southeastern Alberta and is widely available in the till (Grasby et al. 2002: 276, 279, 281). Swan River chert, therefore, is fairly common in the Greater Forks region and would have been obtained locally by the peoples who made basally-thinned triangular points. This emphasis on the use of local lithic materials, and the paucity of extra-regional lithics, indicates a strong orientation to this part of the CPE with limited outside contacts (see also Ives 2006: 16; Hall 2009: 85, 89).

Folsom Complex
On the American Plains, Clovis developed into Folsom which dates ca. 10,900–10,200 BP (Hofman and Graham 1998: 99). Folsom appears to be a direct cultural descendant of Clovis and the projectile points are thin and finely crafted, with full flutes removed from each face. Folsom sites are found from the southern plains of Texas north to the Canadian Plains. On the whole, the Folsom complex falls in the Younger Dryas climatic episode. However, as has been noted, Younger Dryas climatic effects on the plains appears to have been muted and, while winters may have been cold, summers remained relatively warm (Meltzer and Holliday 2010: 26).

In situ Folsom occupations have not been found on the Canadian Plains; however, there have been several surface finds of Folsom points. Folsom points are most common in the southernmost parts of the Prairie Provinces, and it is only here that sites have produced multiple Folsom points. In Alberta, just over a dozen Folsom points have been found (Ives 2006: 17; Gryba 2001; Peck 2011: 41–45), while in Saskatchewan, Hall (2009: 61–66) has reported 24.

CHAPTER 1: Human Ecology of the Canadian Prairie Ecozone ca. 9000 BP

In particular, a site near Bromhead in southeastern Saskatchewan yielded four Folsom points (Hall 2009: 62–63) and sites near Mortlach in south-central Saskatchewan also appear to have produced multiple points (Kehoe 1966: 533–34).

In Manitoba, only the southwestern corner of the province was habitable at this time, since the rest of the area was still inundated by Glacial Lake Agassiz with remaining Laurentide ice to the northeast (Boyd et al. 2003; Dyke 2005: 225–28; Teed et al. 2009). Pettipas (1970; Buchner and Pettipas 1990: 55) has recognized the presence of some Folsom points here and, more recently, Boyd (2000: 33) noted five surface finds of Folsom in Manitoba.

In general, the occurrence of Folsom points decreases to the north in the CPE. It is thought, therefore, that the Folsom occupation is simply a northward extension of that present in the adjacent plains states (Vickers 1986: 35). This interpretation is supported by the lithic materials that compose the Canadian points. In particular, there is a substantial incidence of Knife River flint (Kehoe 1966; Hall 2009: 64), originating in west-central North Dakota, indicating connections with peoples of Folsom culture to the immediate south. Indeed, people from Montana and the Dakotas may simply have moved seasonally into the southern part of the CPE.

One point, here identified as of the Folsom type, has been found at the Shorter site (FeNg-2) in the Greater Forks region (Figure 3g). It is made of brown chalcedony (presumably Knife River flint) and was found on a field surface a few kilometres southwest of the village of Meskanaw (Figure 1.2). Like the Pathlow point discussed above, it was positioned on the northern edge of the Lake Lenore upland. Kehoe (1966: Figure 3i) included this specimen in his discussion of fluted points in Saskatchewan, as known in the 1960s. He (1966: 534) described this as an atypical fluted point, but there is little reason not to identify it as Folsom.[3] Typical of Folsom, it has projecting ears on each side of the base and a basal nipple. It also has the delicacy, the thinness of Folsom and it is made of brown chalcedony, a material not characteristic of the Clovis and basally-thinned triangular points. The main departure from "standard" Folsom are the flutes, neither of which is a classic channel flake. One wavers crookedly up the surface of the point. On the other surface, the initial fluting attempt was unsuccessful, extending only 18 mm up from the point base, and a subsequent attempt was no more successful.

The Meskanaw point is considerably farther north than other Folsom specimens found in Saskatchewan (Kehoe 1966: 531; Hall 2009: 66). However, there was no physical barrier to the northward spread of Folsom at this time. The fact that Folsom is so rare in central Saskatchewan may relate to human

---

3. This is Hall's (2009: 108) specimen #25. He has identified it as a Northwestern Fluted point but it is more likely a Folsom point.

demographic and political factors: the makers of basally-thinned triangular points were already in residence. However, Hall (2009: 84) has proposed that the Folsom population was focused on hunting bison (Blackmar 2001). He, therefore, interprets the northward distribution of these hunters as relating to the presence of grasslands (and bison herds) in southern Saskatchewan and Alberta (Hall (2009: 82–85). On the other hand, Stanford (1999: 301) has noted the diversity of non-bison species also present in Folsom occupations.

Goshen Complex

The Goshen complex was first recognized in eastern Wyoming (Irwin-Williams et al. 1973: 46) and may well be an offshoot of Clovis culture (Frison 1993: 7–11). The artifact assemblage has similarities to Clovis (Irwin-Williams et al. 1973: 46) and also to Folsom (Frison 1991a: 45; Stanford 1999: 308–9). Indeed, the lack of fluting is the main attribute that distinguishes some of the projectile points from Clovis and Folsom points (Frison 1996). The time period of Goshen is not well established (Stanford 1999: 308–9), but at the Hell Gap site Goshen is stratigraphically below Folsom (Irwin-Williams et al. 1973: 46). As well, one set of dates from the Mill Iron site in Wyoming fall in the period 10,900–10,700 BP (Frison 1996; Hofman and Graham 1998: 96–97). On the other hand, there is also evidence that Goshen (and the closely related Plainview complex) may date later than Folsom (Haynes et al. 2007: 320; Hofman and Graham 1998: 97; Holliday 2000: 267).

Yansa (2006: 272) has shown that, beginning before 12,000 BP, white spruce expanded north and northwest from southern refugia that this species had occupied during full glacial times. Following 10,300 BP, a spruce parkland became established on the northern plains, extending from the Dakotas and through southwestern Manitoba and southern Saskatchewan (Yansa 2006: 272–73; see also Teed et al. 2009 and Yansa 2007). It may also have extended into east-central Alberta (Gillespie 2002: 37), although there is no evidence for spruce parkland further south and west in Alberta. Rapid spruce migration was probably promoted by the anticyclonic winds driven by high pressure over the residual Laurentide ice sheet (Ritchie and MacDonald 1986). Yansa has argued that the spruce tended to form a fringe around ponds and lakes, while the drier upland areas supported more typical prairie vegetation. This vegetation assemblage was in place until about 9980 BP (Yansa 2006: 273) and its persistence may have been favoured by the cooler temperatures of the Younger Dryas episode. The development of this spruce parkland can be expected to have had some impact on regional fauna, although it should have been good bison range land. Elk and deer should also have been abundant.

About 10,500 BP the Laurentide front in west-central Manitoba had retreated sufficiently that Glacial Lake Saskatchewan coalesced with Glacial Lake Agassiz (Dyke et al. 2003). The western shoreline of Glacial Lake Agassiz, at 375 m asl, then became positioned on the eastern edge of the Greater Forks

CHAPTER 1: Human Ecology of the Canadian Prairie Ecozone ca. 9000 BP

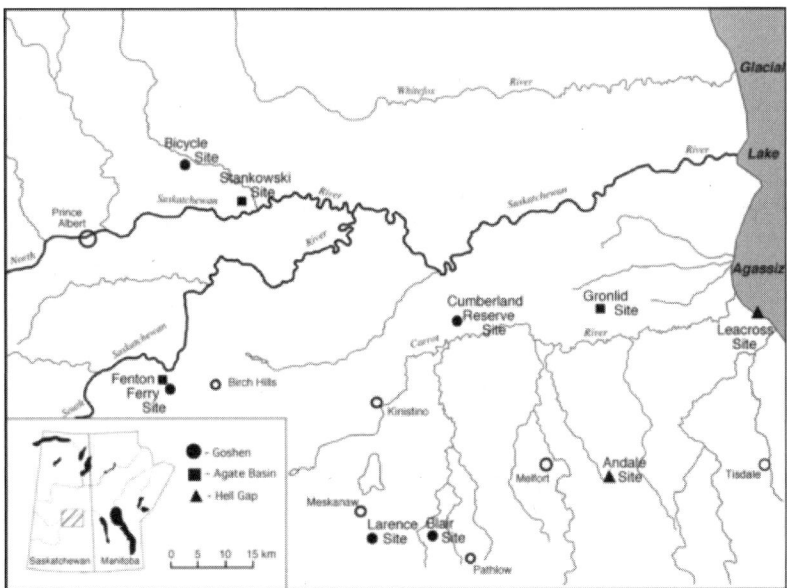

Figure 1.4. The Greater Forks study area with the locations of sites at which Goshen, Agate Basin and Hell Gap points have been found.

region (Figure 1.4). Here, the Saskatchewan River emptied into Glacial Lake Agassiz, forming the Nipawin delta (Christiansen et al. 1995: 346–47). Almost all the Greater Forks region was then available for human occupation.

Goshen points have been recognized as surface finds across the CPE (Pettipas 2004, 2009) and some have been found in the Greater Forks region. In the western part of the Greater Forks region, a projectile point of the Goshen type has been recovered from the Fenton Ferry site (FfNj-1) near Birch Hills (Figure 1.4).[4] This point, made of light gray Swan River chert, has a concave base and fairly prominent ears on each side of the base (Figure 1.3h). The distal edges are abruptly angled to a slightly off-centre tip, evidence that the original tip broke off and the piece was then re-pointed. The maker of this point occupied a well-elevated sandy rise, about 2 km south of the edge of the South Saskatchewan River valley.

Also in the western part of the study region, there is the base of a Goshen point from the Bicycle site (FhNi-97), which is located some 6.5 km north of the North Saskatchewan River (Figure 1.4). This specimen appears to be of Tongue River silicified sediment and the basal concavity and the slightly constricted lower edges are ground.

---

4. This is Hall's specimen #26. While he identifies it as Northwestern Fluted, this is unlikely since it is neither fluted nor strongly basally-thinned.

A Goshen point has also been collected at the Larence site located several kilometres southeast of the village of Meskanaw (Figure 1.4). Made of creamy Swan River chert, the base is slightly concave and lightly ground—as are the lower lateral margins (see also Dyck 1983, Figure 10.3b). An impact spall has been removed from one edge of this broken point (Figure 1.3i). A few kilometres to the east, a complete Goshen point (Figure 1.3j) has been found at the Blair site (FeMe-2) (Figure 1.4). Both of these points were located on well-elevated terrain towards the northern edge of the Lake Lenore Upland.

To the north some 36 km, a Goshen point (Figure 1.3k) has been found at the Cumberland Reserve site (FgNe-3) (Figure 1.4).[5] This point is of fine-grained Swan River chert which is mottled with hues of red and orange—evidence of heat treating. This specimen is ground on its lower margins as well as on the slightly concave base (Campbell and Meyer 1970: 20–21). Stylistically, this point is very similar to some of the Goshen points that Frison (1996) has described from Wyoming.

While the Bicycle, Fenton Ferry, Blair and Larence site points were found outside the ca. 11,000 BP limits of Glacial Lake Saskatchewan, the Cumberland Reserve point was located near the centre of the Fort à la Corne delta. Although it is possible that this hunter traversed sub-aerial parts of the delta while it was active, it is more likely that Glacial Lake Saskatchewan had coalesced with Glacial Lake Agassiz by this time, thus abandoning the delta. As noted previously, the latter coalescence occurred about 10,500 BP and moved the shoreline some 80 km to the east, to the Nipawin area (Christiansen et al. 1995: 346–47). Although almost certainly still the location of a number of lingering ponds, much of this flat expanse of former delta and lakebed would have been blanketed with grasses and sedges. This environmental setting would have been similar to that which Boyd (2000: 33–34, 38; and also Boyd et al. 2003) identified as having attracted Folsom hunters in the Glacial Lake Hind basin of southwestern Manitoba.

Plano Tradition
The Llano tradition is succeeded by the Plano tradition (Dixon 1999: 213–14; Stanford 1999: 326). While some archaeologists (e.g. Frison 1991b) consider that this cultural tradition developed out of the Llano tradition, Stanford (1999: 310, 312) has noted that the characteristic lanceolate points occur as early as Clovis in the American Northwest (see also Bryan 1980, 1988; Beck and Jones 2010). In particular he has proposed that Agate Basin points were "derived from typologically similar early Northern Great Basin/Plateau lanceolate forms that may predate Agate Basin by nearly a millennium." Dixon (1999; 229), however, has set out an alternative hypothesis, noting that the origins may be to

---

5. In Meyer and Campbell (1970), this specimen was incorrectly assigned to a site near the village of Pathlow.

the north, in the lanceolate points of the Denali complex of Alaska. If so, the emphasis on microblade production, so characteristic of Denali, was not transmitted southward although it may be noted that microblade cores are not unknown in Agate Basin assemblages. For instance, such a core was found at the Parkhill site in southern Saskatchewan (Ebell 1980: 114). In any case, the fluting of points was abandoned and subsistence economies on the plains maintained a focus on bison hunting. As well, populations appear to have been greater because Plano sites are fairly common throughout the northern plains.

Agate Basin Complex

The Plano tradition was inaugurated by the Agate Basin complex. Dating ca. 10,500–10,000 BP (Frison 1991b: 57; Hofman and Graham 1998: 105; Irwin-Williams et al. 1973), this complex appears to overlap Folsom and Goshen chronologically. It is characterized by elongated, lanceolate projectile points that were crafted with a very high standard of workmanship. These points generally have a straight to slightly convex base which is ground, as are the lower lateral margins. They have straight edges (no twist), lenticular cross-sections, and are not as thin as Folsom points.

A few *in situ* Agate Basin components have been encountered in Alberta. Peck (2011: 58–64) has described six sites in that province as having intact Agate Basin components (see also Benders 2010). At the most prominent of these, Vermilion Lakes (Ehv-8), located in the Canadian Rockies, Fedje excavated Agate Basin occupation levels in two sections of the site. One of these, at a depth of about a metre, produced a reworked Agate Basin point and three associated radiocarbon dates averaging 9650 BP (Fedje 1986: 34). An Agate Basin point (Fedje 1986: 39) was also recovered from a second area of this site, associated with three radiocarbon dates averaging 9910 ± 95 BP (Fedje 1986: 40). There also are finds of Agate Basin points across the plains region of southern and central Alberta, although the majority of these are surface-collected or lack good provenience (Benders 2010).

In Saskatchewan and Manitoba, intact Agate Basin occupations have not been found, however, there are some major sites, such as Parkhill (EbNj-4), south of Moose Jaw, in cultivated fields (Ebell 1980). As well, there have been scattered finds of Agate Basin points as far north as central Saskatchewan (Benders 2010; Dyck 1983; Meyer and Walker 1999). Several Agate Basin points have also been recovered from fields in southwestern and west-central Manitoba (e.g. Pettipas 1970). By the beginning of Agate Basin times, around 10,500 BP, the Laurentide ice had retreated sufficiently that a northwesterly arm of Glacial Lake Agassiz extended across north-central Saskatchewan (Dyke et al. 2003). Geological interpretations vary as to the timing and the sequence of environmental events that led to episodes of low and high water in Glacial Lake Agassiz during Agate Basin times. On the whole, however, its western shore probably remained in the eastern part of the Greater Forks region (Figure 1.4).

During Agate Basin times, ca. 10,500–10,000 BP, open grassland was present across the southern Alberta plains (Beaudoin and Oetelaar 2003: 200). However, there is evidence that spruce was present at higher elevations in the foothills to the west (MacDonald 1989). As well, spruce parkland persisted across the plains of Manitoba and Saskatchewan. This vegetation zone would have extended north into the Greater Forks region. As in preceding Goshen times, bison numbers should have been high, although substantial numbers of deer and elk would have been present, as well as some moose.

An important Agate Basin component is present at the Fenton Ferry site (FfNj-1) (Figure 1.4) located in a cultivated field, just south of the South Saskatchewan River valley, near the town of Birch Hills. Here, there is a sandy ridge that extends east-west for about 1.3 km. Although this ridge is only elevated some 5 m above the terrain to the south, on the north it is about 10 m above the upper edge of the river valley which lies about 0.5 km away. On the north and west side of the ridge there are several small sloughs surrounded by aquatic vegetation, willows and aspen. This ridge was well drained and provided a good view of the immediate surroundings.

The Fenton Ferry site has yielded the bases of 10 Agate Basin projectile points, six of Swan River chert, two of fused shale (porcellanite) and two of brown chalcedony (one of the latter has been burned) (Figure 1.5a–j). All of these have straight to slightly convex basal edges and have been lightly ground on the lower edges and the bases. One complete point (Figure 1.5k), of gray fused shale, differs stylistically from the others in that is bears regular collateral flaking and the proximal half is slightly constricted. Also present are two carefully worked point midsections, lenticular in cross-section. One is of fused shale and the other of Swan River chert.

There are two other bifaces, both of highly patinated brown chalcedony. One piece has a thick lenticular cross-section and appears to be a broken point preform. The other specimen is also broken and may be part of an asymmetrical knife (Figure 1.5l). However, one edge of the break bears a scar characteristic of the removal of a burin spall. This broken fragment, therefore, appears to have been recycled as a burin.

This site also yielded two drill fragments (Figure 1.5m, n). These both are of patinated brown chalcedony, have ground lateral edges and one (Figure 1.5m) has been made from the midsection of a broken point. There are 17 brown chalcedony endscrapers (Figure 1.5o–ee), and most are highly patinated. Two unpatinated specimens (Figure 1.5aa, cc) may relate to later occupations of this site. Several of these endscrapers have spurs or incipient spurs. One other specimen, of highly patinated brown chalcedony, is a thick, keeled flake that is missing one end. All of its edges bear careful unifacial flaking on the dorsal surface. Also of patinated brown chalcedony is the proximal end of a thick flake. It has nicks around the edges, apparently as a result of use in some cutting task.

These materials almost certainly were left at a base camp. Several lines of

CHAPTER 1: Human Ecology of the Canadian Prairie Ecozone ca. 9000 BP

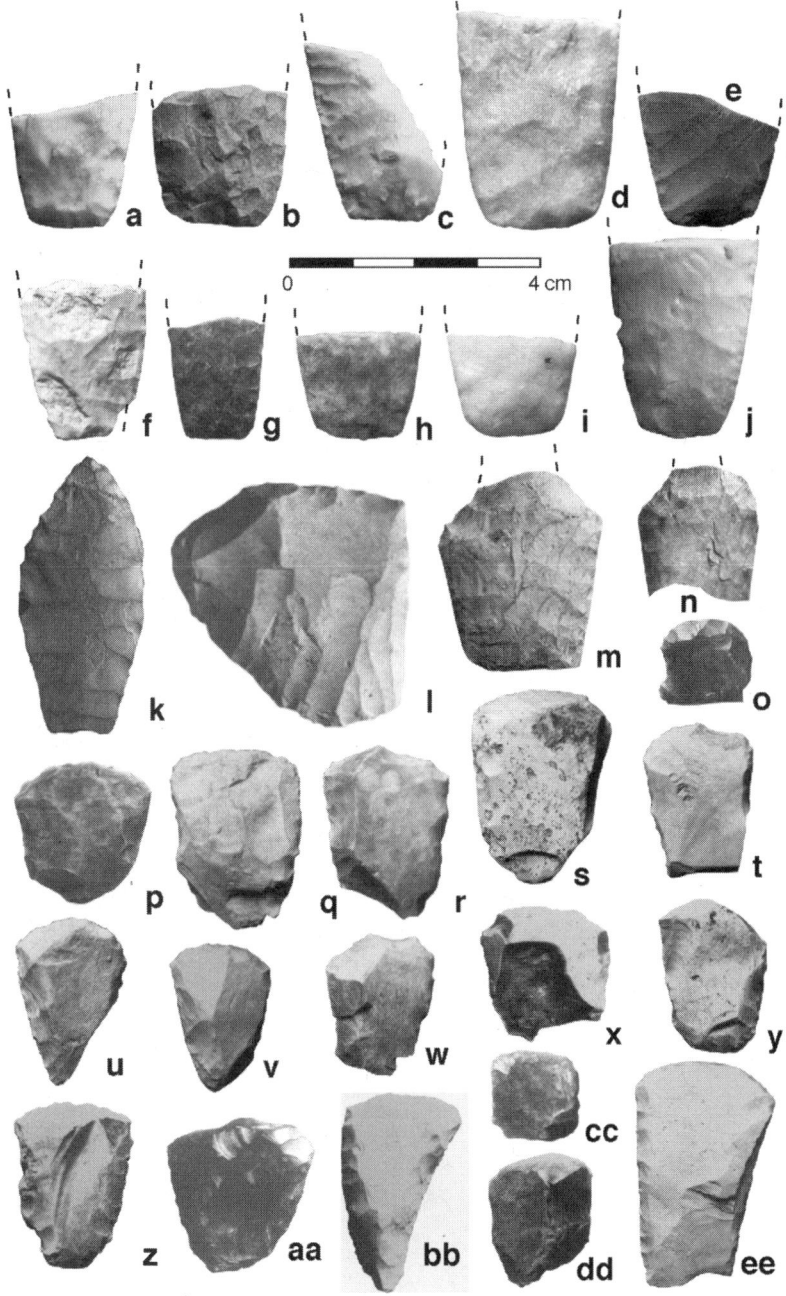

Figure 1.5. Agate Basin artifacts from the Fenton Ferry site.

evidence point to this conclusion. The point bases indicate that the hunters brought foreshafts back to camp following hunting expeditions—foreshafts that still held the bases of points broken in the heat of the hunt. The broken bases were evidently removed from the foreshafts, to be replaced with newly fashioned points. The presence of drill bits also reflects a more settled context, rather than a temporary hunting camp, as do the endscrapers because these tools would have been used by women in the course of preparing skins for clothing, bedding and shelter. In short, whole family units were present.

The Fenton Ferry site, therefore, provides the first evidence of occupation of the Greater Forks region by whole social groups. Presumably, the population was now somewhat greater and these people were regular seasonal occupants of the area. On the other hand, connections to the south were strong, as indicated by the numbers of brown chalcedony and fused shale artifacts. The brown chalcedony is almost certainly Knife River flint from North Dakota, while the nearest sources of fused shale are in far southern Saskatchewan (Johnson 1998: 38–39). Although spruce parkland would have supported substantial numbers of game animals, the climate of this region must still have been rigorous. The Laurentide ice margin was some 250 km to the north by this time, but it was fronted by proglacial Lake Agassiz. The winds would often have been out of the southeast—typically dry cold winds generated by the prevailing high pressure circulation over the Laurentide glacial mass (Ritchie and MacDonald 1986; Yansa 2006: 271).

Elsewhere in the Greater Forks region, Agate Basin points do not seem to be particularly common; however, a few have been collected. One remarkable specimen has been found in the Gronlid area, 25 km north of Melfort (Figure 1.4). This point is of white Swan River chert (Figure 1.6a) and is difficult to distinguish from late Plano points. Indeed, this point has a slight twist and the ventral surface of the flake blank has not been completely removed. Both attributes are more characteristic of late Plano points; however, the straight to slightly convex base is characteristically Agate Basin. This point serves to highlight the fact that it may not be possible to determine whether certain specimens are Agate Basin or later lanceolate points.

The base of another Agate Basin point (Figure 1.6b) was found at the Stankowski site (FhNi-96) which is about a kilometre north of the North Saskatchewan River (Figure 1.4). Composed of fine-grained white quartz, the base and lower edges have been carefully ground.

Hell Gap Complex

On the northwestern American plains the Hell Gap complex follows Agate Basin, out of which it appears to have developed (Frison 1991a: 62; Frison and Stanford 1982: 336–67). Indeed, Hell Gap style points are present in low percentages in some Agate Basin assemblages, such as that from the Agate Basin site (Frison 1991b: 148). The dating of Hell Gap is not well established,

CHAPTER 1: Human Ecology of the Canadian Prairie Ecozone ca. 9000 BP

although Holliday (2000: 227) has proposed 10,500–9500 BP. It is apparent that these peoples regularly conducted large-scale bison kills, as indicated by the excavations of sites such as Casper (Frison 1974), Jones-Miller (Stanford 1978) and Hell Gap (Frison and Stanford 1982) (see also Frison 1991a: 170–77).

Figure 1.6. Plano points from the Greater Forks region: a–b, Agate Basin, c–d, Hell Gap; e–g, Alberta.

– 25 –

The spruce parkland across central Saskatchewan had changed in composition by the beginning of Hell Gap times, with increased abundance of other conifers, signaling the assemblage of an early boreal forest in north and central areas. Farther south, after 9980 BP, deciduous parkland, characterized by aspen, occupied a broad swath across southern Saskatchewan and Manitoba (Yansa 2006: 277). In southern Alberta and southwestern Saskatchewan, grasslands became established, likely with some arboreal vegetation in more sheltered and better watered locales. Isolated uplands, such as the Cypress Hills, retained coniferous vegetation (Sauchyn and Sauchyn 1991), enhancing biodiversity across the CPE. It is from this interval that we see more marked regional differentiation of vegetation. These changes were driven by warmer and drier climatic conditions, the drying of the terrain, and the impact of fire (Yansa 2006: 287), while the effect of the Laurentide Icesheet lessened as retreat continued (see Dyke et al. 2003). Although substantial bison herds would have occupied the spruce parkland, the deciduous parkland should have been even more favourable for bison—as well as other plains species. Of course, bison numbers would have been substantial in the grasslands that appear to have been expanding in southern Alberta at this time (Beaudoin and Oetelaar 2003: 200).

The only *in situ* Hell Gap occupations are in Alberta. One of these is the Eclipse site (EhPv-14), which is located in the Rockies adjacent to the Transcanada Highway, some 100 km west of Calgary (Fedje 1988, in Peck 2011: 60–62). Here, at a depth of 0.5 m a productive occupation level was encountered which produced two complete and four fragmentary Hell Gap points (Peck 2011: 61). Four radiocarbon dates have been obtained, ranging from 9210 to 10,230 BP (Peck 2011: 61). A second Alberta site that has produced *in situ* Hell Gap material is Lindoe (EaOp-9), which is situated on the South Saskatchewan River, in the Medicine Hat region (Bryan 2000, in Peck 2011: 62–63). A single Hell Gap point, in association with very large bison bones was recovered. The bones were partially imbedded in a peat layer, which was dated to 9900 BP (Peck 2011: 63).

Although some Hell Gap type points have been found on field surfaces in the Canadian Plains (e.g. Ebell 1972; Pettipas 1970, 1971; Storck 1973), no concentrations have been encountered. It is uncertain, therefore, what the status of the Hell Gap complex may be in this more northern area. In the Greater Forks region, a Hell Gap point (Figure 1.6c) of Swan River chert has been found at the Andale site, east of Melfort (Figure 1.4). A second Hell Gap point (Figure 1.6d), composed of brown chalcedony, was collected to the northeast, near the village of Leacross (Figure 1.4). Both these points may simply be variants of the Agate Basin lanceolate point type. The latter point was found on or even east of the Campbell Beach—possibly within the bed of Glacial Lake Agassiz. However, about 9900 BP Glacial Lake Agassiz temporarily fell to a much lower level with the opening of an outlet far to the northwest, along the Clearwater River valley (Fisher and Smith 1994; Teller and Leverington 2004: 734–35). As a result, the Nipawin delta would no longer have been active and would have been invaded by flora and fauna, and therefore attractive to regional human bands.

Alberta Complex
The Hell Gap point type, in turn, is considered to have evolved into the large, stemmed Alberta point. The blade of the Alberta point is wide and the shoulder pronounced. The stem is often elongated and sometimes expands at the base, or is constricted below the shoulders and then "balloons" out slightly. Assigned to a complex of the same name, this point type was first recognized in Alberta (Wormington 1957: 134). Indeed, the type site for the Alberta complex is the Fletcher site in south-central Alberta (Hofman and Graham 1998: 111). This site was initially excavated by Forbis in 1963 and 1964 (Forbis 1968), with additional work in 1975 (Quigg 1976) and also excavations in 1987 and 1988 (Vickers and Beaudoin 1989). Dating at this site has proved challenging, but it has been shown that it was occupied not long after 9380 ± 100 BP (TO-1097) (Vickers and Beaudoin 1989: 264). Detailed plant macrofossil analysis at this site suggests primarily open vegetation, with permanent if slightly brackish water sources (Beaudoin 2000). As for other sites across the Canadian plains, the landscape context for the early Holocene occupation here forms a marked contrast to the dryland conditions at present.

Peck (2011: 72–74) has noted a few other possible *in situ* occurrences of Alberta complex occupation in Alberta. In any case, Alberta points are fairly common surface finds across southern Alberta (Wormington and Forbis 1965), Saskatchewan (Dyck 1983; Felton 1971; Pettipas 1975; Phenix, 1964, 1965) and southwestern Manitoba (Pettipas 1970; Pettipas and Buchner 1983).

On the American Plains the Alberta assemblage is best known from sites such as Hell Gap (Irwin-Williams et al. 1973: 48) in Wyoming and Hudson-Meng in Nebraska, where it is dated to 9820 BP (Agenbroad 1978: 116). In general, it appears that the Alberta complex dates ca. 10,200–9400 BP (Holliday 2000).

Several Alberta points have been found in and about the Greater Forks region (Figure 7). Of particular interest is a brown chalcedony specimen (Figure 6e) found at the Riou site (FgMv-4), about 1.5 km northeast of the town of Arborfield (and, therefore, just beyond the eastern edge of the study region). This point was found on the bed of Glacial Lake Agassiz. Indeed, during Alberta complex times, the lake level had temporarily receded and people could have moved onto a location such as this, only 3.5 km from the high water strandline. This point is unusual in that it appears to have been employed in some rough cutting or a chopping chore which nicked and dulled the edges. As well, it is polished on all of its surfaces, as would be expected of a point that has been wave washed—which is what would have occurred as the lake level rose to the Upper Campbell level at 9400 BP. To the northwest, three Alberta points (e.g.

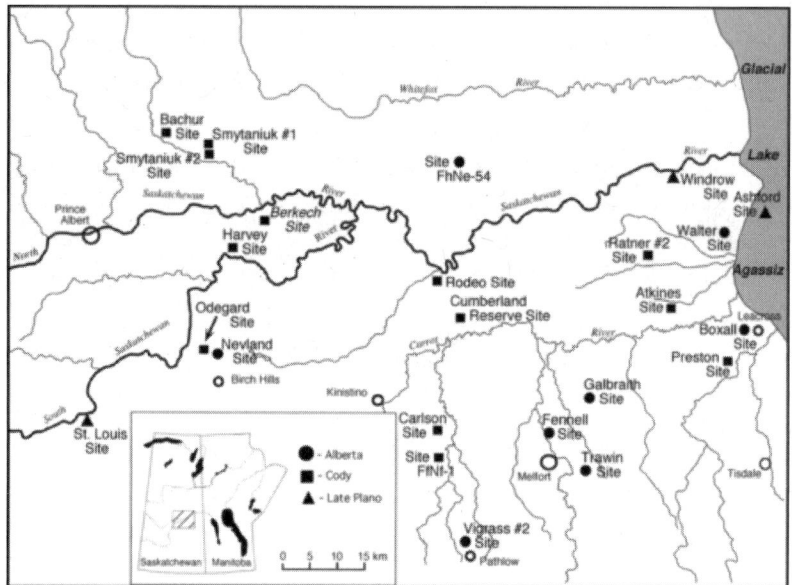

Figure 1.7. The Greater Forks study area with the locations at which Alberta, Cody and late Plano specimens have been found.

Figure 1.6g; Walter site), also of brown chalcedony, have been found, these in the vicinity of the village of Pontrilas (Figure 1.7). To the south and southwest, Alberta points have been found near Leacross (Boxall site), Melfort (Galbraith, Fennell and Trawin sites), Pathlow (Vigrass #2 site) and Birch Hills (Nevland site) (Figure 1.7). In the northern part of the study area, archaeological resource management work in the Fort à la Corne provincial forest has resulted in the recovery of the proximal half of an asymmetrical knife of white quartz from Site FhNe-54 (Golder Associates Ltd. 2006a, 2006b) (Figure 1.7). The stem of this specimen is in the Alberta point style.

The white chert specimen from the Trawin site near Melfort is a fragment of a particularly large point (Figure 1.6f), as is a complete point of brown chalcedony from the Fennell site (Figure 1.8a) (Felton 1971: 9). A specimen from the Nevland site near the town of Birch Hills is of brown chalcedony and also is a large point (Figure 1.8b). Like many Alberta points throughout the CPE, these specimens are mainly of brown chalcedony, evidently Knife River flint. Indeed, of 11 Alberta points known from the Greater Forks region, nine are of brown chalcedony. Almost certainly this is Knife River flint, the quarries for which are over 500 km to the south in western North Dakota. This provides evidence of regular trade connections or travel to the south.

The most northerly known Alberta points in this part of Saskatchewan are two that have been found near the village of Garrick, just north of the Greater Forks study region. By Alberta complex times, boreal forest would have been

CHAPTER 1: Human Ecology of the Canadian Prairie Ecozone ca. 9000 BP

Figure 1.8. Plano artifacts from the Greater Forks study area: a, b, Alberta points; c–l, Cody complex specimens.

established to the north of the Greater Forks study region, albeit with a somewhat different vegetation composition to the present boreal forest. While the northerly limit of the Alberta complex in this part of Saskatchewan is uncertain, it is noteworthy that in northwestern Saskatchewan an Alberta point has been found at a site in the town of Buffalo Narrows (Millar 1997: 104, 106), deep within the present boreal forest.

Yansa (2006: 279) has indicated that following the demise of the spruce parkland, deciduous parkland occupied the southern Canadian Plains for about a millennium—through to about 9000 BP. However, the vegetation record from the Fletcher site and other early Holocene palaeo-environmental sites in southern Alberta suggest a more complex and regionally varied vegetation pattern, with likely more open grassland vegetation established in these areas. Thus the west-east differentiation in vegetation that is apparent at present appears to have been established early in the Holocene. Nevertheless, deciduous parkland would have been prime habitat for many plains species, including bison and it is not surprising, therefore, that there was a substantial occupation by peoples of Alberta culture.

Cody Complex
The Alberta complex is considered to have developed into the Cody complex (e.g. Hofman and Graham 1998: 113) which is characterized by two projectile point types: Scottsbluff and Eden. Also characteristic of the Cody complex is the Cody knife, a stemmed, asymmetrical cutting tool. Cody flint knapping was of a very high order, including remarkably regular collateral flaking of projectile points. The Cody complex dates ca. 9400–8600 BP (Hofman and Graham 1998: 111–13).

The Cody complex is known throughout the Great Plains and, in the northern plains, particularly through excavations at major sites such as Horner (Frison and Todd 1987) and Carter/Kerr-McGee (Frison 1984). Some of the Cody sites contain the remains of large-scale bison kills that almost certainly are the result of well-organized, communal hunting events (Hofman and Graham 1998: 121); however, Stanford (1999: 322) has also emphasized the variety of species that are present in some Cody sites.

During Cody times, climatic conditions in the CPE were becoming somewhat drier and open grassland expanded northward at the expense (presumably) of the deciduous parkland. Increasing evidence of prairie vegetation is also evident in records from southwestern Manitoba (Teed et al. 2009) However, in general, the northern plains climate at this time was conducive to the maintenance of productive plant communities (Beaudoin and Oetelaar 2003: 199–200). In particular, this is reflected in substantial soil development suggesting increasing landscape stability, and marked by the regional occurrence of a distinctive "pre-Mazama paleosol" that is often apparent in cutbanks and exposures (e.g. Reeves and Dormaar 1972; Oetelaar 2002; Waters and Rutter 1984;).

Faunal numbers were almost certainly high during this time and it is not unexpected, therefore, that the human population during Cody times was also higher. Indeed, Cody sites and scattered surface finds are more numerous than those of preceding cultures.

The Cody complex is well evidenced on the Canadian Plains. Scottsbluff and Eden points have been found at numerous sites across southern and central Alberta (Wormington and Forbis 1965: 185; Pettipas and Johnston 1980). Cody complex tools (assigned to the Nezu complex) have also been recovered in northeastern Alberta (Saxberg and Reeves 2003: 308–10). As well, some *in situ* Cody complex occupations have been encountered in Alberta. For instance, the J-Crossing (DjPm-16) site on the Crowsnest River contained an intact Cody complex occupation (Van Dyke et al. 1989). However, Cody complex lithics are concentrated in southern, central, and northwest Alberta, as summarized by Dawe (in press; see also Peck 2011: 80–87).

Scattered finds of Scottsbluff and Eden points have also been made throughout the plains of Saskatchewan (e.g. Novecosky 2002: 52–57; Storck 1973; Tomenchuk and Seib 1973), and some large Cody complex sites have been surface collected, such as Dunn (Ebell 1964, 1988; Dyck 1983: 81–82) and DjNf-8 (Ebell 1975) in south-central Saskatchewan. *In situ* Cody complex components have been excavated at three sites on the Saskatchewan grasslands: Niska (Meyer 1985; Meyer and Liboiron 1991), Heron Eden (Corbeil 1991, 1995; Linnamae and Johnson 1999) and Napao (unreported). The Niska site occupation had been largely disturbed by cultivation, and surface collections from the field included three point stems, two complete stemmed points and four Cody knives (Meyer 1985: 23). We excavated an intact habitation area centred on a hearth and it produced three point stems, five endscrapers, a perforator/concave uniface and numerous flakes of brown chalcedony and fused shale (porcellanite) (Meyer 1985). Only a small amount of bone was recovered, all of which appeared to be large ungulate—presumably bison. Radiocarbon dating proved difficult (Meyer 1985: 28–29), but the most likely assay is 8475 ± 650 BP (S-2510) (Meyer and Liboiron 1990: 299).

The Cody complex component at the Heron-Eden site had also been partially intercepted by cultivation (Linnamae and Johnson 1999: 14). Five complete and two broken points were found on the surface of the field, while one fragmentary and three complete points were found in place, in the course of excavation. Of those complete enough to type, seven have been identified as Scottsbluff and two as Eden points (Linnamae and Johnson 1999: 22). Also recovered were nine complete and fragmentary endscrapers and one burin (Linnamae and Johnson 1999: 22–25).

A substantial number of faunal remains of bison were recovered in the course of excavation and these have been subjected to detailed analysis (Corbeil 1995). These represent a minimum of 35 animals, both cows and bulls, with some juvenile animals. Corbeil's (1995: 83) interpretation is that these animals were killed in mid-winter. The long bones are larger than those of contemporary bison and may be from *Bison antiquus*, although in the absence of skulls this identification cannot be certain (Corbeil 1995: 125–26). Five radiocarbon dates, all on bone, have been obtained. These range from 10,210 ± 100 BP (S-3118) to 8160 ± 200 BP (S-2308) (Linnamae and Johnson 1999: 16), but three that are near 9000 BP most likely date this occupation. The latter is supported by Leyden's (2004: 67, 193) more recent AMS date of 9168 ± 50 BP (NZA-15745).

In situ Cody complex occupations have not been identified in Manitoba, but Scottsbluff and Eden points are fairly common surface finds in southwestern and west-central parts of that province (Pettipas 1970, 1975; Gryba 1976). Similarly, *in situ* Cody complex occupations have not been encountered in the Greater Forks area but Scottsbluff and Eden points are well represented in surface finds (Figure 1.7). These materials have been found in the Birch Hills region, where they include a small Eden point (Figure 1.8c) from the Harvey site and a Cody knife (Figure 1.8d) from the Odegard site, both of patinated brown chalcedony. To the north, between the North and South Saskatchewan Rivers, an assemblage of Cody complex artifacts has been recovered from the Berkech site (FhNh-139) (Figure 1.8e–i). These consist of the stem of a brown chalcedony point (Figure 1.8e), two slightly stemmed points that appear to be recycled from the mid portions of larger points—one of Swan River chert (Figure 1.8f) and the other of brown chalcedony (Figure 1.8g)—the stem of a Swan River chert Cody knife (Figure 8h), and a spurred endscraper of brown chalcedony (Figure 1.8i). To the north of the North Saskatchewan River there are three more Cody complex specimens, all of Swan River chert. One, a proximal point section (Figure 1.8j), is from the Smytaniuk #1 Site (FhNi-86) (Figure 1.7), and that from the adjacent Smytaniuk site #2 (FhNi-85) is a small, rough Cody knife (Figure 1.8k). The third, a nearly complete point (Figure 1.8l), is from the Bachur site (FiNj-5) (Figure 1.7).

Farther to the east, a complete Scottsbluff point (Figure 1.9a) and six stem sections have been found at a site (FgNe-3) on Cumberland Indian Reserve 100A (Figure 1.7). All of these are of Swan River chert. Another Scottsbluff point of Swan River chert was found to the north at the Rodeo site (FgNf-9) on the adjoining James Smith Reserve (Meyer and Klimko 1986: 18, 37). To the east, another complete Scottsbluff point, of fine-grained, white fused shale (Figure 1.9b), comes from the Ratner #2 site (Figure 1.7) while, farther south, in the Melfort area there is a Scottsbluff point (Figure 1.9c), of Swan River chert, from the Fennell site. Some kilometres to the west, a large Scottsbluff point (Figure 1.9d) has been found at the Carlson site. This point, of brown chalcedony, bears a long (49 mm) impact flute on the distal end. An adjacent site, FfNf-1, (Figure 1.7) has also produced a finely crafted Scottsbluff point, this of Swan River chert (Figure 1.9e). In the nearby Pathlow area, numerous Scottsbluff point fragments have been found: a stem (brown chalcedony), a proximal half with stem (Swan River chert), and four bodies without stems

CHAPTER 1: Human Ecology of the Canadian Prairie Ecozone ca. 9000 BP

Figure 1.9. Cody complex specimens from the Greater Forks study area.

Figure 1.10. Scottsbluff points, a, b; late Plano point, c.

(three brown chalcedony, one Swan River chert). A Cody knife of brown chalcedony (Figure 1.9f) has also been collected, this from the Vigrass #2 site (Figure 1.7). A burin spall has been removed from the tip of the latter and the right side (as illustrated) has been unifacially bevelled. The Pathlow area has also produced the proximal half (with stem) of a small Eden point, this of highly patinated brown chalcedony. On the eastern side of the Greater Forks region, two Scottsbluff points are known, both of high quality Swan River chert. One (Figure 1.10a) is from the Atkines site while the other (Figure 1.10b) was found at the Preston site (Figure 1.7).

Like the Alberta complex, the Cody complex occupation of the Canadian Plains differs from later occupations in the widespread presence of high quality lithic materials, often from distant sources. In particular, these tools were frequently of brown chalcedony and fused shale (porcellanite). This scenario must reflect widespread social contacts or long distance travel (or both). Such a lifeway and associated sociopolitical organization may well have been facilitated by the very productive early Holocene environment that characterized the Canadian Plains at this time (Vance et al. 1995: 93).

Late Plano Complexes
Turning to the end of the Plano tradition, around 8500 BP on the American

plains the Cody complex was succeeded by cultural complexes whose hallmark was a lanceolate point, not unlike the much earlier Agate Basin.[6] This same succession extended north through the Canadian Plains. There is a good deal of variation in the style of the lanceolate projectile points, and names applied to point styles during this time include Frederick (Irwin-Williams et al. 1973: 50–51), Jimmy Allen (Mulloy 1959) and Angostura (Wheeler 1954). Given the strictures of formal scientific taxonomy, Hofman and Graham (1998: 114) have proposed a complex named Allen/Frederick and questioned the continued use of the term "Angostura" (Hofman and Graham 1998: 114–15). The Allen/Frederick complex is characterized by diagonally flaked points, usually with concave bases (Irwin-Williams et al. 1973: 50). On the other hand, the points of the Lusk complex are characterized by "haphazard chipping techniques and lower width-to-length ratios (Hofman and Graham 1998: 115). These late Plano materials date in the period 8500–7800 BP.

Late Plano points are common surface finds across the Canadian Prairie Ecozone and a number of intact occupations have been excavated. In Alberta, the latter include the Boss Hill (Doll 1982), Hawkwood (Van Dyke and Stewart 1985) and Tuscany (Oetelaar 1997) sites, all with radiocarbon dates in the 8000 BP range (for an overview, see Peck 2011: 108–17). A late Plano component has also been excavated in (southeastern) Manitoba, at the Sinnock site (dated to 8030 BP) (Buchner 1984). Neither the Alberta nor Manitoba late Plano sites are in SCAPE study areas, but peoples of these cultures would also have occupied these areas.

Late Plano occupation of the CPE would have begun (ca. 8500 BP) during a time when there was open grassland in parts of southern Alberta and, perhaps, southwestern Saskatchewan (Vance et al. 1995: 91–93). It appears that climatic conditions became progressively warmer and drier, signaling the onset of the Hypsithermal, and by 8000 BP grassland had expanded across the Canadian Prairie Ecozone (CPE) (Yansa 2006: 279). At this time the deciduous parkland zone was probably in about the same position as the aspen parkland in historical times. As the Hypsithermal intensified, the open grassland expanded north to encompass the areas now occupied by aspen parkland and even the southern part of the boreal forest (Vance et al. 1995: 89, 94). The late Plano occupation ended, therefore, as the climate of the CPE became increasingly more arid.

In Saskatchewan, points that can be identified as late Plano are common

---

6. Since the Late Plano complexes of the plains evidently did not develop out of the Cody complex, one of the reviewers of this paper questioned whether they are even in the Plano tradition. However, it is clear that the Plano tradition was present more widely in North America than simply the Great Plains. For example, expressions of this tradition are found in such divergent regions as Alaska, the barren grounds of Nunavut and the St. Lawrence River valley of Quebec. In short, the Late Plano complexes are part of a larger North American Plano tradition.

surface finds (e.g. Dyck 1983: 82–83; Meyer and Pettipas 1977; Novecosky 2002: 57–61; Storck 1973: 27). As a result of an extensive cultural resource management project in the Nipawin region in 1976, Meyer (1977: 99–103) proposed that materials such as these be recognized as relating to the "Nipawin complex." This complex is characterized by lanceolate points that often have concave bases and strong basal thinning (see also Meyer 1970; Pettipas 1975: 19). While the majority of the points have concave bases, straight bases also occur (e.g. Meyer 1970: Figure 2a, e, h). The craftsmanship of these points is generally of a lower order than in preceding times and the materials are predominantly local: Swan River chert, white quartz, and Gronlid siltstone.

It is noteworthy that one of the sites recorded in the course of the Nipawin Reservoir Heritage Study, 1981–85,[7] produced fragments of five of these late lanceolate points (Finnigan et al. 1983: 128–29). This site (Windrow, FhNa-93) is in a cultivated field on an upper terrace of the Saskatchewan River (Figure 1.7). This terrace relates to a period when the Saskatchewan River flowed into a high level stand of Glacial Lake Agassiz—the Upper Campbell (Christiansen 1982: 51). The Upper Campbell beach level dates at 9400 BP (Teller and Leverington 2004: 732). As such, this terrace could not have been occupied until Glacial Lake Agassiz dropped to the Lower Campbell (9300 BP) or McCauleyville (9200 BP) levels (Teller and Leverington 2004: 732).

These Nipawin complex points are quite common in the Greater Forks region. A typical specimen is shown in Figure 1.10c. Composed of Swan River chert, it has a concave base, a basal thinning flake has been removed from the illustrated surface, and the base and lower margins are lightly ground. This point was found on the field surface at the Ashford site (Figure 1.7), which is actually on the bed of Glacial Lake Agassiz. Given that this late Plano complex is considered to date from about 8500 BP, Glacial Lake Agassiz would have been at the level of the Burnside beach (Teller and Leverington 2004: 732) at this time. This is a relatively low level and, in the study area, the Nipawin Delta and a large part of the adjacent proglacial lake bed would have been subaerial. Indeed, Meyer (1970) has discussed the presence of numbers of late Plano points on an adjacent section of the Glacial Lake Agassiz bed—an area that is drained by the Carrot River and its tributaries (see also Pettipas 2007).

An *in situ* late Plano component has been excavated in the Greater Forks region, this at the St. Louis site (FfNk-7) (Figure 1.7). This work was funded, in part, by the SCAPE project. The St. Louis site was identified in 2002 by L.J. (Butch) Amundson in the course of a CRM project in the region, funded by the Saskatchewan Ministry of Highways and Infrastructure. It is located on an intermediate terrace within the valley of the South Saskatchewan River (Figure

---

7. The multi-year (1981–85) Nipawin Reservoir Heritage study was funded by the Saskatchewan Power Corporation, as was the preceding reconnaissance in 1976 (Meyer 1977).

CHAPTER 1: Human Ecology of the Canadian Prairie Ecozone ca. 9000 BP

Figure 1.11. Excavation in progress at the St. Louis site, July 2003, looking south.

1.11). This terrace is capped by about 2 m of overbank flood deposits. Each deposit consists of several cm of silty clay sediment, on the surface of which there is a dark organic horizon a few cm thick (see also Cyr et al. 2011). The latter reflect the beginning of soil formation and the presence of a blanket of vegetation at the time the depositional unit was buried. Several of these "paleosols" contain cultural materials, and a series of radiocarbon dates, mainly on bone, have been obtained, ranging from 4590 ± 60 BP (Beta-173608) for the uppermost paleosol to 9150 ± 40 BP (Beta-173611) for one of the deepest. As only 22 of these "couplets" of light silty clay and "paleosols" have been observed, each representing a single overbank flood event, the periodicity of these episodes is approximately 212 years. This suggests that the flood events were not regular but rather extraordinary and that the construction of this terrace and its preservation was a unique circumstance.

In 2002, Amundson, with SCAPE assistance, exposed 67 m^2 of an occupation in the Layer VII paleosol, at a depth below the surface varying around 129–41 cm (Amundson and Meyer 2003). This living floor yielded a scatter of several hundred Swan River chert flakes, fragmentary faunal remains, and some fire-cracked rock, all focussed on a small surface hearth (Figure 1.12). Also present was a biface preform of Swan River chert and the proximal half of a lanceolate projectile point (Figure 1.13a). This point, of Swan River chert, has an irregular, slightly convex base. One of the lower edges of the point has several "nicks," perhaps the result of impact fracture while hafted. The other margin is heavily ground. Amundson also recovered, in the course of backhoe testing, the distal half of a lanceolate point (Figure 1.13b). This point retains some lower

Figure 1.12. Butch Amundson at the late Plano living floor exposed in Layer VII, St. Louis site, July 2002.

edge grinding and likely also originated in the Layer VII occupation. Bone (collagen) from this occupation was dated to 7810 ± 70 BP (Beta-173609).

The 2002 work also led to the discovery of cultural materials in Layer VIII, at a depth of 167–191cm below the surface. Only a small amount of debitage was encountered but a remarkable recovery was a circular shell "sequin," about 4 cm in diameter, with a tiny central hole. Some faunal remains were found, predominantly bison, but the bones of grouse, rabbit and fish were also present. Bone (collagen) from this occupation was dated to 8400 ± 70 BP (Beta-17610).

In Layers IV (6220 ± 70, Beta-173612) through VII (7810 ± 70, Beta-173609), four partial but large bison skulls suggest that the prey species was *Bison antiquus*. Remarkably, the greatest horn core spread (114 cm) is in Layer IV at 6220 BP, a quite recent occurrence for the species (Amundson et al. 2005).

In 2003, Meyer, assisted by Amundson, continued the investigation of this site, exposing an additional section of Layer VII. This work encountered little additional cultural material in Layer VII, but a second sample of bone was dated to 7910 ± 60 BP (TO-11025), thus confirming the previous date. We also excavated a 35m^2 area of the occupation in Layer VIII. Cultural materials were sparse, but included a few Swan River chert flakes and a rough biface, perhaps a preform. As well:

> Particularly noteworthy in Paleosol VIII were numerous flakes of bone, some of which were burned. These exhibit flake attributes such as striking platforms and arris. A good deal of charred wood, apparently branches and small tree trunks, was present in this paleosol. (Meyer 2004: 8)

CHAPTER 1: Human Ecology of the Canadian Prairie Ecozone ca. 9000 BP

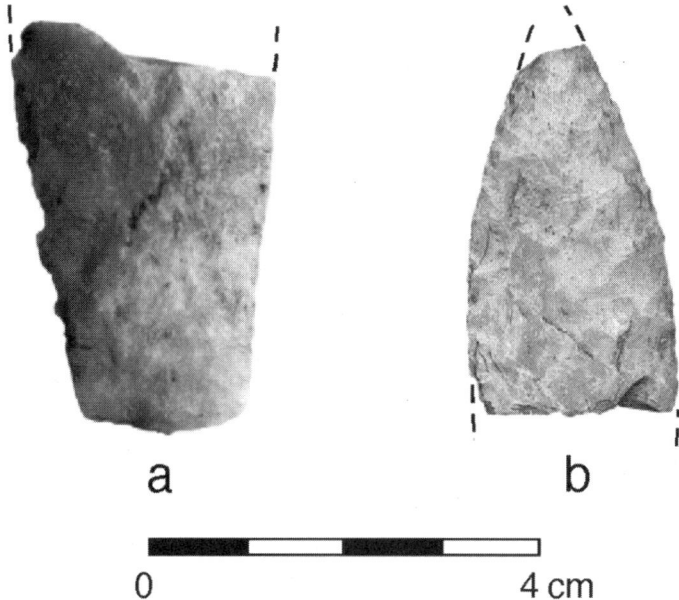

Figure 1.13. Broken late Plano points from the St. Louis site.

A sample of this charred wood was submitted for dating and it assayed at 8320 ± 70 BP (TO-11383), confirming the previous date on this paleosol. Although the Layer VIII occupation is a few centuries older than that in Layer VII, the Swan River chert flakes, the rough biface, and the bone fragments are not unlike those in Layer VII.

Presumably, the Layer VII assemblage can be assigned to the Nipawin complex. Although the lanceolate point found *in situ* has a straight base rather than the usual concave base, as noted above this straight-based variant does occur in the Nipawin complex. Turning to the occupation in Layer VIII, with a date of 8400 BP this could be a Cody complex occupation. However, the lithic materials are the same as those in Layer VII and absent are the higher quality Swan River cherts and exotic materials (e.g. brown chalcedony, fused shale) that would be expected in a Cody complex assemblage. It is likely, therefore, that the Layer VIII occupation is also of late Plano affiliation.

Discussion

During Clovis times, ca. 11,300–10,900, only the southern edge of the Greater Forks region was available for human occupation given the presence of an early stage of Glacial Lake Saskatchewan. At this time, the level of the latter proglacial lake was at about 488 m (asl) and large deltas were formed by the North and South Saskatchewan Rivers (Christiansen et al. 1995: 346). Subsequently, Glacial Lake Saskatchewan dropped to about 457 m and this allowed Clovis descendants, making basally-thinned triangular points, to move onto the previously inundated lands. The vegetation of much of the CPE at this time was a shrub/tundra steppe, and this vegetation would have extended north to the Greater Forks region. This vegetation appears to have supported a substantial faunal population, including herds of a large species of bison. Indeed, the sedges and grasses that would have blanketed the former lakebed must have been particularly attractive to these grazing animals. Although the climate must have remained fairly rigorous, it is clear that this fauna attracted some early hunters, both those who made basally-thinned points and those who made Goshen style points.

Turning to the Plano tradition, from Agate Basin times, beginning 10,500 BP, through to the end of the Cody complex, ca., 8400 BP, it is possible to discern a common cultural trajectory. Most of the technology did not change very much over this 2,000-year span, but projectile point shapes did change, as each style evolved into the next. In general, populations, while well established, do not appear to have been very large and movements and/or trading contacts were maintained over great distances across the plains. In particular, certain high quality lithic materials were sought after and became widely distributed. This preference for good lithic materials was paralleled by a strong emphasis on high quality craftsmanship.

Late Plano culture, therefore, represents a distinct break from the preceding Plano complexes discussed above. The late Plano lanceolate points quite clearly did not develop out of stemmed Scottsbluff or Eden points. As well, the quality of the flint knapping in late Plano times was of a lower order—and poorer quality lithic materials were often used. This cultural disjuncture can be taken as evidence for the movement of new social groups into the northern plains. In particular, technologies with projectile points remarkably like late Plano points are present far to the northwest in Alaska (Kunz and Reanier 1995). Like late Plano points in the CPE, these lanceolate points have (mostly) concave bases and "late stage longitudinal flake removal at the base" (Kunz and Reanier 1995: 15). These materials date to about 10,000 BP (Kunz and Reanier 1995: 17; Hamilton and Goebel 1999: 176), and Dixon (1999: 236–38) has proposed that this culture was taken south through the Rockies, as far as Wyoming and Colorado (but see Hamilton and Goebel 1999: 185). It appears that late Plano groups subsequently expanded eastward onto the plains—at the expense of residents of Cody complex culture.

For late Plano groups to expand onto the already occupied northern Plains, the newcomers must have possessed some technological or other advantages. In particular, changing climatic conditions may have been the stimulus that led to these cultural changes. In the western CPE, the climate became increasingly warm and dry from 9000 BP through to 6000 BP (Vance et al. 1995: 93)—the Hypsithermal climatic episode. By 8500 BP, open grassland was widely established and expanding northward at the expense of parkland. Eventually, grassland even moved north into the southern edge of what is now the boreal forest (Lichti-Fedorovich 1970; Mott 1973: 14; Vance et al. 1995: 89).

While the carrying capacity of the grassland would have been decreased with the onset of Hypsithermal conditions, herds of bison would still have been present and it is difficult to discern why Cody groups would have been under any great stress, especially in the more northerly parts of the CPE. Any advantage possessed by late Plano groups, therefore, is as likely to have involved new forms of sociopolitical organization and ideological orientation, as economic practices. In this regard, it appears that the late Plano social groups were more regionally focused—given there is less evidence for trade and apparent willingness to use local, lower quality lithic materials. In short, the sociopolitical groupings (bands) of the late Plano people may have been more bounded and occupied smaller areas than was the case with preceding peoples. If this was the situation, then the population of each of the groups must have been large enough to provide appropriate spouses for the members as they came to adulthood. Presumably, this related to a somewhat higher population density—perhaps maintained by a more generalized and flexible economic orientation (see also Robertson 2004).

Summary

On the whole, the CPE was, through both Llano and Plano times, simply at the northern extremity of the distribution of cultures that were well established on the adjacent American Plains. By Clovis times, ca. 11,200–10,900 BP, much of the CPE was free of ice, and an herb/shrub steppe had become established. It is clear that late Pleistocene species (many now extinct) were present, including mammoths and horses, and that there was a low density Clovis occupation of much of the CPE.

By 10,500 BP, most of the Late Pleistocene big game had disappeared and the material culture of the somewhat isolated Clovis population that occupied the CPE had changed slightly. In particular, the projectile points became generally smaller, with strong basal thinning rather than fluting. Around this time, 10,300 BP, white spruce migrated onto the Canadian Plains and spruce parkland developed. This parkland should have been good bison habitat and, therefore, it is not surprising that there is evidence of continued human presence. Indeed, this parkland, with its scattering of trees surrounding ponds and potholes, may have provided more resources to its human occupants than the subsequent open grasslands. Certainly, there were other cultural influences from the south at this time, as Goshen points are fairly common across the Canadian Plains. As well, some Folsom occupation occurred in the southern part of the CPE. Indeed, some sites have yielded multiple Folsom points, evidence of larger kills or campsites.

The spruce parkland remained in place through the time span of the Agate Basin complex, ca. 10,500–10,000 BP. This complex is well evidenced throughout the CPE, with some large sites. The presence of a habitation site, Fenton Ferry, in the Greater Forks region is evidence of increasing population and regular occupation of even the northern parts of the Canadian Plains. The Agate Basin complex was followed by a series of descendant cultures: Hell Gap, Alberta and Cody. Around 10,000 BP the spruce essentially died out across much of its former southern range, becoming restricted to the boreal ecoregion further north, leaving a deciduous parkland. Evidently, this remained a productive environment, attractive to human hunter-gatherers since the Alberta and Cody complexes, in particular, are well represented across the CPE. Indeed, numbers of points characteristic of these complexes have been found in the Greater Forks region.

Around 9000 BP, warmer and drier climate began to prevail, marking the onset of the Hypsithermal climatic episode. Arid conditions and droughts became common and, it appears, open grassland expanded north across the CPE. By the height of the Hypsithermal, around 7000 BP, grassland had even become established in what is now the southern part of the boreal forest. Presumably, with extended and more frequent droughts, life became more difficult for Cody complex peoples. It may be for this reason that around 8500 BP a new set of cultures appeared across the northern plains. With projectile point styles variously referred to as Lusk, Frederick, Jimmy Allen or Angostura, these peoples may have moved east out of the Rocky Mountain front. They appear to have formed much more localized bands than those of Cody times, evidently remaining in more restricted regions where they relied on the resources at hand—such as local lithics. As well, their subsistence economies may have been more generalized, oriented more to smaller game and plant foods—although bison evidently remained the staple. These peoples, therefore, had developed lifeways not unlike those of the Middle period cultural groups that followed, beginning ca. 7500 BP.

References

Agenbroad, Larry D. 1978. *The Hudson-Meng Site: An Alberta Bison Kill in the Nebraska High Plains*. Washington, DC: University Press of America.

Amundson, Leslie J., Nathan P. Friesen and Kristen M. Enns-Kavanagh. 2005. Archaeological Investigations at the St. Louis Site FNk-7: An Early to Mid Holocene Occupation of the Lower South Saskatchewan River Valley. Submitted to the Saskatchewan Ministry of Highways and Infrastructure. Copies available from the Heritage Resources Branch, Saskatchewan Tourism, Parks, Culture and Sport, Regina.

Amundson, Leslie J. and David Meyer. 2003. Late-Plano Occupation at the St. Louis Site (FfNk-7), Central Saskatchewan. *Current Research in the Pleistocene* 20: 1–2.

Anderson, David G. and J. Christopher Gillan. 2000. Paleoindian Colonization of the Americas: Implications from an Examination of Physiography, Demography, and Artifact Distribution. *American Antiquity* 65, no. 1: 43–66.

Beaudoin, Alwynne B. 2000. Stop 4: The Fletcher Site (DjOw-1). In *Late Quaternary*

History and Geoarchaeology of Southeastern Alberta and Southwestern Saskatchewan, ed. A.B. Beaudoin and D.S. Lemmen, 21–23. Field Trip Guidebook No. 3. GeoCanada 2000, Calgary, AB.

Beaudoin, Alwynne B. and Gerald A. Oetelaar. 2003. The Changing Ecophysical Landscape of Southern Alberta during the Late Pleistocene and Early Holocene. *Plains Anthropologist* 48, no. 187: 187–207.

Beaudoin, Alwynne B., Milt Wright and Brian Ronaghan. Late Quaternary Landscape History and Archaeology in the "Ice-Free Corridor": Some Recent Results from Alberta. *Quaternary International* 32: 113–26.

Beck, Charlotte, and Tom Jones. 2010. Clovis and Western Stemmed: Population Migration and the Meeting of Two Technologies in the Intermountain West. *American Antiquity* 75, no. 1: 81–116.

Benders, Quinn. 2010. Agate Basin Archaeology in Alberta and Saskatchewan, Canada. MA thesis, University of Alberta.

Berger, W.H. 1990. The Younger Dryas Cold Spell—A Quest for Causes. *Paleogeography, Paleoclimatology, Paleoecology* 8: 219–37.

Blackmar, Jeannette. 2001. Regional Variability in Clovis, Folsom, and Cody Land Use. *Plains Anthropologist* 46, no. 175.

Boyd, Matthew. 2000. Changing Physical and Ecological Landscapes in Southwestern Manitoba in Relation to Folsom (11,000–10,000 BP) and McKean (4,000–3,000 BP) Site Distributions. In *Changing Prairie Landscapes*, ed. Todd A. Radenbaugh and Patrick Douaud, 21–38. Regina: Canadian Plains Research Centre, University of Regina.

———. 2003. Paleoecology of an Early Holocene Wetland on the Canadian Prairies. *Géographie physique et Quaternaire* 57, nos. 2–3: 139–49.

Boyd, Matthew, Garry L. Running IV and Karen Havholm. 2003. Paleoecology and Geochronology of Glacial Lake Hind During the Pleistocene Holocene Transition: A Context for Folsom Surface Finds on the Canadian Prairies. *Geoarchaeology: An International Journal* 18, no. 6: 583–607.

Broecker, Wallace S. 2006. Was the Younger Dryas Triggered by a Flood? *Science* 312: 1146–48.

Bryan, Alan L. 1980. The Stemmed Point Tradition in Western North America. In *Anthropological Papers in Memory of Earl H. Swanson*, ed. L.B. Harten, Claude N. Warren, and Donald R. Tuohy, 78–107. Special Publication of the Idaho State Museum of Natural History, Pocatello, Idaho.

———. 1988. The Relationship of the Stemmed Point and Fluted Point Traditions in the Great Basin. In *Early Human Occupation in Far Western North America: The Clovis-Archaic Interface*, ed. Judith A. Willig, ca. Melvin Aikens and John L. Fagan, 53–74. Anthropological Papers No. 21. Nevada State Museum, Carson City.

———. 2000. The Lindoe Site, Southeastern Alberta. Non-permit. Archaeological Survey of Alberta, Edmonton, AB.

Buchanan, Briggs, Mark Collard and Kevan Edinborough. 2008. Paleoindian Demography and the Extraterrestrial Impact Hypothesis. *Proceedings of the National Academy of Sciences* 105, no. 33: 11651–54.

Buchner, Anthony P. 1984. *Investigations at the Sinnock Site, 1980 and 1982*. Papers in Manitoba Archaeology, Final Report 17. Historic Resources Branch, Manitoba Culture, Heritage and Recreation, Winnipeg.

Buchner, Anthony P. and Leo F. Pettipas. 1990. The Early Occupations of the Glacial Lake Agassiz Basin in Manitoba: 11,500 to 7,700 BP. In *Archaeological Geology of North America*, ed. Norman P. Lasca and Jack Donahue, 51–59. Geological Society of America, Boulder.

Burns, James A. 1996. Vertebrate Paleontology in the Alleged Ice-Free Corridor: the Meat of the Matter. *Quaternary International* 32: 107–12.

Campbell, Archibald and David Meyer. 1970. Three Early Man Points from the Melfort Area. *Saskatchewan Archaeology Newsletter* 30: 18–21.

Christiansen, Earl A. 1982. Quaternary Geology of the Nipawin Area, Saskatchewan. E.A. Christiansen Consulting Ltd., Report 0075-002, Saskatoon.

Christiansen, Earl A., E. Karl Sauer and Brian T. Schreiner. 1995. Glacial Lake Saskatchewan and Lake Agassiz Deltas in East-central Saskatchewan with Special Emphasis on the Nipawin Delta. *Canadian Journal of Earth Sciences* 32: 334–48.

Clark, Donald W. 1984. Northern Fluted points: Paleo-Eskimo, Paleo-Arctic, or Paleo-Indian. *Canadian Journal of Anthropology* 4, no. 1: 65–81.

———. 1991. The Northern (Alaska-Yukon) Fluted Points. In *Clovis Origins and Adaptations*, ed. Robson Bonnichsen and Karen L. Turmire, 35–48. Center for the Study of the First Americans, Oregon State University, Corvallis.

Clark, Donald W. and A. MacFadyen Clark. 1983. Paleo-Indians and Fluted Points; Subarctic Alternatives. *Plains Anthropologist* 28, no. 102: 283–92.

Corbeil, Marcel. 1991. The Heron Eden Site—1991 Update. *Saskatchewan Archaeological Society Newsletter* 12, no. 6: 106.

———. 1995. The Archaeology and Taphonomy of the Heron Eden Site, Southwestern Saskatchewan. MA thesis, University of Saskatchewan.

Cyr, Howard, Calla McNamee, Leslie Amundson and Andrea Freeman. 2011. Reconstructing Landscape and Vegetation through Multiple Proxy Indicators: A Geoarchaeological Examination of the St. Louis Site, Saskatchewan, Canada. *Geoarchaeology: An International Journal* 26, no. 2: 165–88.

Dawe, Robert J. In press A Review of the Cody Complex in Alberta. In *Paleoindian Lifeways of the Cody Complex*, ed. Edward J. Knell and Mark P. Muniz. University of Utah Press.

Dixon, James E. 1999. Bones, Boats and Bison: *Archeology and the First Colonization of Western North America*. The University of New Mexico Press, Albuquerque.

Doll, Maurice F.V. 1982. *The Boss Hill Site (FdPe-4) Locality 2: Pre-Archaic Manifestations in the Parkland of Central Alberta, Canada*. Provincial Museum of Alberta Occasional Paper 2, Edmonton.

Driver, Jonathan C., Martin Handly, Knut R. Fladmark, E. Erle Nelson, Gregg M. Sullivan and Randall Preston. 1996. Stratigraphy, Radiocarbon Dating and Culture History of Charlie Lake Cave, British Columbia. *Arctic* 49, no. 3: 265–77.

Dyck, Ian G. 1983.The Prehistory of Southern Saskatchewan. In *Tracking Ancient*

Hunters, ed. Henry T. Epp and Ian G. Dyck, 63–139. Saskatchewan Archaeological Society, Regina.

Dyke, Arthur S. 2005. Late Quaternary Vegetation History of Northern North America Based on Pollen, Macrofossil, and Faunal Remains. *Géographie physique et Quaternaire* 59, nos. 2–3: 211–62.

Dyke, Arthur S., Andrew Moore and Louis Robertson. 2003. *Deglaciation of North America*. Geological Survey of Canada Open File 1574. Natural Resources Canada, Ottawa.

Ebell, S. Biron. 1964. An Eden and Scottsbluff Site in South-Central Saskatchewan. *Saskatchewan Archaeology Newsletter* 6: 1–3.

———. 1972. Two Early Man Recoveries. *Saskatchewan Archaeology Newsletter* 37: 9–10.

———. 1975. A Cody Complex Site in South-Central Saskatchewan (DjNf-8). *Saskatchewan Archaeology Newsletter* 49: 1–6.

———. 1980. *The Parkhill Site: An Agate Basin Surface Collection in South-Central Saskatchewan*. Pastlog No. 4, Saskatchewan Museum of Natural History, Regina.

———. 1988. The Dunn Site. *Plains Anthropologist* 33: 505–30.

Fedje, Daryl. 1986. Banff Archaeology 1983–1985. In *Eastern Slopes Prehistory: Selected Papers*, ed. Brian Ronaghan, 25–62. Archaeological Survey of Alberta Occasional Paper 30, Edmonton.

———. 1988. *The Norquay and Eclipse Sites: Trans-Canada Highway Twinning Mitigation in Banff National Park*. Parks Canada Microfiche Report Series No. 286, Ottawa, Ontario.

Fedje, Daryl W., James M. White, Michael C. Wilson, D. Earl Nelson, John S. Vogel and John R. Southon. 1995. Vermilion Lakes Site: Adaptations and Environments in the Canadian Rockies During the Latest Pleistocene and Early Holocene. *American Antiquity* 60: 81–108.

Felton, Orly. 1971. Scottsbluff Points from North Battleford, Blaine Lake and Melfort Area. *Saskatchewan Archaeology Newsletter* 33: 8–9.

Finnigan, James T., David Meyer and Jean Prentice. 1983. *Resource Inventory, Assessment and Evaluation*. Nipawin Reservoir Heritage Study Vol. 5, ed. David Meyer. Saskatchewan Research Council Publication No. E-903-9-E-83, Saskatoon.

Firestone, R.B., A. West, J.P. Kennett, L. Becker, T.E. Bunch, Z.S. Revay, P.H. Schultz, T. Belgya, D.J. Kennett, J.M. Erlandson, O.J. Dickenson, A.C. Goodyear, R.S. Harris, G.A. Howard, J.B. Kloosterman, P. Lecher, P.A. Mayewski, J. Montgomery, R. Poreda, T. Darrah, S.S. Que Hee, A.R. Smith, A. Stich, W. Topping, J.H. Wittke and S. Wolbach. 2007. Evidence for an Extraterrestrial Impact 12,900 Years Ago that Contributed to the Megafaunal Extinctions and the Younger Dryas Cooling. *Proceedings of the National Academy of Sciences* 104, no. 41: 16016–21.

Fisher, Timothy and Derald G. Smith. 1994. Glacial Lake Agassiz: Its Northwest Maximum Extent and Outlet in Saskatchewan (Emerson Phase). *Quaternary Science Reviews* 13: 845–58.

Fladmark, Knut R., Jonathan C. Driver and Diana Alexander. 1988. The Paleoindian Component at Charlie Lake Cave (HbRf 39), British Columbia. *American Antiquity* 53, no. 2: 371–84.

Forbis, Richard G. 1968. Fletcher: A Paleo-Indian Site in Alberta. *American Antiquity* 33: 1.

Frey, Douglas. 1993. A Find from North Central Saskatchewan. *Saskatchewan Archaeological Society Newsletter* 14, no. 2: 54.

Frison, George C. 1974. *The Casper Site: A Hell Gap Bison Kill on the High Plains*. Academic Press, New York.

———. 1984 The Carter/Kerr-McGee Paleoindian Site: Cultural Resource Management and Archaeological Research. *American Antiquity* 49, no. 2: 288–314.

———. 1991a. *Prehistoric Hunters of the High Plains*, 2nd ed. Toronto, ON: Academic Press.

———. 1991b. The Goshen Paleoindian Complex: New Data for Paleoindian Research. In *Clovis Origins and Adaptations*, ed. Robson Bonnichsen and Karen L. Turnmire, 133–51. Cornvallis, OR: Center for the Study of the First Americans, Oregon State University.

———. 1993. The North American Paleoindian a Wealth of New Data but Still Much to Learn. In *Prehistory and Human Ecology of the Western Prairies and Northern Plains*, ed. Joseph A. Tiffany, 5–16. *Plains Anthropologist Memoir* 27.

———. 1996. *The Mill Iron Site*. Albuquerque, NM: University of New Mexico Press.

———. 1999. The Late Pleistocene Prehistory of the Northwestern Great Plains, the Adjacent Mountains, and Intermontane Basins. In *Ice Age People of North America*, ed. Robson Bonnichsen and Karen Turnmire, 264–80. Cornvallis, OR: Oregon State University Press.

Frison, George C. and Dennis J. Stanford. 1982. Summary and Conclusions. In *The Agate Basin Site: A Record of the Paleoindian Occupation of the Northwestern Plains*, ed. George C. Frison and Dennis J. Stanford, 361–70. New York: Academic Press.

Frison, George C. and Lawrence C. Todd. 1987. *The Horner Site: The Type Site of the Cody Cultural Complex*. New York: Academic Press.

Gill, Jacquelyn L., Jeremiah P. Marsicek, J.P. Donnelly, Bruce Simonson and Jack W. Williams. 2009. *Do Lake Sediment Records Show Evidence of a Younger Dryas Impact Event or its Potential Ecological Effects?* Abstract. 94th Ecological Society of America Meeting, Albuquerque, New Mexico.

Gillespie, Jason D. 2002. Archaeological and Geological Evidence for the First Peopling of Alberta. MA thesis, University of Calgary.

Golder Associates Ltd. 2006a. Heritage Resources Impact Assessment: De Beers Canada Inc. Fort à la Corne 2005 Diamond Exploration Program (Permit 05-038). Heritage Resources Branch, Saskatchewan Tourism, Parks, Culture and Sport, Regina.

———. 2006b. Heritage Resources Impact Assessment: Fort à la Corne Joint Venture Advanced Exploration Program (Permit 06-064). Copies available from the Heritage Resources Branch, Saskatchewan Tourism, Parks, Culture and Sport, Regina.

Grasby, Stephen E., Eugene M. Gryba and Ruth K. Bezys. 2002. A Bedrock Source of Swan River Chert. *Plains Anthropologist* 47, no. 182: 275–81.

Grayson, Donald K. and David J. Meltzer. 2002. Clovis Hunting and Large Mammal Extinction: A Critical Review of the Evidence. *Journal of World Prehistory* 16, no. 4: 313–59.

Green, F.E. 1963. The Clovis Blades: An Important Addition to the Llano Complex. *American Antiquity* 29, no. 2: 145–65.

Gryba, Eugene M. 1976. The Prehistoric Occupation of the Lower Trout-Hubble Creek Drainage Area in the Swan River Valley of Manitoba. *Napâo* 7, nos. 1 and 2: 11, 23.

———. 1983. *Sibbald Creek: 11,000 Years of Human Use of the Alberta Foothills*. Archaeological Survey of Alberta. Archaeological Survey of Alberta Occasional Paper 22. Alberta Culture, Edmonton.

———. 1985. Evidence of the Fluted Point in Alberta. In *Contributions to Plains Prehistory: The 1984 Plains Symposium*, ed. David Burley, 22–38. Archaeological Survey of Alberta Occasional Paper 26, Edmonton.

———. 1988. An Inventory of Fluted Point Occurrences in Alberta. Manuscript on file with the Archaeological Survey of Alberta, Edmonton.

———. 2001. Evidence of the Fluted Point Tradition in Western Alberta. In *On Being First: Cultural Innovations and Environmental Consequences of First Peopling*, ed. Jason Gillespie, Susan Tupakka and Cristy de Mille, 251–84. Chacmool, AB.

Hall, Jonathan B. 2009. Pointing It Out: Fluted point Distributions and Early Human Populations in Saskatchewan. MA thesis, Simon Fraser University.

Hamilton, Thomas D. and Ted Goebel. 1999. Late Pleistocene Peopling of Alaska. In *Ice Age People of North America*, ed. Robson Bonnichsen and Karen Turnmire, 156–99. Cornvallis, OR: Oregon State University Press.

Haynes, Gary, David G. Anderson, C. Reid Ferring, Stuart J. Fiedel, Donald K. Grayson, C. Vance Haynes Jr., Vance T. Holliday, Bruce B. Huckell, Marcel Kornfeld, David J. Meltzer, Julie Morrow, Todd Surovell, Nicole M. Waguespack, Peter Wigand and Robert M. Yohe II. 2007. Comment on "Redefining the Age of Clovis: Implications for the Peopling of the Americas." *Science* 317: 320.

Hofman, Jack L. and Russell W. Graham. 1998. The Paleo-Indian Cultures of the Great Plains. In *Archaeology on the Great Plains*, ed. W. Raymond Wood, 87–139. Lawrence: University Press of Kansas.

Holliday, Vance T. 2000. The Evolution of Paleoindian Geochronology and Typology on the Great Plains. *Geoarchaeology* 15, no. 3: 227–90.

Holliday, Vance T. and David J. Meltzer. 2010. The 12.9-ka ET Impact Hypothesis and North American Paleoindians. *Current Anthropology* 51, no. 5: 75–85.

Hutchings, K.W. 1997. The Paleoindian Fluted Point: Dart or Spear Armature? The Identification of Paleoindian Delivery Technology Through the Analysis of Lithic Fracture Velocity. PhD dissertation, Simon Fraser University.

Irwin-Williams, Cynthia, Henry Irwin, George Agogino and C. Vance Haynes. 1973. Hell Gap: Paleo-Indian Occupation on the High Plains. *Plains Anthropologist* 18, no. 59: 40–53.

Ives, John W. 2006. 13,001 Years Ago: Human Beginnings in Alberta. In *Alberta Formed Alberta Transformed*, ed. Michael Payne, Donald Wetherall and Catherine Cavanaugh, 1–34. Edmonton, AB: The University of Alberta Press.

Jass, Christopher N., Alwynne B. Beaudoin and James A. Burns. 2009. Perspectives on Paleontological Change in Ice Age Alberta: Past, Present, and Future. *9th North American Paleontological Convention Abstracts*: 298. Cincinnati Museum Center Scientific Contributions Number 3.

Johnson, Eldon A. 1998. Properties and Sources of Some Saskatchewan Lithic Materials of Archaeological Significance. *Saskatchewan Archaeology* 19: 1–45.

Kehoe, Thomas F. 1966. The Distribution and Implications of Fluted Points in Saskatchewan. *American Antiquity* 31: 530–39.

Kooyman, Brian P., Leonard V. Hills, Paul McNeil and Shayne Tolman. 2006. Late Pleistocene Horse Hunting at the Wally's Beach site (DhPg-8), Canada. *American Antiquity* 71: 101–21.

Kooyman, Brian, Margaret E. Newman, Christine Cluney, Murray Lobb and Shayne Tolman. 2001 Identification of Horse Exploitation by Clovis Hunters Based on Protein Analysis. *American Antiquity* 66, no. 4: 686–91.

Kunz, Michael L. and Richard E. Reinier. 1995. The Mesa Site: A Paleoindian Hunting Lookout in Arctic Alaska. *Arctic Anthropology* 32, no. 1: 5–30.

Lahren, Larry and Robson Bonnichsen. 1974. Bone Foreshafts from a Clovis Burial in Southwestern Montana. *Science* 186: 147–50.

LeBanc, Raymond J. and Milton J. Wright. 1990. Macroblade Technology in the Peace River Region of Northwestern Alberta. *Canadian Journal of Archaeology* 14: 11.

Leyden, Jeremy J. 2004. Paleoecology of Southern Saskatchewan Bison: Changes in Diet and Environment as Inferred through Stable Isotope Analysis of Bone Collagen. MA thesis, University of Saskatchewan.

Lichti-Federovich, Sigrid. 1970. The Pollen Stratigraphy of a Dated Section of Late Pleistocene Lake Sediment from Central Alberta. *Canadian Journal of Earth Sciences* 7, no. 3: 938–45.

Linnamae, Urve and Eldon Johnson. 1999. An Analysis of the Lithic Collection from the Heron Eden Site: A Cody Complex Manifestation in Saskatchewan. *Saskatchewan Archaeology* 20: 14–32.

MacDonald, Glen M. 1989. Postglacial Paleoecology of the Subalpine Forest-Grassland Ecotone of Southwestern Alberta: New Insights on Vegetation and Climate Change in the Canadian Rocky Mountains and Adjacent Foothills. *Paleogeography, Paleoclimatology, Paleoecology* 73: 155–73.

MacDonald, Glen M. and T.K. McLeod. 1996. The Holocene Closing of the "Ice-Free Corridor": A Biogeographical Perspective. *Quaternary International* 32: 87–95.

Mandryk, Carole A.S. 1992. Paleoecology as Contextual Archaeology: Human Viability of the Late Quaternary Ice-Free Corridor, Alberta, Canada. PhD dissertation, University of Alberta.

———. 1996. Late Wisconsinan Deglaciation of Alberta: Process and Palaeogeography. *Quaternary International* 32: 79–85.

Marlon, J.R., P.J. Bartlein, M.K. Walsh, S.P. Harrison, K.J. Brown, M.E. Edwards, P.E. Higuera, M.J. Power, R.S. Anderson, C. Briles, A. Brunelle, C. Carcaillet, M. Daniels, F.S. Hu, M. Lavoie, C. Long, T. Minckley, P.J.H. Richard, A.C. Scott, D.S. Shafer, W. Tinner, C.E. Umbanhowar, Jr. and C. Whitlock. 2009. Wildfire Responses to Abrupt Climate Change in North America. *Proceedings of the National Academy of Sciences* 106, no. 8: 2519–24.

Meltzer, David J. and Vance T. Holliday. 2010 Would North American Paleoindians have Noticed Younger Dryas Age Climate Changes? *Journal of World Prehistory* 23: 1–41.

Meyer, David. 1970. Plano Points in the Carrot River Valley. Saskatchewan Archaeology Newsletter 29: 8–21.

———. 1977. *The Nipawin Archaeological Survey for the Saskatchewan Power Corporation.* Saskatchewan Research Council Publication C 77-6, Saskatoon, Saskatchewan.

———. 1985. A Component in the Scottsbluff Tradition: Excavations at the Niska Site. *Canadian Journal of Archaeology* 9, no. 1: 1–37.

———. 2004. *Excavations at the St. Louis Site (FfNk-7): Interim Report on the 2003 Season.* Heritage Resources Branch, Saskatchewan Culture, Youth and Recreation, Regina.

Meyer, David and Olga Klimko. 1986. *The James Smith Archaeological Survey.* Saskatchewan Research Council Publication E-903-5-E-86. Saskatoon, Saskatchewan.

Meyer, David and Henry Liboiron. 1990. A Paleoindian Drill from the Niska Site in Southern Saskatchewan. *Plains Anthropologist* 35, no. 129: 299–312.

Meyer, David and Leo Pettipas. 1977. Angostura Observations. *Saskatchewan Archaeology Newsletter* 52, no. 2: 9–11.

Meyer, David and Ernest G. Walker. 1999. Glacial Retreat and Population Expansion. In *Atlas of Saskatchewan*, ed. K.I. Fung, 20. University of Saskatchewan.

Millar, James F.V. 1997. *The Prehistory of the Upper Churchill River Basin, Saskatchewan, Canada.* BAR International Series 668, Oxford.

Mott, Robert J. 1973. *Palynological Studies in Central Saskatchewan.* Geological Survey of Canada Paper 72-49. Department of Energy, Mines and Resources. Ottawa.

Mulloy, T. 1959. The James Allen Site, Near Laramie, Wyoming. *American Antiquity* 25: 112–16.

Novecosky, Bradley J. 2002. Archaeological Investigations in the Quill Lakes Region, East Central Saskatchewan. MA thesis, University of Saskatchewan.

Oetelaar, Gerald A. 1997. *Interim Report on the 1995 and 1996 Archaeological Excavations at Tuscany* (Permits 95-40 and 96-29). Submitted to Carma Developers, Ltd. Calgary. Department of Archaeology, University of Calgary, Alberta.

———. 2002. River of Change: A Model for the Development of Terraces Along the Bow River, Alberta. *Géographie physique et Quaternaire* 56: 155–69.

Paquay, François S,. Steven Goderis, Greg Ravizza, Frank Vanhaeck, Matthew Boyd, Todd A. Surovell, Vance T. Holliday, C. Vance Haynes, Jr. and Philippe Claeys. 2009. Absence of Geochemical Evidence for an Impact Event at the Bølling-Allerød/Younger Dryas Transition. *Proceedings of the National Academy of Sciences* 106, no. 51: 21505–10.

Peck, Trevor R. 2011. *Light from Ancient Campfires: Archaeological Evidence for Native Lifeways on the Northern Plains.* Edmonton: Athabasca University Press.

Pendree, Wayne. 1981. A Clovis Point from Medstead, Saskatchewan (FhNx-1). *Saskatchewan Archaeological Society Newsletter* 2, no. 4: 82–85.

Pettipas, Leo F. 1969. Early Man in the Swan River Valley, Manitoba. *Manitoba Archaeological Newsletter* 6, no. 3: 3–22.

———. 1970. Early Man in Manitoba. In *Ten Thousand Years: Archaeology in Manitoba*, ed. Walter M. Hlady, 5–28. Manitoba Archaeological Society.

———. 1971. Possible Early Man Artifacts from Manitoba. *Saskatchewan Archaeology Newsletter* 32: 6–17.

———. 1975. The Paleo-Indian Prehistory of Saskatchewan. *Saskatchewan Archaeology Newsletter* 50: 1–32.

———. 2004. "The Goshen Question" in Manitoba. *Manitoba Archaeological Journal* 14, no. 2: 1–15.

———. 2007. How Archaeology is Science: a Case in Point. *Saskatchewan Archaeological Society Newsletter* 28, no. 4: 122–24.

———. 2009. An Alternative to "Milnesand." *Saskatchewan Archaeology Newsletter* 30, no. 2: 40–41.

Pettipas, Leo F. and Anthony P. Buchner. 1983. Paleo-Indian Prehistory of the Glacial Lake Agassiz Region in Manitoba, 11,500–6,500 BP. In *Glacial Lake Agassiz*, ed. James T. Teller and Lee Clayton, 421–51. Geological Association of Canada Special Paper 26. St. John's, Newfoundland.

Pettipas, Leo F. and Russell A. Johnston. 1980. The Little Gem Complex. *Saskatchewan Archaeology* 1, no. 2: 3–81.

Phenix, Thomas S. 1964. The Alberta Point in Time and Space. *Saskatchewan Archaeology Newsletter* 5: 4.

———. 1965. Alberta Point Distribution in Saskatchewan. *Saskatchewan Archaeology Newsletter* 10: 4.

Pinter, Nicholas and Scott E. Ishman. 2008. Impacts, Mega-tsunami, and Other Extraordinary Claims. *GSA Today* 18, no. 1: 37–38.

Pohorecky, Zenon S. and Dennis E. Anderson. 1968. Agassiz Archaeology in Saskatchewan. *Napao: A Saskatchewan Anthropology Journal* 1, no. 1: 48–70.

Quigg, J. Michael. 1976. A Note on the Fletcher Site. In *Archaeology in Alberta, 1975*, ed. J. Michael Quigg and William J. Byrne, 108–15. Archaeological Survey of Alberta Occasional Paper 1, Edmonton.

Reeves, Brian O.K. and John Dormaar. 1972. A Partial Holocene Pedological and Archaeological Record from the Southern Alberta Rocky Mountains. *Arctic and Alpine Research* 4: 325–36.

Richards, J. Howard. 1969. Physical Features of Saskatchewan. In *Atlas of Saskatchewan*, ed. J. Howard Richards and Kai-Iu Fung, 40–41. Saskatoon, SK.

Ritchie, James C. 1987. *Postglacial Vegetation of Canada*. Cambridge University Press.

———. 1989. History of the Boreal Forest of Canada. In *Quaternary Geology of Canada and Greenland*, vol. 5, ed. R.J. Fulton, 508–12. Geological Society of Canada.

Ritchie, James C. and Glen M. MacDonald. 1986. The Patterns of Post-Glacial Spread of White Spruce. *Journal of Biogeography* 13: 527–40.

Robertson, Elizabeth. 2004. Communal Hunting as a Social Model for the Paleoindian to Early Archaic Transition on the Plains. In *Archaeology on the Edge: New Perspectives from the Northern Plains*, ed. Brian Kooyman and Jane H. Kelley, 211–29. Canadian Archaeological Association Occasional Paper 4. Calgary: University of Calgary Press.

Ronaghan, Brian. 1993. The James Pass Project: Early Holocene Occupation in the Front Ranges of the Rocky Mountains. *Canadian Journal of Archaeology* 17: 85–91.

Sauchyn, Mary A. and David J. Sauchyn. 1991. A Continuous Record of Holocene Pollen from Harris Lake, Southwestern Saskatchewan, Canada. *Palaeogeography, Palaeoclimatology, Palaeoecology* 88: 13–23.

Saxberg, Nancy and Brian O.K. Reeves. 2003. The First 2000 Years of Oil Sands History: Ancient Hunters at the Northwest Outlet of Glacial Lake Agassiz. In *Archaeology in Alberta: A View from the New Millennium*, ed. Jack. W. Brink and John F. Dormer, 290–322. Medicine Hat, AB: Archaeological Society of Alberta.

Smith, Thomas R. 1964. Early Man in Eastern Saskatchewan. *Saskatchewan Archaeology Newsletter* 7: 8.

———. 1967. The Clovis Problem. *Saskatchewan Archaeology Newsletter* 18: 3–4

———. 1972. Early Man in Terms of Glaciation in East Central Saskatchewan. *Saskatchewan Archaeology Newsletter* 36: 5–12.

Stanford, Dennis. 1978. The Jones-Miller Site: An Example of Hell Gap Bison Procurement Strategy. In *Bison Procurement and Utilization: A Symposium*, ed. Leslie B. Davis and Michael Wilson, 90–97. Plains. Anthropologists Memoir 14. Plains Anthropological Society.

———. 1990. Clovis Origins and Adaptations: An Introductory Perspective. In *Clovis Origins and Adaptations*, ed. Robson Bonnichsen and Karen Turnmire, 1–15. Cornvallis, OR: Oregon State University Press.

———. 1996. Foreshaft Sockets as Possible Clovis Hafting Devices. *Current Research in the Pleistocene* 13: 44–46.

———. 1999 Paleoindian Archaeology and Late Pleistocene Environments in the Plains and Southwestern United States. In *Ice-Age Peoples of North America: Environments, Origins, and Adaptations*, ed. Robson Bonnichsen and Karen Turnmire, 281–339. Corvallis, OR: Oregon State University Press.

Storck, Peter L. 1973. A Description of some Paleo-Indian and Archaic Projectile Points and Knives from Saskatchewan, Manitoba and Alberta in Collections of the Royal Ontario Museum, Toronto. *Saskatchewan Archaeology Newsletter* 41: 1–28.

Strong, Wayne L. and Leonard V. Hills. 2005 Late-glacial and Holocene Palaeovegetation Zonal Reconstruction for Central and North-central North America. *Journal of Biogeography* 32, no. 6: 1043–62.

Surovell, Todd, Vance T. Holliday, Joseph Gingerich, Caroline Ketron, C. Vance Haynes, Ilene Hilman, Daniel Wagner, Eileen Johnson, Philippe Claeys. 2009. An Independent Evaluation of the Younger Dryas Extraterrestrial Impact Hypothesis. *Proceedings of the National Academy of Sciences* 106: 18155–58.

Teed, Rebecca, Charles Umbanhower and Philip Camill. 2009. Multiproxy Lake Sediment Records at the Northern and Southern Boundaries of the Aspen Parkland Region of Manitoba, Canada. *The Holocene* 19, no. 6: 937–48.

Teller, James T. and David W. Leverington. 2004. Glacial Lake Agassiz: A 5000 Year History of Change and Its Relationship to the Delta18O Record of Greenland. *Geological Society of America Bulletin* 116: 729–42.

Turner, Mort D., Edward J. Zeller, Gisela A. Dreschoff and Joanne C. Turner. 1999. Impact of Ice-related Plant Nutrients on Glacial Margin Environments. In *Ice Age People of North America: Environments, Origins, and Adaptations*, ed. Robson Bonnichsen and Karen L. Turnmire, 42–77. Cornvallis, OR: Oregon State University Press.

Tomenchuk, John W. and Gary Seib. 1973. Scottsbluff Points from East Central Saskatchewan. *Saskatchewan Archaeology Newsletter* 43: 11–14.

Turner, M.D., E.J. Zeller, G.A. Dreschoff and J.C. Turner. 1999. Impact of Ice-Related Plant Nutrients on Glacial Environments. In *Ice Age People of North America: Environments, Origins and Adaptations*, ed. Robson Bonnichsen and Karen L. Turnmire, 42–77. Cornvallis, OR: Oregon State University Press.

Vance, Robert E., Alwynne B. Beaudoin and Brian H. Luckman. 1995. The Paleoecological Record of 6 KA BP Climate in the Canadian Prairie Provinces. *Géographie Physique et Quaternaire* 49, no. 1: 81–98.

Van Dyke, Stanley, Thomas Head and Barbara Neal. 1989. Oldman River Dam Prehistoric Archaeology Mitigation Program Campsites Component. Section 3.0 1988. Permit 88-039. Report on file, Archaeological Survey of Alberta, Provincial Museum of Alberta, Edmonton, Alberta.

Van Dyke, Stanley and Sally Stewart. 1985. *Hawkwood Site (EgPm-179): A Multicomponent Prehistoric Campsite on Nose Hill*. Archaeological Survey of Alberta Manuscript Series 7, Edmonton.

Vickers, J. Roderick. 1986. *Alberta Plains Prehistory: A Review*. Archaeological Survey of Alberta, Occasional Paper No. 27. Alberta Culture Historical Resources Division, Edmonton.

Vickers, J. Roderick and Alwynne B. Beaudoin. 1989. A Limiting AMS Date for the Cody Complex Occupation at the Fletcher Site, Alberta, Canada. *Plains Anthropologist* 34, no. 125: 261–64.

Waters, Michael R. and Thomas W. Stafford. 2007. Redefining the Age of Clovis: Implications for the Peopling of the Americas. *Science* 315: 1122–26.

Waters, Pamela L. and Nathaniel W. Rutter. 1984. Utilizing Paleosols and Volcanic Ash in Correlating Holocene Deposits in Southern Alberta. In *Correlation of Quaternary Chronologies*, ed. W.C. Mahaney, 203–23. GeoBooks, Norwich, England, UK.

Wheeler, R.P. 1954. Selected Projectile Points of the United States II. *Bulletin of the Oklahoma Anthropological Society* 2: 1–6.

Wilmeth, Roscoe. 1968. Fossilized Bone Artifact from Southern Saskatchewan. *American Antiquity* 33: 100-101.

Wilson, Michael. 1983. *Once Upon a River: Archaeology and Geology of the Bow River Valley at Calgary, Alberta, Canada*. Archaeological Survey of Canada Paper 114, National Museum of Man Mercury Series, Ottawa, Ontario.

Wilson, Michael C. and James A. Burns. 1999. Searching for the Earliest Canadians: Wide Corridors, Narrow Doorways, Small Windows. In *Ice Age People of North America*, ed. Robson Bonnichsen and Karen L. Turnmire, 213–48. Oregon State University Press.

Wolfe, Stephen A., Jeff Ollerhead, David Huntley and Olav B. Lian. 2006. Holocene Dune Activity and Environmental Change in the Prairie Parkland and Boreal Forest, Central Saskatchewan, Canada. *The Holocene* 16: 17–29.

Wormington, H. Marie. 1957. *Ancient Man in North America.* Denver Museum of Natural History, Popular Series, No. 4. Denver Museum, Denver.

Wormington, H. Marie and Richard G. Forbis. 1965. *An Introduction to the Archaeology of Alberta, Canada. Denver Museum of Natural History Proceedings, No. 11.* Denver Museum.

Wright, James V. 1995. *A History of the Native People of Canada: Volume I (10,000–1000 B.C.).* Archaeological Survey of Canada, Mercury Series Paper 152. Canadian Museum of Civilization, Hull.

Yansa, Catherine H. 2006. The Timing and Nature of Late Quaternary Vegetation Changes in the Northern Great Plains, USA and Canada: A Re-assessment of the Spruce Phase. *Quaternary Science Reviews* 25: 263–81.

———. 2007. Lake Records of Northern Plains Paleoindian and Early Archaic Environments: The "Park Oasis" Hypothesis. *Plains Anthropologist* 52: 109–44.

Chapter 2
Human Ecology of the Canadian Prairie Ecozone ca. 6000 BP: Hypsithermal Adaptations to the Canadian Prairie Ecozone?
Gerald A. Oetelaar

KEYWORDS: Hypsithermal, adaptive strategies, geomorphology, settlement patterns

On the Great Plains, the paucity of sites dating to this time interval is generally attributed to the negative impact of the Hypsithermal on the human occupation of the Canadian Prairie Ecozone (CPE) (Dyck and Morlan 2001; Frison 2001; Vehik 2001). Generally interpreted as an episode of increased aridity, the Hypsithermal is assumed to have negatively impacted the carrying capacity of the Plains with concomitant changes in the adaptive strategies of the resident populations. Given the current north-to-south and east-to-west aridity gradients on the Great Plains and the temporal variation in the onset of the Hypsithermal, the timing and effect of this climatic episode varied somewhat across the region. Even though there is much regional and temporal variation, archaeologists from Texas to Alberta working with assemblages dating to this time interval tend to focus on similar research questions. At the regional level, researchers are trying to quantify and explain the paucity of sites dating to this time interval, whereas locally they are attempting to identify changes in adaptive strategies relating to the change in climate.

Even though this discussion focuses primarily on the CPE, I will be comparing the results of our work with those of other researchers working in other areas. More specifically, I will briefly summarize the impact of the inferred climate change on the ecology of the Great Plains generally before proceeding to a more detailed discussion of the constraints imposed on the human populations living on the Northern Plains ca. 6000 BP (years before present). For purposes of this discussion, the Great Plains is subdivided into three large regions identified as the Southern Plains, the Central Plains and the Northern Plains (Figure 2.1). The Southern Plains closely approximates the regions so defined

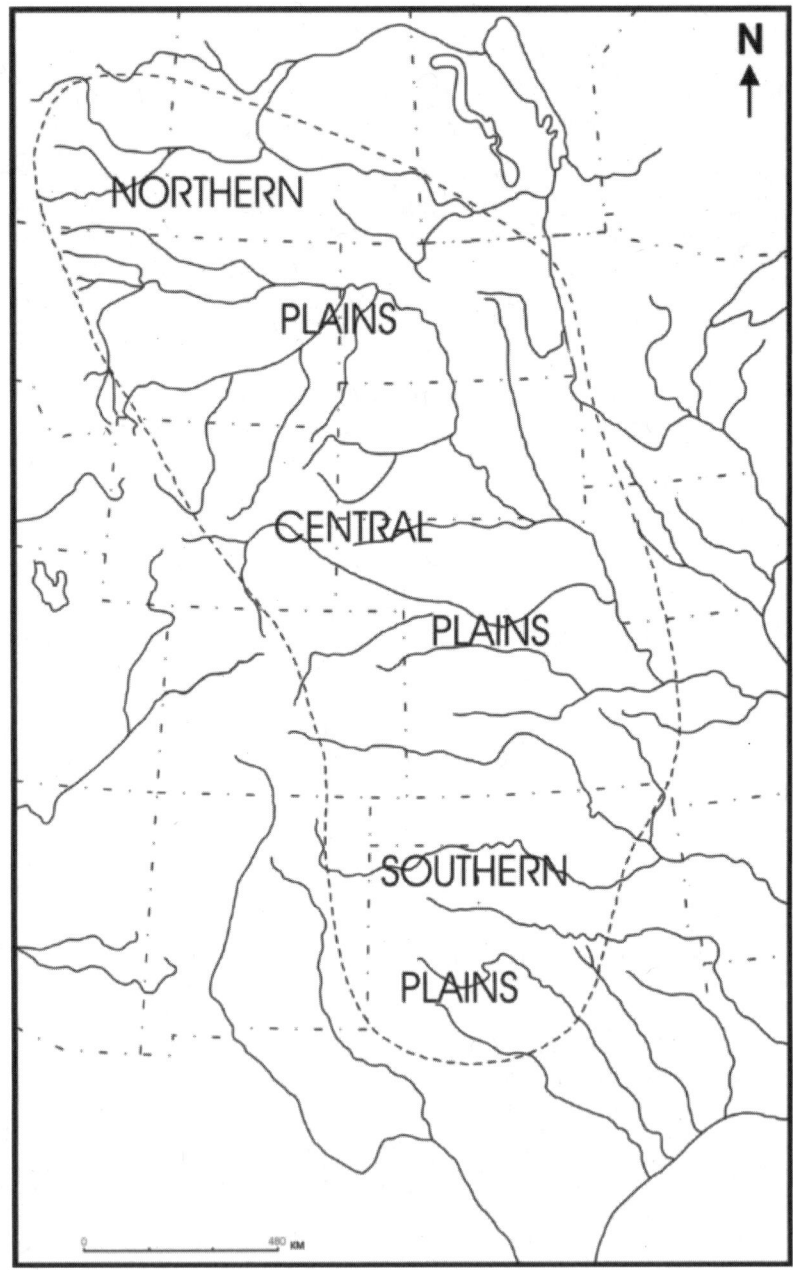

Figure 2.1. Map of the Great Plains Showing the Subdivisions Identified as the Northern, Central and Southern Plains.

by Vehik (2001) and includes portions of eastern New Mexico, most of Texas, western Oklahoma, southern Kansas and southern Colorado. The Central Plains combines Frison's (2001) Central Plains with most of his northwestern Plains and includes eastern Colorado and Wyoming, all of South Dakota, Nebraska and Kansas, and extreme western Iowa and Missouri. Finally, the Northern Plains, as defined here, consists of eastern Montana and most of North Dakota as well as southern Alberta, southern Saskatchewan and southwestern Manitoba.

The Hypsithermal and Its Impacts
The Hypsithermal, also referred to as the Altithermal or mid-Holocene thermal maximum, is generally characterized as an episode of aridity identified in numerous paleoenvironmental proxy records across North America and Europe. Even though the effects of the arid climate were manifest across the Great Plains, the dates for the onset and termination of this climatic interval are time-transgressive across the Northern Plains. In Alberta, for example, the Hypsithermal generally is assumed to have lasted from 9200 to 5900 BP or slightly later (Anderson et al. 1989; Vance et al. 1995), whereas in southwestern Manitoba and North Dakota the interval extended from 8500 to 4800 BP (Barnosky et al. 1987; Yansa 2007). The decreased precipitation and increased temperatures during this interval lowered water tables, increased salinity in ponds and lakes, expanded grasslands, decreased vegetation cover and increased fire frequency (Anderson et al. 1989; Vance et al. 1995). The sparse vegetation cover, in turn, influenced the nature and distribution of bison herds which apparently completely abandoned the Southern Plains (Vehik 2001), moved into the mountainous terrain of the Central Plains (Frison 2001) and appear to have moved to the peripheries of the Northern Plains whose boundaries expanded northward at this time (Reeves 1973). Together, these aspects of the Hypsithermal climate influenced the habitability of the Plains environment.

The decrease in vegetation cover also accelerated the rate of erosion and sediment delivery to the drainage systems and activated a number of dune fields scattered across the Great Plains (e.g. Eckerle 1997; Havholm and Running 2005; Meltzer 1999; Oetelaar 2004; Sauchyn 1990; Wolfe et al. 2002). Of course, the mobilization of sediments entails the removal of material from one part of the landscape and its subsequent deposition elsewhere. The former process can destroy or modify culture-bearing deposits (e.g. Frison 2001: 134; Seebach 2002) whereas the latter often buries and thus preserves cultural materials, including some redeposited artifacts. Of particular interest to archaeologists are the contexts of deposition which, in most of the western Great Plains, can be identified by the presence of Mazama ash. This tephra, which was deposited 6730 ± 45 BP (Hallett et al. 1997) or 7627 ± 150 BP (Zdanovich et al. 1999), has been found in alluvial sediments along major rivers and their tributaries (Davis and Greiser 1992; Oetelaar 2002; Waters and Rutter 1984); in lakes, wetlands, and prairie potholes (e.g. Sauchyn and Sauchyn 1991; Vreeken 1994); in bluff edge dunes (David 1970; Oetelaar 2004); in alluvial fans (e.g. Beaudoin and King 1994; Roed and Wasylyk 1973), and in colluvial settings (e.g. Reeves and Dormaar 1972). Together, these geomorphological processes influenced the differential preservation and visibility of the archaeological remains dating to this time interval.

The paucity of sites on the Great Plains during the Hypsithermal is thus attributed to the inhospitable nature of the environment or to the destructive nature of geomorphological processes operative at this time. Forbis (1992: 59), for example, believes that the lower frequency of sites dating to this interval cannot be attributed to geological processes or failure to recognize particular point types. Instead, he maintains that continuous human settlement on the Northern Plains was possible only after the Hypsithermal (ca. 5000 BP) because of (1) climatic amelioration, (2) the emergence of the modern species of *Bison bison*, (3) the use of the dog and travois to travel across the arid sea of grass, (4) the use of the tipi and ceremonial structures "built of native field stone ... leaving remains of tipi rings, cairns, boulder effigies and possibly other stone alignments, and (5) the development of an innovative method of cooking by stone boiling. The latter strategy allowed the preparation of bone grease and marrow to be used for pemmican, a reliable, storable, portable and nutritious foodstuff. Reeves (1973), by contrast, attributes the poor representation of archaeological sites to geomorphological processes and the failure of archaeologists to identify Middle Prehistoric projectile points in surface collections. Archaeological sites investigated as part of the SCAPE project allow us to address many of the issues relating to the differential preservation and visibility of cultural materials dating to this time interval as well as evaluate some of the suggested changes in adaptation. Each one of these topics is reviewed and evaluated in light of this new evidence.

Intensity of Human Occupation

Faced with the challenges of coping with scarce resources during the Hypsithermal, human groups changed their lifestyles and implemented a variety of adaptive strategies. Discussions of changes in adaptive strategies during this interval run the gamut from total abandonment of the Plains to essentially no change in subsistence and settlement practices. One of the key issues in evaluating human responses to the Hypsithermal then is determining the extent of human occupation within the Great Plains. The magnitude of human occupation can be measured at the level of the site or the region. Regionally, the intensity of human use of the landscape is measured by the number of sites present within a study area and this is the topic which has garnered the greatest amount of debate. In an early summary of Plains prehistory, Mulloy (1958: 208–09) noted a general paucity of sites dating between 7000 and 5000 BP and proposed the hypothesis that the Plains area might have been abandoned at this time due

CHAPTER 2: Human Ecology of the Canadian Prairie Ecozone ca. 6000 BP

to the unfavourable climate, although he did acknowledge the possibility of sampling biases. This proposal was soon challenged by Hurt (1966) who argued instead for a reduction in human populations, especially during the early part of the Hypsithermal, and a greater use of refuges located along the northern, eastern and western peripheries of the Great Plains as well as in the vicinity of rivers and springs originating in the mountainous areas. By 1973, Reeves even challenged the proposed reduction in human populations arguing that sampling biases were largely responsible for the marked decrease in the number of sites dating to this interval. The sampling biases were attributed to the differential preservation and visibility of sites and the failure of archaeologists to recognize Early Middle Prehistoric projectile points in surface collections.

Instead of resolving the issue, these studies have simply served to establish the terms of reference for the debate. There is general consensus that the number of sites dating to the early Middle Prehistoric Period (ca. 7500–5000 BP) is small when compared to those from the preceding or succeeding periods (Dyck and Morlan 2001; Frison 2001; Vehik 2001) but the reason for the disparity is still contested. For example, Wedel (1978: 199) suggested that only the short grass Plains were abandoned in favour of the mountains during this interval whereas Forbis (1992) and Albanese and Frison (1995) argued that the lower frequency of occupation during the Hypsithermal cannot be attributed to geological processes or failure to recognize particular points types. Buchner (1980) and Sheehan (1994, 2002) favour a change in settlement pattern with a greater emphasis on refugia which now include not only the margins of the Plains but also springs, major river valleys and localized uplands within the Great Plains. By contrast, Husted (2002) redefines the Northwestern Plains to exclude all mountainous terrain, including the Black Hills of South Dakota and isolated mountain groups in central Montana, to assert his position concerning the Hypsithermal abandonment of the high western Plains. Finally, Meltzer (1991, 1999) argues that different strategies may have been used by different groups depending on the severity of the environmental changes. Thus, groups may have totally abandoned the Southern Plains (e.g. Vehik 2001), moved toward refugia in the Central Plains (e.g. Sheehan 1994) and changed their settlement strategies only slightly, if at all, in the Northern Plains (e.g. Dyck and Morlan 2001).

Regardless of the strategies adopted by the groups occupying the different regions of the Great Plains, the number of sites dating to the Hypsithermal interval is still consistently lower than that of preceding or succeeding episodes, even in the Northern Plains (e.g. Albanese and Frison 1995; Greiser 1985; Forbis 1992; Vehik 2001; Walker 1992; but see Larson 1997). Perhaps then, the paucity of sites reflects a number of taphonomic processes which conspire either to destroy a large number of sites or to bury the cultural deposits beneath several metres of sediment as suggested by Reeves (1973). That is, the lack of sites may be the product of natural processes, not the result of changes in human use of the landscape. The biases engendered by these mid-Holocene geomorphological processes have been described and discussed in a number of geoarchaeolgical publications (e.g. Albanese 2000; Artz 2000; Bettis 1995; Mandel 1992; Waters and Kuehn 1996; Wilson 1983). Further, cultural deposits dating to this interval are frequently discovered in a variety of deeply buried contexts including alluvial terraces (e.g. Cyr 2006; Walker 1992; Wilson 1974; Zurburg 1991), alluvial fans (e.g. Gryba 1975), bluff edge dunes (e.g. Oetelaar 2004), sand dunes (e.g. Doll 1982), hummocky moraine (e.g. Van Dyke and Stewart 1985), and colluvial settings (e.g. Reeves and Dormaar 1972). Therefore, archaeologists can no longer rely on the results of surface surveys to establish the intensity of human occupation during different time periods (e.g. Artz 1996; Sheehan 1995, 1996).

Although not designed to address the regional intensity of landscape use, the results of the SCAPE project nonetheless offer some interesting new insights on the differential preservation of mid-Holocene archaeological deposits (e.g. Kasstan 2004; Klassen 2003, 2004; Meyer 2003, 2004; Nicholson and Playford 2009; Oetelaar 2004, 2006; Roskowski 2004). At all three localities, deposits dating to the 6000-year-old time interval were uncovered beneath several metres of alluvial, colluvial and aeolian sediments (Figure 2.2). Although some of these sites had been the subject of earlier investigations (e.g. Gryba

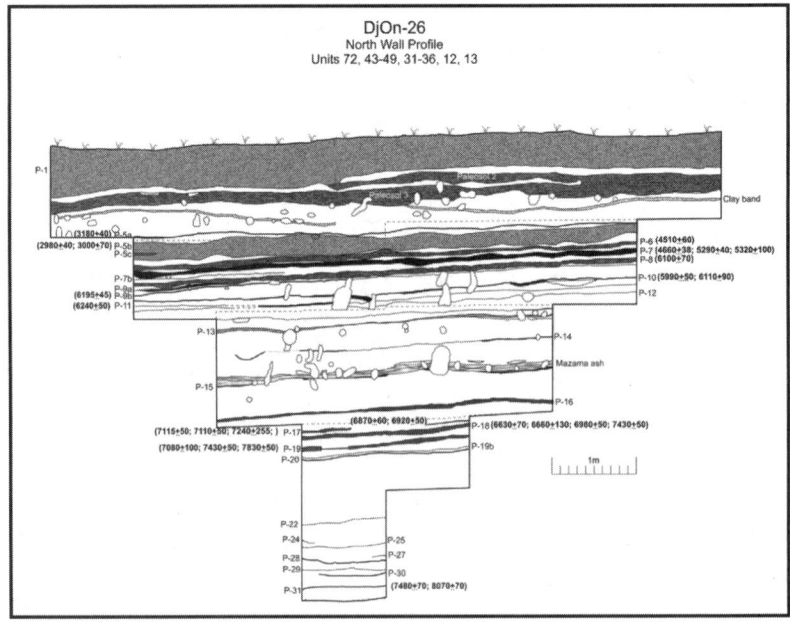

Figure 2.2: Profile of the Stampede Site Showing the 6000-Year-Old Cultural Deposits at Depths Ranging from 1.5 to 4 Metres Below Surface (dates listed derive from Gryba 1975; Meyer et al. 2009; Oetelaar 2004, 2006; Vivian et al. 2008).

Figure 2.3. Projectile Points Recovered from Cultural Deposits Dating Between 3000 and 6100 BP. Numbers Correspond to Paleosols Identified on Figure 2.2.

1975; Meyer 1990; Wilson 1982), others were discovered by chance and by design. Perhaps the most significant contribution of the SCAPE project in this area was the detailed geoarchaeological work associated with the identification of landforms which had the potential of yielding cultural deposits dating to this time period. For example, Robertson (2002, 2006) used the bucket auger and geoprobe to identify a number of alluvial fans and terraces in the Cypress Hills with deeply buried cultural materials comparable to those uncovered at the Stampede site. Similarly, Oetelaar (2002) outlined a model of terrace development along the major rivers and their tributaries which allows researchers to identify landforms of an appropriate age, most of which show a succession of overbank deposits spanning the interval from 9000 to 5000 BP. Further, Havholm and Running (2005) note that dunes were more active during the mid-Holocene climatic optimum which has resulted in the better preservation of deposits formed near the end of this phase in southwestern Manitoba.

In addition to the effects of geomorphological processes, the lack of sites dating to this time period has also been attributed to the failure of archaeologists to recognize and correctly assign many of the associated points (Reeves 1973). This argument essentially holds that many of the diagnostic projectile points dating to this time period are incorrectly identified as more recent side- or corner-notched types such as Hanna, Pelican Lake and Besant. In an attempt to resolve the typological confusion for this period, Walker (1992) used discriminant function analysis to define five point types that overlap spatially and temporally but form a sequence spanning more than 2,500 years. As a result of the SCAPE project, the number of points from datable contexts has increased significantly (e.g. Kasstan 2004; Oetelaar 2004), including material from the first excavated component in southwestern Manitoba (Nicholson and Playford 2009). Although no attempt was made to use Walker's (1992) discriminant function, the morphological variety in the sample of points from dated contexts at Stampede, Below Forks and Atkinson clearly exceeds the five types defined for this period. More importantly, several of the points from the Stampede site would, if found on the surface, be identified as Besant, Hanna, or even Pelican Lake (Figure 2.3). Therefore, the point typology for this time period is in need of substantive revision but archaeologists must also acknowledge the very real possibility that many of the established types actually persist for much longer intervals than previously accepted.

Changes in Settlement and Subsistence Strategies

Although total abandonment of the Northern Plains is rarely accepted as an explanation for the paucity of sites dating to the Hypsithermal, changes in settlement strategies are still invoked. To the majority of researchers, for example, surface water became rare, unpredictable, and generally non potable whereas the discharge in rivers and springs decreased substantially. Further, the entire region is assumed to have experienced "a reduction in the total amount of plants and animals available for harvest and an overall concentration of the remaining resources in areas with permanent water" (Bamforth 1997: 36). Variously identified as oases or refugia, these concentrations of resources presumably occurred along the peripheries of the Plains proper or along major river valleys, near perennial springs and near localized uplands within the CPE proper (e.g. Buchner 1980; Meltzer 1999; Sheehan 1994, 2002; Walker 1992). As noted by Sheehan (1994: 117, emphasis in original), however, "we cannot assume that *all* river basins represented potential refugia" because even some of the larger rivers on the Plains sometimes run dry during the summer months. Further, on the Southern High Plains, even "seeps and springs declined or

CHAPTER 2: Human Ecology of the Canadian Prairie Ecozone ca. 6000 BP

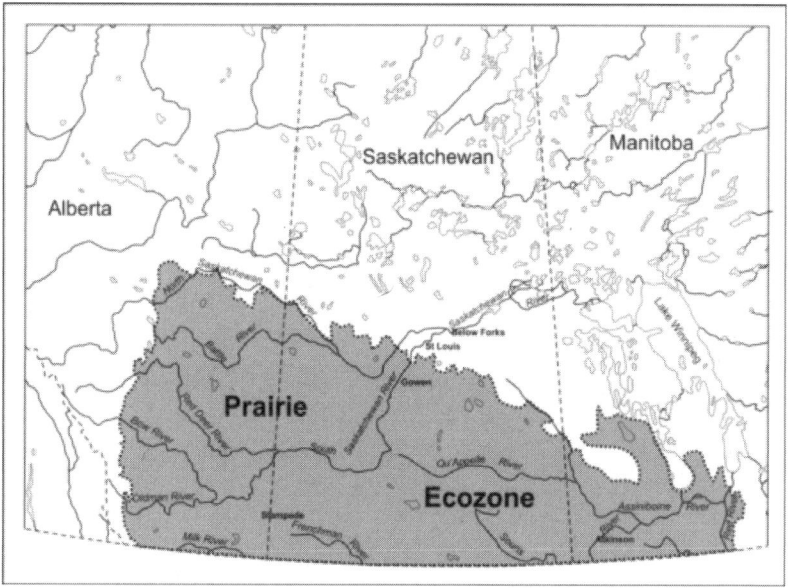

Figure 2.4. Map of the Canadian Prairie Ecozone Showing the Location of Sites Relative to the Prairie Soils and Associated Vegetation.

disappeared in places as aquifer recharge failed to keep pace with discharge" (Meltzer 1999: 405).

On the Southern High Plains or Llano Estacado the water table was lowered by an estimated three metres, prompting groups in New Mexico and Texas to dig wells in the bottom of drainages to access ground water (Evans 1951; Meltzer 1991; Meltzer and Collins 1987). In the Central and Northern Plains, major aquifers such as the Ogallala may have been able to sustain springs and ground water seeps because of the higher recharge rates, storage capacity and overall volume (Meltzer 1999; Sheehan 1994). In addition, the rivers originating in the Rocky Mountains, especially the major rivers on the Northern Plains, were probably able to maintain discharge over most if not all of their courses (Hurt 1966; Meltzer 1999). Human responses to the decreasing availability of potable water on the Central and Northern Plains thus involved increasing use of refugia along the margins of the Plains or near major rivers and springs.

Of the sites examined as part of the SCAPE project, the Below Forks site is located along the Saskatchewan rivers near the northern limits of the modern parkland whereas the St. Louis site is located along the South Saskatchewan near the southern limits of the modern parkland (Figure 2.4). However, both of these sites would have been situated within the grassland environment during the Hypsithermal (Johnston 2005: 46). Although currently buried beneath the sands of the Lauder Sand Hills, the Atkinson site is today (and was at the time of occupation) situated within the CPE along the shores of the Souris River. The Stampede site, in turn, is located within the Cypress Hills near a small spring-fed stream emptying into Elkwater Lake although the lake may have been dry at this time because the oldest date obtained from the basal sediments of numerous cores is only 5000 BP. Nonetheless, the springs along the north face of the Cypress Hills are fed by very strong aquifers which, given the orographic effect of the hills (e.g. Holmes 1969), would have been replenished almost every year. Thus, Middle Prehistoric camp sites on the Northern Plains, including those investigated as part of the SCAPE project, tend to occur in the vicinity of reliable sources of water. Whether or not such settlement strategies represent a departure from those used by previous or succeeding occupants of the area is a topic in need of further study. Certainly, the occupations at three of the sites (Below Forks, St. Louis and Stampede) continued well beyond the end of the Hypsithermal, whereas occupations at the Stampede and St. Louis sites may well have started before the onset of arid conditions.

The arid conditions of the Hypsithermal not only caused a decrease in the availability of potable water but also a reduction in biomass, particularly the number of bison. Although Bamforth (1997) identifies a number of human responses to the changes in the resource base, only the increase in diet breadth will be considered here. Evidence for a change in diet on the Southern Plains is limited given the paucity of sites dating to this interval but the data currently available suggest increased reliance on plants and a wide variety of smaller animals (Bamforth 1997; Vehik 2001). In the Central Plains, the predicted increase in diet breadth, particularly the focus on plants, is not supported even though the earliest evidence of preserved floral remains comes from components dating to this interval (e.g. Greiser 1985; Creasman and Thompson 1997). Frison (1997, 2001), however, argues for a decreased reliance on bison and a greater concentration on small mammals and plants because the sophisticated methods of communal bison hunting developed during Paleoindian times were no longer sustainable except in refugia such as the Black Hills. Dyck and Morlan (2001), by contrast, suggest that diet breadth remained unchanged on the Northern Plains and that the reliance on bison did not abate during the Hypsithermal.

Although a number of taxa are represented in the faunal assemblages from the Stampede, Below Forks and Atkinson sites, bison is, by far, the dominant species being hunted at this time. Additional taxonomic groups represented in the assemblages from these sites include canids, cervids, waterfowl, and perhaps rodents. At the same time, there is very little evidence for increased reliance on plant resources even though flotation and wet screening were used during the excavation of these sites. Although the samples are no doubt biased by the differential preservation of unburned materials, the few charred plant remains recovered from the deposits derive from species which could have entered the archaeological record through various means (e.g. Siegfried 2002). For example, the plants may have been charred as the occupants of the site cleared the living space by burning the vegetation. Alternatively, the taxa may have been used as fuel for the domestic fires or they may have been discarded during an episode of site maintenance. The latter botanical materials may have been brought into camp for use as tools or medicine, or they may simply have been collected incidentally during the episode of maintenance. Finally, the species in question may have been specifically collected for use as food. Either way, the botanical resources available in the immediate vicinity of the sites do not appear to have contributed significantly to the diet of the occupants although we recognize the inevitable biases which tend to conspire against the importance of plants as food resources in the past.

Even though bison remained the dominant prey for groups occupying the Northern Plains during the Hypsithermal, hunting strategies may have been adjusted to accommodate changes in the foraging behaviour of this species. Given the sparse vegetation cover on the grasslands, bison populations would have congregated along major drainages and localized uplands such as the Cypress Hills. In these selected locales, communal bison procurement may still have been feasible but elsewhere on the Northern Plains bison hunting "probably was carried out on an encounter basis by small groups of people taking small numbers of animals at any one time" (Bamforth 1997: 38). To date, only one communal kill site, Hawken, has been identified (Frison et al. 1976) whereas other kill sites have been interpreted as opportunistic hunts where small herds or individual animals were driven into snowdrifts, ambushed at water holes or mired in mud (e.g. Landals 1986, 1990; Walker 1992: 130; Wilson 1974, 1983; Zurburg 1991). Significantly, all of these sites occur within refugia suggesting that encounter strategies were preferred at this time. Although Landals (1986: 214–16) notes the advantages of using such strategies in mountainous environments, the evidence from other sites suggests that similar opportunistic hunting also occurred in the major river valleys. Perhaps then, the number of animals actually did decrease during the Hypsithermal and the concentration of bison in refugia was substantively less than expected.

Alternatively, the opportunistic hunting strategies may have been designed to exploit a species of bison whose behaviour was markedly different from the modern *Bison bison*. The species identified at most of the kill sites on the Northern Plains was *Bison bison occidentalis*. These animals were very large with particularly massive horn cores, especially among the males (Frison et al. 1976). Wilson (1978) defines a chronoclinal trend in dwarfing throughout the Holocene which may have accelerated somewhat during the Hypsithermal and defines an arbitrary point in time (5000 BP) when the transition from *Bison bison occidentalis* to *Bison bison bison* occurs. Despite the number of taxonomic analyses including recent mtDNA studies (Shapiro et al. 2004), there are very few attempts to explain potential differences in the behaviour of the animals. Larger horns and increased sexual dimorphism are sometimes viewed as characteristic of animals living in smaller herds. If so, *Bison bison occidentalis* may have been better suited to opportunistic hunting, although such behavioural differences fail to account for the communal hunts at Hawken, for example.

The increased incidence of pathologies has also been used as evidence for bison populations under stress during the Hypsithermal. On the Southern Plains, the increased incidence of dental anomalies on bison killed at this time suggests the presence of a species under stress or one whose diet includes a great deal of grit (Meltzer 1999; Vehik 2001). By contrast, the limited number of pathologies observed in the skeletal remains at the Hawken site suggests that the animals on the Central Plains were in good health (Frison et al. 1976). On the Northern Plains, Zurburg (1991: 159–64) identifies a bison population under stress based on the high attrition rate for the molars, the incidence of dental anomalies, and the shorter lifespan for the animals at the Norby site. The faunal assemblages from other sites do not exhibit comparable signs of stress and none of the animals represented at the Stampede, Below Forks or Atkinson site show pathologies suggestive of a species under stress, although sample sizes are small and most of the bone is highly fragmented.

Changes in Social Organization
Using examples from the Southern and Central Plains, Bamforth (1997) identifies two possible social responses to resource stress including an increase in mobility or a decrease in group size to fit the resource base. To infer mobility patterns from the archaeological data, he uses the density of artifacts and the nature of the features present to determine the duration of site occupation and the sourcing of lithic raw materials to estimate the size of the area over which groups moved. For his sample, artefact density as measured by the number of pieces of worked stone per square metre of excavation suggests increasingly transient camps. Similarly, the lower proportion of extremely heavily fired hearths at the Allen site indicates shorter residence times for the Early Archaic occupants. Bamforth (1997) also views the shift from post moulds to stone circles at Hell Gap as an indication of a change toward increasingly temporary site occupations. Finally, raw materials used in the production of projectile points recovered from communal kill sites in Wyoming indicate a reduction in the reliance on exotic stone and, by extension, a decrease in range size. In short, Bamforth (1997) argues for more ephemeral occupations by smaller residence groups during the Hypsithermal.

On the Northern Plains, Dyck and Morlan (2001) use the variety in point types and the preponderance of local raw materials to argue for a sparse population with little opportunity for frequent communication and trade. By contrast, Greiser (1985) attributes the significant increase in technological variability evident in early Archaic assemblages to the increased interaction among various cultures as these groups congregated in refugia along the margins of the Central Plains. The data from the Stampede, Below Forks and Atkinson site tend to support some aspects of these models while challenging others. For example, local raw materials appear to have been used by groups occupying all three sites with only a limited number of exotic sources represented. The density of artifacts at Stampede and Below Forks clearly exceeds the levels postulated above but the differences could be attributed to differential recovery. At the Stampede site, for example, wet screens with 2 mm openings were used to recover the small debris normally associated with the drop zone around a hearth. Not surprisingly, very dense concentrations of small (<1 cm) lithic and faunal remains were uncovered in the immediate vicinity of these features. Similar recovery levels were obtained during the excavation of the lower component at the Below Forks site. These data suggest that occupations at Stampede and at Below Forks cannot be considered ephemeral although the different interpretation may reflect recovery bias more than a change in social organization.

Changes in Architecture and Facilities

The ethnological data and models used by Bamforth (1997) predict an increase in range size with a decrease in biomass but his archaeological data, namely the proportion of exotic materials, suggest otherwise. Similarly, the density of artifacts from the Stampede and Below Forks site indicates more prolonged use of these locations, contrary to the expectations for the mobility patterns of these groups. Although the archaeological data are not consistent with the models derived from ethnological data, they may indicate that human groups were limiting their travels to areas with reliable sources of water and were remaining within these refugia for extended periods of time. The concentration of human activities within refugia has obvious implications for the patterned use of space and the conservation of resources. People planning to stay in an area over a prolonged period of time select places where resources are plentiful and devise strategies which allow them to remain at the locus of occupation over a longer interval. Archaeologists have developed a number of strategies to identify sites with intensive occupation including evidence for the construction of more durable facilities, the periodic maintenance of the living space, the management of local resources, and the accommodation of potential social conflicts (e.g. Binford 1983; Camilli 1983; Dewar and McBride 1992; Oetelaar 2006; Smith and McNees 1999; Wandsnider 1992). Many of these changes in the patterned use of space and the conservation of resources entail changes in architecture and technology which can be identified in the archaeological record.

The primary evidence for long-term land use of refugia involves the repeated and prolonged occupation of particular sites. On the Southern Plains there is, as noted earlier, very little evidence of human occupation, let alone prolonged or repeated occupations of specific locations. On the Central Plains, many caves and rockshelters include signs of repeated use whereas open sites with good stratified sequences of Early Archaic materials are rare (Frison 2001:

133). On the Northern Plains, caves and rockshelters are comparatively rare whereas open sites tend to have the stratified sequences with occupations dating to this interval (Gryba 1975). However, the number of sites with evidence of repeated and prolonged occupation during the Hypsithermal does not exceed that of preceding or succeeding periods, especially when one includes sites with compressed stratigraphy. In the Cypress Hills, for example, the Stampede site, located on the eastern margin of the lake, is deeply stratified with the main occupations spanning the interval between 8000 and 5000 BP whereas DjOn-8, which is situated on the western margin of the lake, has evidence of intensive human use from 5000 BP to the time of contact (Brumley et al. 1981). If anything, the repeated use of specific sites, including kill sites, is far more common after 5000 BP on the Northern Plains (e.g. Reeves 1990).

Within refugia, the repeated use of a particular location may not be as important as the duration of individual occupations (Oetelaar 2006). Prolonged occupation of a site generally entails the construction of more durable facilities as indicated by the nature of house remains and the associated storage facilities (e.g. McGuire and Schiffer 1983). Bamforth (1997), for example, interprets the shift from post moulds to stone circles at Hell Gap as indicative of a change toward increasingly temporary occupations from Paleoindian to Early Archaic times. On the Southern Plains, no architectural facilities have been identified (Meltzer 1999; Vehik 2001) whereas caves, rockshelters and pit house structures with internal hearths, storage facilities and post moulds are common in the Central Plains during this interval (e.g. Frison 1991: 83–86; Metcalf and Black 1997; Waitkus and Eckles 1997). Human groups apparently sought shelter from the summer heat in the caves and rockshelters (Greiser 1985) whereas they used the pit houses primarily during the winter months (Creasman and Thompson 1997). On the Northern Plains, the architectural remains uncovered to date are limited to partial stone circles (e.g. Van Dyke and Stewart 1986), a rectangular arrangement of four post moulds at the Gowen 2 site (Walker 1992: 119) and an arc of shallow post moulds, presumably the remains of a structure, from the Stampede site. In this case, however, the more durable structures with post moulds occur in Early Archaic contexts whereas the stone circles tend to be associated with later occupations. Using Bamforth's (1997) logic, the evidence from the Northern Plains would suggest more prolonged occupations during the Hypsithermal, a conclusion consistent with the inferred reliance on refugia. However, both types of architectural facilities continue to be used well after the end of the Hypsithermal by groups whose mobility strategies varied substantively from one region to the next. Perhaps then, the different types of architectural facilities should be defined on the basis of more data than a simple distinction between the arrangement of post moulds and the presence of stone circles. Obviously, the pit houses identified at Central Plains sites represent a much larger investment of time and energy in the construction of a shelter than do either stone circles or circular arrangements of post moulds.

Prolonged occupation of a site may also entail the design, construction, and repeated use of facilities such as wells, hearths and pit features. On the Southern Plains, for example, the construction and use of wells to access water indicates a prolonged use and attachment to place (e.g. Meltzer 1991). Pit features filled with fire-cracked rock do occur in this area but large storage pits comparable to those from the Central Plains have yet to be identified. In addition to the winter and summer camps with their hearths and storage cists, the temporary and logistical camp sites on the Central Plains often include pits filled with fire cracked rock and charcoal, many of which exhibit signs of repeated use. As noted by Frison (2001: 135), the easiest way to preserve a pit for later use is to fill the feature with debris between episodes of use. On the Northern Plains, hearths and, to a lesser extent, pit features do occur on sites dating to this interval but there are relatively few signs that these facilities were designed or constructed for prolonged or repeated use. Hearths and pit features uncovered at the Stampede, Below Forks, and Atkinson site are certainly consistent with this observed trend although the presence of a sand layer covering the hearth at Atkinson may have served to preserve the feature for later use much as filling the pits with debris between episodes of use at Central Plains sites.

The wells, pit houses, earth ovens and stone boiling pits appear to represent innovations introduced during the Hypsithermal but such conclusions may be spurious. In terms of the wells, for example, only the most recent episodes of use will tend to be represented in the sample of datable materials recovered from these features. Further, the Early Archaic as well as possible Late Paleoindian surfaces may have eroded away, leaving only the preserved basal remnants of some of these features. Similarly, earth ovens and stone boiling pits have a long tradition of use by late Paleoindian Foothill-Mountain groups (Frison 2001) but they have also been found at Paleoindian sites on the Northern Plains (e.g. Armstrong 1993). Thus, the evidence does not support the introduction of these innovations although the data do suggest an increased reliance on these facilities. At the same time, the majority of these architectural innovations continue to be used until the time of contact, suggesting that prolonged occupation of specific site locations was not restricted to refugia used during the Hypsithermal.

Prolonged occupation of a site also entails careful organization and regular maintenance of the living space. Periodic maintenance of the living space can be assessed from the size and density of debris present on the occupation surface. That is, intensively used and regularly maintained work spaces tend to accumulate high concentrations of very small debris but comparatively little obtrusive refuse (e.g. Hayden and Cannon 1983; Oetelaar 1993). However, determining the intensity of site maintenance necessitates the use of fine-scale recovery procedures. Unfortunately, such excavation strategies are rarely used on the Great Plains and, not surprisingly, there is very little information on this aspect of site use. However, the dense concentrations of very small debris around the hearths uncovered at the Stampede site suggest relatively prolonged occupation of this site between 7500 and 4500 BP. A similar pattern was observed at the Below Forks site where substantive quantities of small lithic debitage occur in the vicinity of features associated with the earliest component at the site. Perhaps, then, this aspect of spatial organization is in need of further examination in the future.

Changes in Food Preparation and Storage Strategies

Given the lack of evidence for a change in the composition of the diet, several authors have argued for a change in food preparation strategies, particularly a shift toward a more intensive use of the limited resources available at this time (e.g. Hofman 1997). For example, Forbis (1992) argues that hunters killed a limited number of animals at any one time but butchered their prey very efficiently. Further, innovative cooking techniques such as stone boiling allowed the preparation of bone grease and marrow for the production of pemmican—a reliable, storable, portable, and nutritious foodstuff. However, Forbis (1992) believes that these innovations did not appear until the end of the Hypsithermal ca. 5000 BP (see also Reeves 1990). Similarly, the increased emphasis on plant resources, especially grass seeds, would have permitted greater reliance on storage and, by extension, a more intensive use of the landscape (Eckerle 1997). The best residential strategy under these circumstances would be to build an efficient shelter near a reliable source of firewood and water, collect and efficiently process as many resources as possible, store as much food as practicable, and use these supplies to tide the group through episodes of scarcity.

Archaeological evidence for the preparation of bone grease and the production of pemmican includes hearths showing traces of prolonged use, stone-boiling pits, quantities of fire-cracked rock, and extremely comminuted bones (e.g. Leechman 1951; Quigg 1997; Vehik 1977). On the Southern Plains, evidence for the preparation of bone grease and pemmican is generally limited to sites of more recent age (e.g. Quigg 1997), presumably reflecting the absence of bison during the Hypsithermal. On the Central Plains, Frison (2001) identifies basin-shaped fire pits, some of which contained stones to hold the heat, as well as pits filled with fire-fractured rock and charcoal but interprets these as features designed for the preparation of vegetable food products. Although stone boiling was used to prepare a variety of foods including soups, stews, and bone grease, the function of archaeological features should be inferred based on the nature of the associated refuse. In this case, there is no indication as to whether or not these features were surrounded by scatters of bone fragments or botanical remains. Even though Forbis (1992) and Reeves (1990) identify the production of pemmican as an important innovation in the preparation of food on the Northern Plains, they place the introduction of this technology at the end of the Hypsithermal ca. 5000 BP. Certainly, the bone beds at the Maple Leaf, Mona

Lisa, and Norby sites (Landals 1986, 1990; Wilson 1974, 1983; Zurburg 1991) indicate the selective removal of carcass components rather than the efficient use of the entire animal. However, highly fragmented bones tend to occur at campsites where they are normally associated with features such as hearths, suggesting the possible production of pemmican (e.g. Walker 1992).

Evidence for the intensive processing of animal carcasses occurs at all three sites investigated as part of the SCAPE project. However, since all three sites have been identified as campsites, the presence of hearths and highly fragmented bone is hardly surprising. At the Atkinson site, the degree of fragmentation is, at least in part, attributable to the poor preservation of the faunal remains (Nicholson and Playford 2009). Further, a hearth is present but there is no associated pit feature and very little evidence of fire-broken rock. The assemblage from the early component at the Below Forks site also includes a number of hearths, some highly fragmented though poorly preserved bones, some fire-broken rock, but no pit features. Finally, the relevant occupations at the Stampede site have yielded hearths and associated pit features, one of which contained a sample of fire-broken rock. Although the number of identifiable pieces of fire-broken rock is generally quite small, the sample of pebble-sized rock fragments with evidence of heat alteration recovered by wet screening is quite large, suggesting the intensive re-use of the local rock for this purpose (*sensu* Brink and Dawe 2003). Further, the sample of faunal remains is very highly fragmented, with the majority of the pieces measuring less than one centimetre in maximum dimension. In this case, however, the concentration of small bone splinters, tiny pieces of debitage, and fragments of fire-broken rock is interpreted as evidence for the periodic maintenance of the work space around the hearths whereas the fireplaces and the associated pit features are inferred to be evidence of stone boiling. Whether or not the features were used for the preparation of bone grease or plant remains is open to debate pending further analysis of the data.

The importance of floral resources in the diet of the occupants may not be accurately reflected by the quantity of plant remains at sites dating to this period because of preservation biases (e.g. Kornfeld 1997). As a result, archaeologists have used the presence of specific tools and facilities to infer the nature and intensity of plant use. On the Central Plains, for example, more sophisticated grinding tools, such as manos and grinding slabs, were introduced at this time to process plant resources (see also Bamforth 1997; Frison 2001: 134) although Greiser (1985) actually reports a decrease in the proportion of milling stones for this interval, especially when compared to earlier and subsequent components. At the same time, manos and grinding stones are extremely rare on Early Archaic sites from the Northern Plains (Dyck and Morlan 2001), the few nondescript milling stones from Boss Hill notwithstanding (Doll 1982). None of the sites investigated as part of the SCAPE project yielded lithic artifacts identifiable as grinding stones or manos, although "hammerstones" occur in each one of the assemblages. Hammerstones generally include cobbles with evidence of pecking along the margins or on surfaces. However, as noted by Zarrillo and Kooyman (2006), such artifacts may actually have been used to process plant remains but such functions will remain undetected until archaeologists examine the surfaces for residues such as starch grains or phytoliths. Therefore, some of the artifacts identified as hammerstones at sites across the Great Plains may actually have been used for the preparation of plant foods.

Storage is identified as another strategy designed to cope with the unpredictable nature of resources available to the inhabitants of the Great Plains at this time (Larson 1997). Archaeological evidence of storage behaviour is generally based on the presence of storage facilities, primarily large underground pits. Such features have only been identified in caves, rockshelters and house pits on the Central Plains. No storage pits or comparable facilities have been reported from Early Archaic sites on the Southern or the Northern Plains. However, pits represent but one type of facility used for plant storage; others include ceramic containers, bins, internal or external racks, or bags suspended from architectural elements in the lodge. Although ceramic containers can be excluded for the Early Archaic, all other storage strategies could have been used. However, given the paucity of evidence for architectural facilities, inferences for the use of such facilities remain largely conjectural. Certainly, no evidence of storage facilities was uncovered at any of the sites examined during the SCAPE project.

Conclusion

In summary then, investigations at the Stampede, Below Forks, and Atkinson sites have provided interesting new insights on the impact of the Hypsithermal on human occupation of the CPE. For example, the cultural deposits at all three sites occur beneath several metres of sediment, indicating that the paucity of sites dating to this interval may indeed be a product of poor visibility as originally suggested by Reeves (1973). Geoarchaeological research at each of the sites, however, has generated a series of models which will help future archaeologists identify landforms which have a high potential of containing sites dating to this interval. At the same time, the diversity in the point assemblages recovered from the three sites suggests that the typology for this time period is in desperate need of revision before we will be able to identify these diagnostic artifacts in surface collections. Only then will we be in a position to determine more accurately the degree of human occupation of the Great Plains during the Hypsithermal.

In addition, the archaeological investigations at the Stampede, Below Forks and Atkinson sites have supported some—and challenged other—inferences on the adaptive responses of human groups to the effects of the Hypsithermal. Although far from conclusive, the data currently available suggest that occupations were by no means ephemeral even though the ranges of individual human groups may have been somewhat limited when compared to their predecessors. Similarly, there is at least some evidence in support of intensification in the preparation and storage of some foodstuffs. Whether or not these responses were the result of prolonged use of refugia remains a question in need of further research. Finally, our work suggests that archaeologists must change their recovery procedures in the future should they wish to increase their samples of botanical remains or to derive better assessments of site maintenance activities, particularly as these relate to the duration of site *occupation*.

Acknowledgements

The ideas for this paper developed through discussions with members of the SCAPE (Study of Cultural Adaptations in the Canadian Prairie Ecozone) project, particularly Bev Nicholson, Gary Running IV, Dion Wiseman, David Meyer, Alwynne Beaudoin and Andrea Freeman. I would also like to thank the two anonymous reviewers for their critical evaluations of the manuscript. Finally, none of this research would have been possible without the generous support of SSHRC through MCRI Grant #412-99-1000, the Alberta Historical Resources Foundation, Alberta Community Development, the University of Calgary, and the Archaeological Society of Alberta

References

Albanese, J. 2000. Resumé of Geoarchaeological Research on the Northern Plains. In *Geoarchaeology in the Great Plains*, ed. R.D. Mandel, 199–249. Norman, OK: University of Oklahoma Press.

Albanese, J.P. and G.C. Frison. 1995. Cultural and Landscape Change during the Middle Holocene, Rocky Mountain Area, Wyoming and Montana. In *Archaeological Geology of the Archaic Period in North America*, ed. E.A. Bettis III, 1–19. Boulder, CO: Geological Society of America, Special Paper 297.

Anderson, T.W., R.W. Mathewes and C.E. Schweger. 1989. Holocene Climatic Trends in Canada with Special Reference to the Hypsithermal Interval. In *Quaternary Geology of Canada and Greenland*, ed. R.J. Fulton, 520–28. Geology of Canada No. 1, Geological Survey of Canada.

Armstrong, S.W. 1993. Alder Complex Kitchens: Experimental Replication of Paleoindian Cooking Facilities. *Archaeology in Montana* 34, no. 2: 1–66.

Artz, J.A. 1996. Cultural Response or Geological Process? A Comment on Sheehan. *Plains Anthropologist* 41, no. 158: 383–93.

———. 2000. Archaeology and the Earth Sciences on the Northern Plains. In *Geoarchaeology in the Great Plains*, ed. R.D. Mandel, 250–85. Norman, OK: University of Oklahoma Press.

Bamforth, D. 1997. Adaptive Change on the Great Plains at the Paleoindian/Archaic Transition. In *Changing Perspectives of the Archaic on the Northwest Plains and Rocky Mountains*, ed. M.L. Larson and J.E. Francis, 14–54. Vermillion, SD: University of South Dakota Press.

Barnosky, C.W., E.C. Grimm and H.E. Wright, Jr. 1987. Towards a Postglacial History of the Northern Great Plains: A Review of the Paleoecologic Problems. *Annals of the Carnegie Museum* 56: 259–73.

Beaudoin, A.B. and R.H. King. 1994. Holocene Palaeoenvironmental Record Preserved in a Paraglacial Alluvial Fan in Sunwapta Pass, Jasper National Park, Alberta, Canada. *Catena* 22: 227–48.

Bettis III, E.A. 1995. *Archaeological Geology of the Archaic Period in North America*. Boulder, CO: Geological Society of America, Special Paper 297.

Binford, L.R. 1983. Long Term Land Use Patterns: Some Implications for Archaeology. In *Lulu Linear Punctated: Essays in Honor of George Irving Quimby*, ed. R.C. Dunnell and D.K. Grayson, 27–53. Ann Arbor, MI: Anthropological Papers, Museum of Anthropology, University of Michigan, No. 72.

Brink, J.W. and B. Dawe. 2003. Hot Rocks as Scarce Resources: The Use, Re-Use and Abandonment of Heating Stones at Head-Smashed-In Buffalo Jump. *Plains Anthropologist* 48, no. 186: 85–104.

Brumley J.H., B.J. Dau, M. Greene, L. Heikkila, J.M. Quigg, C. Rushworth and S. Saylor. 1981. Archaeological Salvage Investigations Conducted in 1979 and 1980 Within Cypress Hills Provincial Park. Manuscript on file (Permits 79–91 and 80–108c), Alberta Culture, Edmonton.

Buchner, A.P.1980. *Cultural Responses to Altithermal Climate Along the Eastern Margins of the North American Grasslands: 5,500 to 3,000 B.C.* Ottawa, ON: National Museum of Man Mercury Series Paper 97.

Camilli, E. 1983. Interpreting Long-Term Land-Use Patterns from Archaeological Landscapes. *American Archaeology* 7, no. 1: 57–66

Creasman, S.D. and K.W. Thompson. 1997. Archaic Settlement and Subsistence in the Green River Basin of Wyoming. In *Changing Perspectives of the Archaic on the Northwest Plains and Rocky Mountains*, ed. M.L. Larson and J.E. Francis, 242–304. Vermillion, SD: The University of South Dakota Press.

Cyr, T.J. 2006. The Dog Child Site (FbNp-24): A 5500 Year-Old Multi-component Site on the Northern Plains. MA thesis, University of Saskatchewan.

David, P.P. 1970. Discovery of Mazama Ash in Saskatchewan. *Canadian Journal of Earth Sciences* 7: 1579–83.

Davis, L.B. and S.T. Greiser. 1992. Indian Creek Paleoindians: Early Occupation of the Elkhorn Mountains' Southeast Flank, West-Central Montana. In *Ice Age Hunters of the Rockies*, ed. D.J. Stanford and J.S. Day, 225–83. Denver CO: Denver Museum of Natural History and University Press of Colorado.

Dewar, R.E. and K.A. McBride. 1992. Remnant Settlement Patterns. In *Space, Time, and Archaeological Landscapes*, ed. J. Rossignol and L. Wandsnider, 227–55. New York: Plenum Press.

Doll, M.V. 1982. *Boss Hill Site (FdPe4) Locality 2: Pre-Archaic Manifestations in the Parkland of Central Alberta, Canada*. Edmonton, AB: Human History, Occasional Paper 2, Provincial Museum of Alberta.

Dyck, I. and R.E. Morlan. 2001. Hunting and Gathering Tradition: Canadian Plains. *Handbook of North American Indians, Volume 13, Part I: Plains*, ed. R.J. DeMallie, 115–30. Washington, DC: Smithsonian Institution Press.

Eckerle, W.P. 1997. Eolian Geoarchaeology of the Wyoming Basin: Changing

Environments and Archaic Subsistence Strategies in the Holocene. In *Changing Perspectives of the Archaic on the Northwest Plains and Rocky Mountains*, ed. M.L. Larson and J.E. Francis, 138–67. Vermillion, SD: The University of South Dakota Press.

Evans, G. 1951. Prehistoric Wells in Eastern New Mexico. *American Antiquity* 17: 1–9.

Forbis, R.G. 1992. The Mesoindian (Archaic) Period in the Northern Plains. *Journal of American Archaeology* 5: 27–70.

Frison, G.C. 1991. *Prehistoric Hunters of the High Plains*. New York: Academic Press.

——. 1997. The Foothill-Mountain Late Paleoindian and Early Plains Archaic Chronology and Subsistence. In *Changing Perspectives of the Archaic on the Northwest Plains and Rocky Mountains*, ed. M.L. Larson and J.E. Francis, 84–104. Vermillion, SD: The University of South Dakota Press.

——. 2001. Hunting and Gathering Tradition: Northwestern and Central Plains. *Handbook of North American Indians, Volume 13, Part I: Plains*, ed. R.J. DeMallie, 131–45. Washington, DC: Smithsonian Institution Press.

Frison, G.C., M. Wilson and D.J. Wilson. 1976. "Fossil Bison and Artifacts from an Early Altithermal Period Arroyo Trap in Wyoming. *American Antiquity* 41: 28–57.

Greiser, S.T. 1985. *Predictive Models of Hunter-Gatherer Subsistence and Settlement Strategies on the Central High Plains*. Plains Anthropologist, Memoir 20.

Gryba, E.M. 1975. *The Cypress Hills Archaeological Site DjOn-26*. Edmonton, AB: Alberta Department of Recreation and Parks.

Hallett, D.J., L.V. Hills and J.J. Clague. 1997. New Accelerator Mass Spectrometry Radiocarbon Ages for the Mazama Tephra Layer from Kootenay National Park, British Columbia, Canada. *Canadian Journal of Earth Sciences* 34: 1202–09.

Havholm, K.G. and G.L. Running IV. 2005. Stratigraphy, Sedimentology, and Environmental Significance of Late Mid-Holocene Dunes, Lauder Sand Hills, Glacial Lake Hind Basin, Southwestern Manitoba. *Canadian Journal of Earth Sciences* 42: 847–63.

Hayden, B. and A. Cannon. 1983. Where the Garbage Goes: Refuse Disposal in the Maya Highlands. *Journal of Anthropological Archaeology* 2: 117–63.

Hofman, J.L. 1997. Preface: Changing the Plains Archaic. In *Changing Perspectives of the Archaic on the Northwest Plains and Rocky Mountains*, ed. M.L. Larson and J. E. Francis, xi–xxvi. Vermillion, SD: The University of South Dakota Press.

Holmes, R.M. 1969. A Study of the Climate of the Cypress Hills. *Weather* 24, no. 8: 324–30.

Hurt, W.R. 1966. The Altithermal and the Prehistory of the Northern Plains. *Quaternaria* 8: 101–14.

Husted, W.M. 2002. Archaeology in the Middle Rocky Mountains: Myopia, Misconceptions and Other Concerns. *Plains Anthropologist* 47, no. 183: 379–86.

Johnston, J.S. 2005. The St. Louis Site (FfNk-7) and the Below Forks Site (FhNg-25): The Faunal Analysis of Two Mummy Cave Series and Oxbow Complex Sites in Central Saskatchewan. MA thesis, University of Saskatchewan.

Kaastan, S.C. 2004. Lithic Technology at the Below Forks Site, FhNg-25: Strategems of Stone Tool Manufacture. MA thesis, University of Saskatchewan.

Klassen, J.A. 2003. Paleoenvironmental Interpretation of the Soils and Sediments of the Stampede Site (DjOn-26), Cypress Hills, Alberta. MA thesis, University of Calgary.

———. 2004. Paeloenvironmental Interpretations of the Paleosols and Sediments at the Stampede Site (DjOn-26), Cypress Hills, Alberta. *Canadian Journal of Earth Sciences* 41: 741–53.

Kornfeld, M. 1997. Affluent Foragers of the Western Black Hills: A Settlement and Subsistence Model. In *Changing Perspectives of the Archaic on the Northwest Plains and Rocky Mountains*, ed. M.L. Larson and J.E. Francis, 57–83. Vermillion, SD: The University of South Dakota Press.

Landals, A. 1986. The Maple Leaf Site: An Interpretation of Prehistoric Hunting and Butchering Strategies in the Southern Alberta Rockies. MA thesis, University of Calgary.

———. 1990. The Maple Leaf Site: Implications of the Analysis of Small-Scale Bison Kills. In *Hunters of the Recent Past*, ed. L.B. Davis and B.O.K. Reeves, 122–52. London, UK: Unwin Hyman.

Larson, M.L. 1997. Rethinking the Early Plains Archaic. In *Changing Perspectives of the Archaic on the Northwest Plains and Rocky Mountains*, ed. M.L. Larson and J.E. Francis, 106–36. Vermillion, SD: The University of South Dakota Press.

Leechman, D. 1951. Bone Grease. *American Antiquity* 16: 355–56.

Mandel, R. 1992. Soils and Holocene Landscape Evolution in Central and Southwestern Kansas: Implications for Archaeological Research. In *Soils in Archaeology: Landscape Evolution and Human Occupation*, ed. V.T. Holliday, 41–100. Washington, DC: Smithsonian Institution Press.

McGuire, R.H. and M.B. Schiffer. 1983. The Determinants of Architectural Desgin: A General Formulation. *Journal of Anthropological Archaeology* 2: 277–301.

Meltzer, D.J. 1991. Altithermal Archaeology and Paleoecology at Mustang Springs on the Southern High Plains of Texas. *American Antiquity* 56, no. 2: 236–67.

———. 1999. Human Responses to Middle Holocene (Altithermal) Climates on the North American Great Plains. *Quaternary Research* 52: 404–16.

Meltzer, D.J. and M.B. Collins. 1987. Prehistoric Water Wells on the Southern High Plains: Clues to Altithermal Climates. *Journal of Field Archaeology* 14: 9–28.

Metcalf, M.D. and K.D. Black. 1997. Archaic Period Logistical Organization in the Colorado Rockies. In *Changing Perspectives of the Archaic on the Northwest Plains and Rocky Mountains*, ed. M.L. Larson and J.E. Francis, 168–209. Vermillion, SD: The University of South Dakota Press.

Meyer, D. 1990. Test Excavation at the Below Forks Site (FhNg-25), 1989. Manuscript on file at the Heritage Branch of Saskatchewan Culture, Multiculturalism and Recreation, Regina.

———. 2003. Excavations at the Below Forks Site: The 2002 Season Interim Report. Manuscript on file at the Saskatchewan Heritage Branch, Regina.

———. 2004. Excavations at the St. Louis Site (FjNk-7): Interim Report on the 2003 Season. Manuscript on file at the Saskatchewan Heritage Branch, Regina.

Meyer, D.A., J. Blakey and J. Roe. 2009. Stampede Site (DjOn-26) Archaeological

Excavations 2008 Phase 2 Investigations, Final Report Permit 2008-257. Manuscript prepared for the Archaeology and History Section, Alberta Tourism, Parks, Recreation and Culture, Edmonton.

Mulloy, W.B. 1958. *A Preliminary Historical Outline for the Northwestern Plains*. University of Wyoming Publications 22.

Nicholson, B.A. and T. Playford. 2009. The Atkinson Site—A 6400 Year Old Gowen (Mummy Cave) Occupation near Lauder, Manitoba. *Plains Anthropologist* 54, no. 209: 29–48.

Oetelaar, G.A. 1993. Identifying Site Structure in the Archaeological Record: An Illinois Mississippian Example. *American Antiquity* 58, no. 4: 662–87.

———. 2002. River of Change: A Model for the Development of Terraces Along the Bow River, Alberta, *Géographie Physique et Quaternaire* 56: 155–69.

———. 2004. Six Meters Below Surface and Beyond: The Record of Human Occupation during the Archaic at the Stampede Site (DjOn-26), Cypress Hills, Alberta. Paper presented at the 62th Plains Anthropological Conference, October 13–16, 2004, Billings, Montana.

———. 2004. Landscape Evolution and Human Occupation during the Archaic Period on the Northern Plains. *Canadian Journal of Earth Sciences* 41: 725–40.

———. 2006. "Mobility and Territoriality on the Northwestern Plains of Alberta, Canada: A Phenomenological Approach." In *Notions de territoire et de mobilité exemples de l'Europe et des Premières Nations en Amérique du Nord avant le contact européen*, ed. C. Bressy, A. Burke, P. Chalard et H. Martin, 137–41. Liège, FR: Études et Recherches Archéologiques de l'Université de Liège, Numéro 116.

Quigg, J.M. 1997. Bison Processing at the Rush Site, 41TG346, and Evidence for Pemmican Production in the Southern Plains. *Plains Anthropologist* 42, no. 159: 145–61.

Reeves, B.O.K. 1973. The Concept of an Altithermal Cultural Hiatus in Northern Plains Prehistory. *American Anthropologist* 75, no. 5: 1221–53.

Reeves, B.O.K. and J.F. Dormaar. 1972. A Partial Holocene Pedological and Archaeological Record from the Southern Alberta Rocky Mountains. *Arctic and Alpine Research* 4, no. 4: 325–36.

Robertson, E.C. 2002. Depositional Environments and Archaeological Site Formation in the Cypress Hills, Southeastern Alberta. *Géographie Physique et Quaternaire* 56, nos. 2–3: 261–77.

———. 2006. Late Quaternary Landform Development, Paleoenvironmental Reconstruction and Archaeological Site Formation in the Cypress Hills of Southeastern Alberta. PhD dissertation, University of Calgary.Roed, M.A. and D.G. Wasylyk. 1973. Age of Inactive Alluvial Fans—Bow River Valley, Alberta. *Canadian Journal of Earth Sciences* 10: 1834–40.

Roskowski, L. 2004. The Geoarchaeology of the Below Forks Site (FhNg-25), Saskatchewan. M.A. thesis, University of Calgary.

Sauchyn, D.J. 1990. A Reconstruction of Holocene Geomorphology and Climate, Western Cypress Hills, Alberta and Saskatchewan. *Canadian Journal of Earth Sciences* 27: 1504–10.

Sauchyn, M.A. and D.J. Sauchyn. 1991. A Continuous Record of Holocene Pollen from Harris Lake, Southwestern Saskatchewan, Canada." *Palaeogeography, Palaeoclimatology, Palaeoecology* 88: 13–23.

Seebach, J.D. 2002. Stratigraphy and Bonebed Taphonomy at Blackwater Draw Locality No. 1 during the Middle Holocene (Altithermal). *Plains Anthropologist* 47, no. 183: 339–58.

Shapiro, B., A.J. Drummond, A. Rambaut, M.C. Wilson, P.E. Matheus, A.V. Sher, O.G. Pybus, M. Thomas, P. Gilbert, I. Barnes, J. Binladen, E. Willerslev, A.J. Hansen, G.F. Baryshnikov, J.A. Burns, S. Davydov, J.C. Driver, D.G. Froese, C.R. Harington, G. Keddie, P. Kosintsev, M.L. Kunz, L.D. Martin, R.O. Stephenson, J. Storer, R. Tedford, S. Zimov and A. Cooper. 2004. The Rise and Fall of the Beringian Steppe Bison. *Science* 306: 1561–65.

Sheehan, M.S. 1994. Cultural Responses to the Altithermal: The Role of Aquifer-Related Water Resources. *Geoarchaeology* 9, no. 2: 113–37.

———. 1995. Cultural Responses to the Altithermal or Inadequate Sampling? *Plains Anthropologist* 40, no. 153: 261–70.

———. 1996. Cultural Responses to the Altithermal or Inadequate Sampling Reconsidered. *Plains Anthropologist* 41, no. 158: 395–97.

———. 2002. Dietary Responses to Mid-Holocene Climatic Change. *North American Archaeologist* 23, no. 2: 117–43.

Siegfried, E.V. 2002. Paleoethnobotany on the Northern Plains: The Tuscany Archaeological Site (EgPn-377), Calgary. Ph.D. dissertation, University of Calgary.

Smith, C.S. and L.M. McNees. 1999. Facilities and Hunter-Gatherer Long-Term Land Use Patterns: An Example from Southwest Wyoming. *American Antiquity* 64, no. 1: 117–36.

Vance, R.E., A.B. Beaudoin and B.H. Luckman. 1995. The Paleoecological Record of 6 ka BP Climate in the Canadian Prairie Provinces. *Géographie Physique et Quaternaire* 49: 81–98.

Van Dyke, S. and S. Stewart. 1985. *Hawkwood Site (EgPm-179): A Multicomponent Prehistoric Campsite on Nose Hill*. Archaeological Survey of Alberta, Manuscript Series No. 7. Edmonton.

Vehik, S.C. 1977. Bone Fragments and Bone Grease Manufacturing: A Review of Their Archaeological Use and Potential. *Plains Anthropologist* 22, no. 77: 169–82.

———. 2001. Hunting and Gathering Tradition: Southern Plains. In *Handbook of North American Indians, Volume 13, Part I: Plains*, ed. R.J. DeMallie, 146–58. Washington, DC: Smithsonian Institution Press.

Vivian, Brian C., Dan Meyer, Jason Roe and Janet Blakey. 2008. 2007. *Historical Resource Excavations at the Stampede Site (DjOn-26) Final Report (Permit 2007-382)*. Manuscript prepared for the Archaeology and History Section, Alberta Tourism, Parks, Recreation and Culture, Edmonton.

Vreeken, W.J. 1994. A Holocene Soil-Geomorphic Record from the Ham Site near Frontier, Southwestern Saskatchewan. *Canadian Journal of Earth Sciences* 31: 532–43.

Waitkus, B. and D.G. Eckles. 1997. Semi-Subterranean Pithouse Structures in Wyoming.

In *Changing Perspectives of the Archaic on the Northwest Plains and Rocky Mountains*, ed. M.L. Larson and J.E. Francis, 306–32. Vermillion, SD: The University of South Dakota Press.

Walker, E.G. 1992. *The Gowen Sites: Cultural Responses to Climatic Warming on the Northern Plains (7500-5000 B.P.)*. Archaeological Survey of Canada, Mercury Series Paper 145. Ottawa, ON: Canadian Museum of Civilization.

Wandsnider, L. 1992. The Spatial Dimension of Time. *Space, Time, and Archaeological Landscapes*, ed. J. Rossignol and L. Wandsnider, 257–82. New York: Plenum Press.

Waters, M.R. and D.D. Kuehn. 1996. The Geoarchaeology of Place: The Effect of Geological Processes on the Preservation and Interpretation of the Archaeological Record. *American Antiquity* 61: 483–97.

Waters, P.L. and N.W. Rutter. 1984. Utilizing Paleosols and Volcanic Ash in Correlating Holocene Deposits in Southern Alberta. In *Correlation of Quaternary Chronologies*, ed. W.C. Mahaney, 203–23. Norwich, England, UK: GeoBooks.

Wedel, W.R. 1978. The Prehistoric Plains. In *Ancient Native Americans*, ed. J.D. Jennings, 183–219. San Francisco, CA: W.H. Freeman.

Wilson, J.S. 1982. Archaeology and History. In *Environmental Baseline Study of the Saskatchewan River, Saskatchewan, in the Vicinity of Choiceland and the "Forks,"* ed. A.E. Pipe, 743–975. Saskatchewan Research Council Report No. C-805-25-E-80. Saskatoon.

Wilson, M.C. 1974. Fossil Bison and Artifacts from the Mona Lisa Site, Calgary, Alberta. Part 1: Stratigraphy and Artifacts. *Plains Anthropologist* 19, no. 63: 34–45.

———. 1978. Archaeological Kill Site Populations and the Holocene Evolution of the Genus Bison. *Plains Anthropologist* 14, no. 82, part 2: 9–22.

———. 1983. *Once Upon a River: Archaeology and Geology of the Bow River Valley at Calgary, Alberta, Canada*. Archaeological Survey of Canada, Paper No 114. National Museums of Canada, Ottawa.

Wolfe, S.A., A. Aitken, I. Dyck and E. Walker. 2002. *Holocene Geomorphology, Archaeology, and Environmental Change in South-Central Saskatchewan*. Geological Association of Canada/Mineralogical Association of Canada, Saskatoon, Saskatchewan, Field Trip A4 Guidebook.

Yansa, C.H. 2007. Lake Records of Northern Plains Paloeindian and Early Archaic Environments: The Park Oasis Hypothesis. *Plains Anthropologist* 52, no. 201: 109–44.

Zarrillo, S. and B. Kooyman. 2006. Evidence for Berry and Maize Processing on the Canadian Plains from Starch Grain Analysis. *American Antiquity* 71, no. 3: 473–99.

Zdanowich, C.M., G.A. Zielinski and M.S. Germani. 1999. Mount Mazama Eruption: Calendrical Age Verified and Atmospheric Impact Assessed. *Geology* 27, no. 7: 621–24.

Zurburg, S.C. 1991. The Norby Site: A Mummy Cave Complex Bison Kill on the Northern Plains. MA thesis, University of Saskatchewan.

Chapter 3
Human Ecology of the Canadian Prairie Ecozone ca. 3000 BP: Post Hypsithermal Adaptations to the Canadian Prairie Ecozone

B.A. Nicholson and Sean Webster

KEYWORDS: Oxbow, McKean, Duncan, Hanna, Pelican Lake, burials

In this chapter, the discussion which began in chapter two, dealing with the cultures and events centred on the period 6000 BP in the Canadian Prairie Ecozone (CPE) (Figure 3.1), resumes. At this point in time, the Hypsithermal

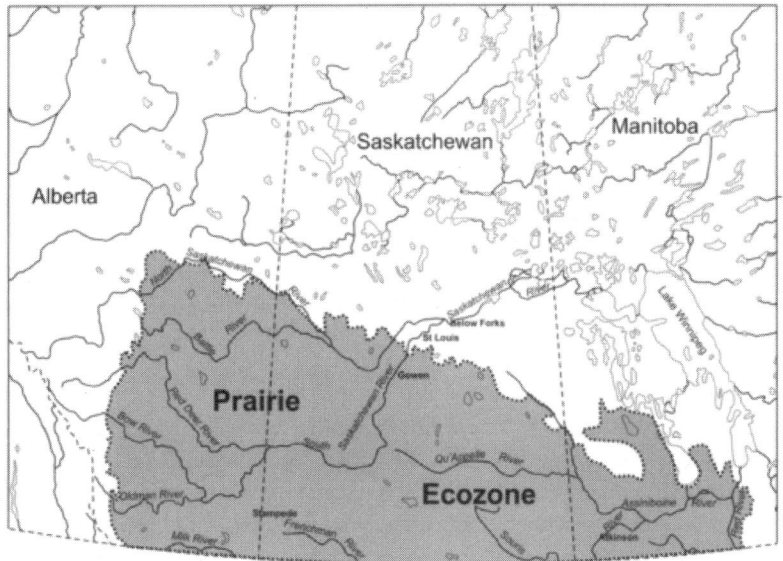

Figure 3.1. Canadian Prairie Ecozone map.

drought had begun to abate and by 4000 BP (years before present) conditions were similar to modern climatic parameters. It is generally accepted that the Hypsithermal, a period of warmer climate and drought conditions, began ca. 8500 BP and began to ameliorate ca. 4800 BP (Buchner 1980; Walker 1992; Webster 2004: 99). Others (Oetelaar in this volume) place the onset of the Hypsithermal somewhat earlier, ca. 9200 BP to 5900 BP (Barnosky et al. 1987; Yansa 2007) in the western part of the CPE. This time period brackets the emergence and decline of the Mummy Cave/Bitteroot/Gowen culture. The Oxbow culture emerges ca. 5000 BP and is closely followed by the McKean Complex, which persists until ca. 3000 BP (Webster 2004). The Pelican Lake Complex then replaces the McKean Complex, and then disappears ca. 1700 BP. These replacements are not rapid and there is evidence for a measure of co-existence. In some cases, the lithics indicate shared technologies and occasionally there are similarities in stylistic elements. However, there is no convincing evidence for jointly shared occupations of sites, and the while artifacts may share similarities, it appears that these complexes had very little sustained interaction with each other.

Oxbow

The Oxbow complex is believed to have emerged in the mountain valleys and adjacent high plains as a variant of the preceding Mummy Cave/Bitteroot/Gowen Series (Green 2005: 103; Walker 192: 144). Wright (1995: 300) states that, "The chipped stone tool assemblage of the Mummy Cave complex continues into the Oxbow complex with the distinction between the two complexes being based upon the attributes of their respective side-notched projectile points" and this view is supported by Dyck (1983: 96). Their "eared bases," resulting from corner-notching, coupled with a strongly concave base distinguish the projectile points (Figure 3.2). It is noted there is significant overlap in radiocarbon dates of the occupations of both complexes (Wright 1995: 300), and projectile points from early components at the Oxbow Dam and Long Creek sites in southern Saskatchewan appear to be transitional in form (Dyck and Morlan 2001). Similarly, sites such as the Hawkwood site in Calgary contain occupations that have been referred to as "Late Mummy Cave/Oxbow" (Van Dyke and Stewart 1985). The Oxbow complex extends from the edge of the boreal forest in the north and into the edge of this forest biome in eastern Manitoba and northern Minnesota (Figure 3.3). In the west it extends from the foothills of Alberta and Montana into Wyoming and eastward into North and South Dakota (Millar 1980; Webster 2004). Radiocarbon dates indicate that the Oxbow people abandoned the central grasslands (earliest dates) and migrated into the northern peripheries of their known range (most recent dates)—possibly displaced by the influx of McKean complex people (Spurling and Ball 1981; Webster 2004: 102). There has been some discussion of an eastern origin for the Oxbow culture (Spurling and Ball 1981: 91–100) but others have

CHAPTER 3: Human Ecology of the Canadian Prairie Ecozone ca. 3000 BP

Figure 3.2. Oxbow points from Manitoba.

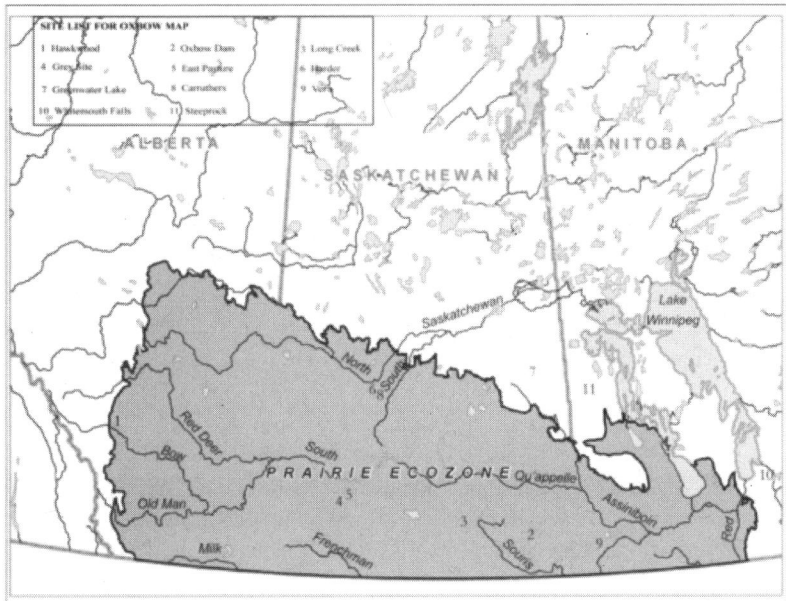

Figure 3.3. Oxbow area map.

indicated that the origins are in western North America, possibly related to Mummy Cave (Kooyman 2000: 212; Millar 1981a: 85, 1981b: 156), and this latter view appears to be most widely accepted.

Oxbow lithic technology is similar to the preceding Mummy Cave complex, including the continued use of bipolar split-pebbles (Dyck and Morlan 2001). Wright (1995: 306) notes that "[t]he bone and shell technology of the Oxbow and McKean complexes is quite rudimentary in terms of quality and variety. Bone awls and beads are present in both complexes as are shell beads and pendants. Bone beamers and antler flakers have been reported from Oxbow complex sites in the boreal forest (Buchner et al. 1983) and unilateral barbed harpoons have been recovered from the subsequent McKean complex (Syms 1970)." Wright (1995: 306) also makes the observation that "[s]imple utilized bone sections and fragments, unrecognized until recently, were likely the most common bone tools in Middle Plains culture."

Of interest is the possible association of Oxbow Complex materials with copper artifacts typical of the Old Copper Industry of the Great Lakes Region. Green (2005: 99) notes that, "the strongest evidence of an Oxbow/Old Copper association comes from the Gray Burial site in southwestern Saskatchewan where copper artifacts, including tube beads, were placed as grave goods with human interments." In addition, the inclusion of shell beads in several of the interments, identified as belonging to mollusk species from the Atlantic Coast (Millar 1978: 332), is indicative of influence from, and possibly well-developed trade networks with, cultural groups from eastern Canada.

Although bison remains clearly dominate Oxbow sites, no Oxbow bison kill sites have been reported. Bison remains are common in campsites, but typically represent a relatively low number of animals, with canids such as wolf and coyote being a weak second runner up (Dyck and Morlan 2001: 120; Green 2005: 100; Wright 1995: 310). Such evidence suggests the use of a hunting strategy that did not include large-scale bison kills (Green 2005: 101), with Oxbow subsistence strategies appearing to have been quite opportunistic, making use of locally available resources including small mammals. This is particularly the case in sites on the margins of the Plains or those extending into the boreal forest. The Near Norbert site, north of the Churchill River, and estimated to have been occupied ca. 3000 BC (5000 BP) (Meyer et al. 1981), is a fishing station where extensive flint-knapping activities dominated the tool assemblage (Wright 1995: 307). In contrast to earlier Paleo-Indian reliance on mass-kill communal bison procurement, the practice of opportunistic "broad spectrum foraging" of local plants and animals was established during the early Middle Precontact time period, when the Hypsithermal climatic shift brought a dramatic change, and the local availability of bison became less certain (Robertson 2004: 219). Robertson (2004: 219) notes "that Early Archaic subsistence practices may have been geared toward a wider range of food species. Furthermore, this emphasis on individual procurement of plants and animals may not have been restricted to species other than bison. Instead the exploitation of bison also may have become an individual pursuit." The absence of Oxbow mass-kills of bison is consistent with this scenario (Dyck 1983: 96). Similarly, this pattern is consistent with the following Middle Precontact period McKean subsistence patterns. Oxbow sites tend to be small and probably represent the activities of small family groups within the social context of a larger set of related people spread across the Plains and parklands and into the foothills.

Oxbow mortuary patterns typically include extended burials and the use of red ochre (Walker 1984). Burials are not associated with campsites and are often isolated. An exception is the Gray burial site, located in southwestern Saskatchewan, where excavated remains represent as many as 304 individuals in 99 burial units (Millar 1978, 1981). Although Oxbow points are only associated with seven of the burial units (Dyck and Morlan 2001: 119), many of the burials are represented by primary extended interments with heavy use of red ochre, consistent with the Oxbow mortuary style recorded elsewhere (Walker 1984). The presence of a number of secondary bundle burials that have disturbed earlier interments may indicate continued use of the Gray burial site by later complexes. Morlan (1993: 19) notes two clusters of radiocarbon dates from the Gray burial site. The first includes nine dates from 5150 to 4340 BP, four of which are associated with Oxbow projectile points. The second cluster, ranging from 3755 to 3415 BP, is not associated with diagnostic projectile points and seems to support the idea of a separate period of use; however, the methods used to obtain the dates have been questioned.

McKean Complex

The McKean Complex, popularly defined by the presence of McKean Lanceolate, Duncan and Hanna projectile points (Figures 3.4 and 3.5), was originally thought to have emerged from the Desert Culture in the Great Basin and subsequently these people migrated north into the Plains (Mulloy 1958; Wedel 1961). This hypothesis was supported by faunal materials in sites such as Leigh Cave where plants, small mammals and even insects dominated the McKean assemblages to the near exclusion of bison. Frison and Huseas (1968: 26) concluded that "[t]he occupation at Leigh Cave is more reminiscent of a desert culture orientation than that of Plains Indian hunters." Others (Wright 1995) believed that McKean evolved in situ from earlier Oxbow peoples living on the Northern Plains. However, as has been pointed out by Webster (2004), while McKean and Oxbow are frequently identified in sites in Saskatchewan and elsewhere, there is no evidence for any co-occurrence of Oxbow and McKean points within the occupations, where excavations have been conducted in undisturbed sites. In all cases, the Oxbow materials were recovered below the McKean occupations. This observation is supported by the stratigraphic column at the Vera site in southwestern Manitoba, where a single Oxbow point was recovered below a more extensive Duncan/Hanna occupation (Nicholson

Figure 3.4. Duncan points from Manitoba.

Figure 3.5. Hanna points from Manitoba.

CHAPTER 3: Human Ecology of the Canadian Prairie Ecozone ca. 3000 BP

and Hamilton 1997; Watt 2003: 41, and Figs. 7a and 8). Duncan and Hanna points are common in Manitoba sites and collections, but the McKean Lanceolate point is rarely found either in surface collections or in excavated components. More recent work strongly indicates that the McKean Complex is derived from Early Archaic cultures, possibly Mummy Cave-related traditions, in the High Plains and adjacent mountains in Wyoming and Montana (Webster 2004: 95–99).

The earliest dates for McKean cluster around 4900 BP in and around the Bighorn Basin with somewhat later dates falling between 4700–4500 BP in the Black Hills region of Wyoming and South Dakota (Webster 2004: 96). Webster (204: 101) notes that "[i]n Saskatchewan, acceptable Oxbow radiocarbon dates range from 5500 to 3869 RCYBP (Morlan 1993 [in Webster 2004: 101]), while McKean dates range from 4410 to 3150 BP." By the end of the Hypsithermal, 4,000 to 5,000 years ago, there was a return to the cooler and moister conditions of the sub-boreal period (Webster 2004: 99). This observation is supported by work done in the Glacial Lake Hind Basin in southwestern Manitoba. Boyd (2000: 38) states that "[s]ince there is also strong evidence for development of a high water table prior to the late Holocene, by at least 4000 BP the region had probably developed into a large mosaic of wetland and prairie." The radiocarbon dates indicate that the McKean complex people expanded out of the Bighorn Basin area into the surrounding grasslands and northward into the plains of Alberta, Saskatchewan and Manitoba. It has been suggested that this McKean expansion displaced the Oxbow people northwards into the margins of the boreal forest where the most recent Oxbow dates have been recorded.

It is probable that the large river networks, such as those of the Missouri and Saskatchewan rivers, facilitated the rapid expansion of the McKean culture into the northern plains (Syms 1969: 175; Webster 2004: 43). These riverine networks would have provided wood for winter fuel, water sources in summer, and would also have served to attract bison in from the dry plains surrounding these river networks. Similarly, a wide range of plants and other animal resources would have been present in and adjacent to these riverine systems.

In addition to the diagnostic McKean projectile points, Webster (2009) lists a wide range of lithic tools associated with the processing of animals and animal skins that have been recovered from McKean Complex sites. These include bifacial knives, side-scrapers, end scrapers, unifaces and marginally utilized or retouched lithics (MURLs). Tools for working wood or bone include spokeshaves, wedges and grooved abraders (Webster 2004). At the Vera site in southwestern Manitoba, a beautifully crafted stone drill with a concave base was recovered (Watt 2003: 37). This tool could have been used to drill soapstone, bone or wood. The tool shows no evidence of wear and may have been resharpened immediately prior to its loss. Similarly, mano and metate grinding stones are common, particularly in the southern part of the McKean range. These milling stones likely indicate the processing of seeds, and edible seeds have been recovered in sites where fine screening or floatation of soil matrix has been conducted. Webster (2004: 66) notes the presence of plant remains in several sites in the southern portion of the McKean range. In addition, grinding stones at the George Hey site appear to be pecked and pitted rather than polished and ground, indicating probable usage for pounding dried meat during pemmican manufacture (Tratebas 1998: 291). Few instances of bone tools have been reported but this may be largely a result of these items being overlooked by excavators and collectors at McKean sites.

The McKean complex subsistence strategy, while utilizing the bison resource extensively, also appears to have made regular use of plant and small animal resources. They have been described in the literature as hunter-foragers (Webster 2009). In Saskatchewan and Alberta, Webster (2004: 77) notes that "[t]he limited data on seasonality indicate that many of these sites were occupied in the warmer months of the year. Of the 23 McKean occupations at Thundercloud, Redtail, Crown and Cactus Flower only three appear to have been occupied in winter." Sites such as Vera in Manitoba, where organic remains have not been preserved in the lower occupations, do not provide reliable indictors for seasonality. In this respect it should be noted that this area meets the criteria for the presence of critical resources, that is, wood and water, as outlined by Vickers and Peck (2004). It is noted that late precontact period Mortlach and Vickers Focus sites in this locale—*Makotchi-Ded Dontipi*—have been shown to include both warm season and cold season occupations (Playford and Nicholson 2006: 419).

The known McKean sites (Figure 3.6) provide evidence for a wide range of subsistence strategies that focus on local resources to maximum effect. These range from the Scoggin site in Wyoming, where a pound structure was employed to procure large numbers of bison, to Leigh Cave in Wyoming, where plant remains dominated the assemblage. Webster (2004: 64–66) notes that, at Leigh Cave, the presence of large amounts of plant material, grinding stones and evidence for hundreds of roasted Mormon crickets indicate a broad-based forager strategy where large mammals were of minimal importance. Other "McKean component sites in the southern portion of the northwestern plains, such as Carbella, Dead Indian Creek, Lissolo Cave, Belle Rockshelter, and Lightning Spring, reveal evidence of small-scale hunting activities that are more clearly focused on one or more species of medium to large artiodactyls" (Webster 2004: 66).

On the Canadian Plains, the same diversity in subsistence practice is evident. However, the interpretation of subsistence strategies in the CPE is hampered by a number of factors. In the first instance, few Middle Prehistoric period sites have been fully reported, if they have been published at all. Secondly, fine mesh screens or floatation of samples from the small number of excavated sites has either not been employed or reported on. Thirdly, in many cases, the preservation of organic materials in sites deposited during the post-Hypsithermal

CHAPTER 3: Human Ecology of the Canadian Prairie Ecozone ca. 3000 BP

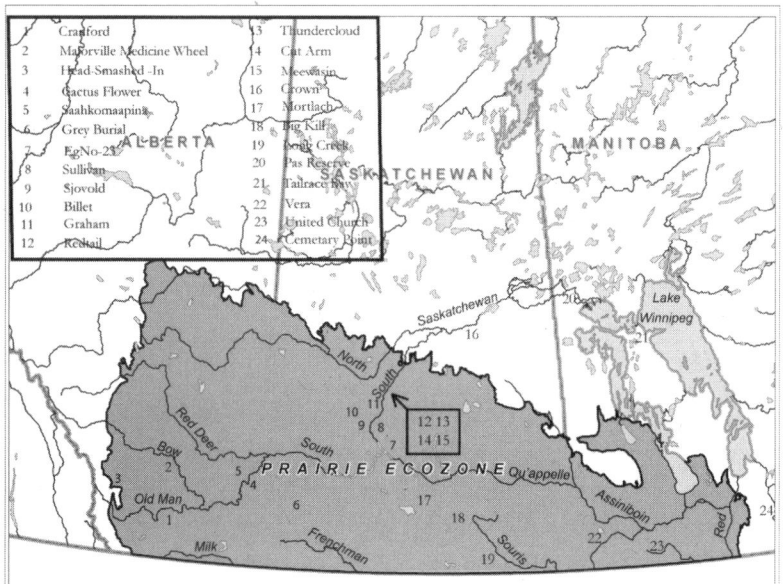

Figure 3.6. McKean area map.

period has frequently been unfavourable. In the case of the Vera site a high, fluctuating water table has led to the complete destruction of organic material for all occupations prior to the Pelican Lake occupation, where a single severely leached tibia fragment yielded a late date of 2065 ± 105 BP.

In Alberta and Saskatchewan, sites such as the Cactus Flower site, located in a high, dry prairie environment, are dominated almost exclusively by bison (Brumley 1975; Webster 2004: 70). At the Crown site, an increased reliance on elk and moose reflects proximity to the boreal forest (Webster 2004: 69). In occupations such as those in the Redtail and Thundercloud sites, there are small numbers of bison and a number of small animals, including rodents and frogs that were being utilized as dietary items (Webster 2004: 69). Further, with the exception of Leigh Cave, the Redtail site has the largest seed assemblage of any McKean site on the Northern Plains and, "[m]ore importantly, this is the first site in the Canadian Plains that has definitive evidence of McKean plant utilization" (Webster 2004: 72). Similarly, Webster (2004: 72) notes that

> The Thundercloud site faunal assemblage also revealed evidence of a more diverse subsistence base. The McKean component includes the remains of at least 16 species of mammals, four species of birds, and two amphibians. Fine screen samples taken from hearth features reveal a number of burned and calcined specimens, several small mammals, a microtine rodent and a small bird.

Fish remains are associated with McKean occupations at several sites in Manitoba. Webster (2004: 73) notes that,

> At the Pas Reserve site (Tamplin 1977) Duncan and Hanna projectile points were associated with burbot (*Lota lota*), canids and bison. The Tailrace Bay site (Lukens Jr. 1967) also revealed a diverse faunal assemblage. Faunal remains recovered from the gravel zone (associated with McKean Lanceolate points) include elements from bison, sturgeon (*Acipenser fulvescens*) and northern pike (*Esox luscious*) (Syms 1969).

The McKean components that contain a wider spectrum of animal species are located outside, or on the fringes of, the grassland environment and include sites in the boreal forest, aspen parkland and in tributary valleys of the major river systems (Webster 2004: 73). Bison-dominated McKean assemblages characterize sites in the open Plains where populations of these animals are ubiquitous. Many of these sites are located adjacent to natural landforms such as dune fields and arroyos, which may have aided in ambush or entrapment of small numbers of animals. Webster (2004: 75–76) states that most McKean occupations have relatively small faunal assemblages where the remains of one or two bison are found among the elements from a variety of medium-to-large size mammals including deer, pronghorn, elk, canids, and several species of leporids. He further notes that these small assemblages do not indicate communal hunting and are better interpreted as the result of successful opportunistic kills. It is probable that these sites represent the activities of small, family-based hunter-gatherer bands.

Webster (2004: 76–77) indicates that many McKean complex sites are situated in transitional environments allowing for the potential utilization of a variety of local flora and fauna. This pattern is consistent with the results of the Study of Cultural Adaptations in the Canadian Prairie Ecozone (SCAPE) Project, where areas of high biodiversity within the CPE were chosen for investigation (Nicholson and Wiseman 2006). During this five-year project, four areas were chosen for site excavations. These were the Tiger Hills and the Lauder Sandhills in Manitoba, the Greater Forks area surrounding the junction of the North and South Saskatchewan rivers in Saskatchewan, and the Stampede site and surrounding area in the Cypress Hills of Alberta. McKean materials were found in each of these site locales, as well as older and more recent cultural occupations. In short, these areas of high biodiversity tend to be more stable in terms of subsistence resources (Nicholson and Wiseman 2007: 2)—and for critical resources such as wood and water—essential resources for winter and summer occupations respectively (Vickers and Peck 2004), than the surrounding grasslands. The excavations in these locales confirmed that these areas were used repeatedly over the centuries by a succession of groups, particularly as wintering sites.

The evidence strongly indicates that the McKean Complex people were flexible hunter-foragers who adapted themselves to a wide range of local conditions. They also favoured areas with high biodiversity for their campsites and often reoccupied these locales. For the most part, they appear to have traveled and camped as small social groups. It is likely that these groups were composed of close relatives—probably extended family groupings. In addition to excavated sites, there are large numbers of "find spots" in cultivated fields where collectors have recovered the diagnostic McKean projectile points. In most cases the numbers of points are small, indicating small transitory occupations that are typical of nomadic hunter-gatherer extended family groups.

McKean mortuary practices differ substantially from those of the preceding Oxbow complex. Although the sample is small, McKean burials are often located in shallow pits located directly below the living floor (Webster 2009). Grave goods are absent and burials are not associated with red ochre pigment.

The McKean occupation of the Northern Plains appears to have terminated rather rapidly by ca. 3000 BP. The reasons for this are not known. It may be that other more efficient bison hunting groups simply out-competed the McKean hunter-foragers and either absorbed these people, or that they were compelled by competition for resources to modify their material assemblages and procurement technology in order to compete for the bison resource. The last remnants of the McKean people may have been the Pelican Lake bison hunters who, in turn, were replaced by the highly efficient Sonota and Besant bison hunters who employed a well-demonstrated mass-kill technology, including regular use of bison pounds.

Pelican Lake
The Pelican Lake Complex follows the McKean Complex on the Northern Plains. The distinctive corner-notched projectile points are generally believed to have been dart points, although smaller versions may have been arrow points. The points are shaped somewhat like a "Christmas tree" with sharp, tanged shoulders and slightly concave to slightly convex basal shape (Figure 3.7). Similar points have been identified in the US Midwest and extend from circa 3000 BP until the contact period when smaller versions were likely arrow points. A late occurrence of these smaller corner-notched points was demonstrated at the Vera site, where a small cluster (five points) was identified overlying the Besant occupation (Watt 2003: 24–26 and Fig. 4). A similar point was recovered from within a small cobble pavement at the *Na-ha-stew-in* site, which overlooks Rock Lake in south-central Manitoba (Nicholson 1995: 74). Aside from the similarity in the shape of these small points, there is little to suggest that they are lineal descendants of the Late Archaic or Middle Period Pelican Lake Culture. Watt (2003) has named these small corner-notched points Vera points. In Montana and Wyoming, Frison (1978) places Pelican Lake points between 3300 and 1800 BP. Dyck and Morlan (2001: 121) place their first appearance slightly

Figure 3.7. Pelican Lake points from Manitoba.

earlier, between 1850 BCE and AD 350. They (Dyck and Morlan (2001: 12) note that:

> The question of Pelican Lake origins is perplexing. The evidence that Pelican Lake was adapted to bison hunting from the beginning opens an argument for in situ development on the plains. Continuities between certain Hanna and Pelican Lake tool forms—drills, ovate bifaces, pointed unifaces and dome shaped side-scrapers—and the common use of basin-shaped rock filled hearths provide support for this idea (Reeves 1970, 1983).

Kooyman (2000: 122) notes that "Yonkee projectile points from Wyoming and southern Montana are similar and probably related, perhaps being a local development from McKean in the area of the Powder River Basin." While the origins of Pelican Lake still remain uncertain, there is a well-demonstrated presence of these points across the CPE in the indicated time period (Figure 3.8). Reeves (1983: 7) offered an alternative explanation for Pelican Lake origins, postulating that Pelican Lake was intrusive from the west and arose out of interaction between Plains and Mountain cultures. Dyck and Morlan (2001: 123) note that "[t]his idea receives some support from the grouping of early and late Pelican Lake dates on the western half of the Northern Plains."

CHAPTER 3: Human Ecology of the Canadian Prairie Ecozone ca. 3000 BP

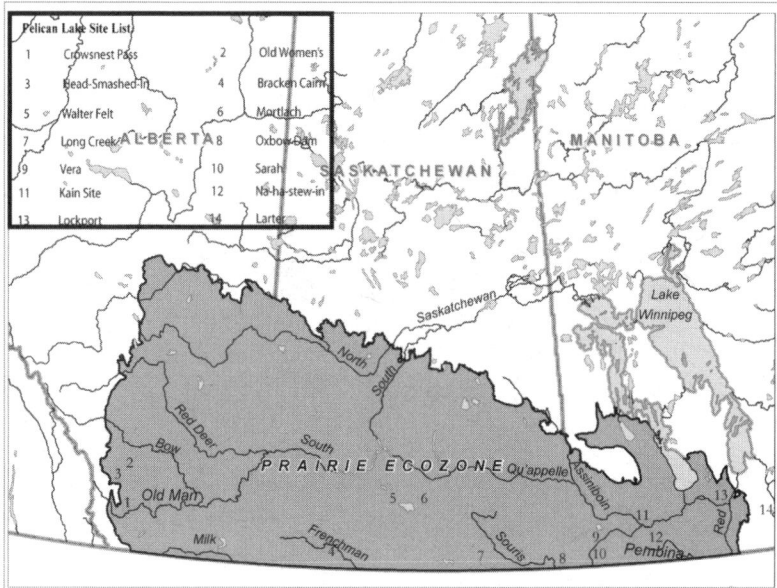

Figure 3.8. Pelican Lake area map.

Dyck (1983: 107) has provided a useful list of tools associated with Pelican Lake occupations on the Northern Plains:

> In addition to the diagnostic points, Pelican Lake chipped stone tools include plano-convex and keeled end-scrapers, large and small ovoid bifaces, elongated drills with convex butts, and miscellaneous uniface tools. Sharp pointed bone splinter awls are present. Carved ornaments such as simulated elk tooth pendants and bear claws made of bone and distinctive rectangular shell gorgets with circular projections on one side are also found. Shell beads and a small folded copper bead have also been found with a Pelican Lake burial at the Bracken Cairn (King 1961).

The shell ornaments and the copper bead suggest a connection, possibly through trade, to contemporary groups such as the Adena, Hopewell or Laurel cultures living in the Eastern Woodlands. These groups all fall within or overlap the time period that Pelican Lake was present in the CPE.

In the Crowsnest Pass, Duke (1986: 8) identified 51 Pelican Lake sites at the time of writing and stated that "[t]he Palaeoeconomy apparently revolved around the heavy utilization of Bison, supplemented by exploitation of a wide range of ungulate, plant, fish and small animal species." He further indicates that "[s]ubsistence strategies identified with Pelican Lake sites range from widespectrum hunting, fishing and gathering in the west (Turnbull 1973) to communal bison hunting on the Plains (Reeves 1983)."

Duke (1986: 11) postulates that bison tended to be present in summer throughout the valley and wintered in the valley bottom, and shifted eastward into the chinook belt towards the lower end of the valley where herds from the plains would also congregate. He proposes a settlement pattern that would have seen people using the western and central section of the valley in summer and autumn, with a shift eastward into the chinook zone in the late fall, where there would have been an influx of bison from the plains as well as a shift into the valley bottoms and into the chinook zone from the west. This pattern closely resembles that of the Plains where bison hunters wintered where there was wood and shelter, in an expectation that the bison herds would also drift into these locales (Hamilton and Graham 2007; Hamilton et al. 2006; Vickers and Peck 2004).

In southwestern Manitoba two sites contain securely dated Pelican lake occupations. Both of these are small, short-term campsites. The Kain site occupation dates to 2065 ± 105 BP and the Vera site occupation is dated to 2530 ± 80 BP. The Kain site faunal remains are dominated by well-preserved bison bone and the Pelican Lake occupation at the Vera site had only one very poorly preserved bison radius with a low collagen yield. A third site in the Crepeele locale may be a Pelican Lake component but no closely associated diagnostics were recovered. This occupation, at the Sarah site, appears to have been a wintering site, including a small bison kill (Ansell 2008), with two dates of 2810 ± 80 BP and 3120 ± 130 BP from levels 20 and 21. These four dates would indicate an extended, although sparse, Pelican Lake occupation in southwestern Manitoba throughout the Pelican Lake time period. In Manitoba, Reeves' Pelican Lake Larter Phase includes the Larter and Lockport sites (Reeves 1983: 316).

In Saskatchewan, Dyck (1983: 105) notes that Pelican Lake occupations include campsites, a bison pound and, at the Bracken Cairn (King1961), a cairn-covered grave containing secondary burials. He goes on (1983: 107) to state that [a]lthough they were not the inventors of bison jumps and pounds, Pelican Lake peoples were the first to use some mass kill locations that were used repeatedly. Examples are the Old Women's Buffalo Jump, Alberta and the Walter Felt site, Saskatchewan. Dyck and Morlan (2001: 122) state that

> Pelican Lake burials are usually secondary bundle interments, placed in shallow pits, infused with red ochre, accompanied by a diverse assemblage of grave goods, sometimes covered with rock cairns, and usually situated in prominent spots overlooking water or on high hill slopes (Brink and Baldwin 1988: 131). The Wind River Canyon burial is a mountain variant placed at the base of a steep sandstone wall on a low terrace 10 meters above the River.

Reeves (1983: 135–36) notes that flexed burials are characteristic of the Pelican Lake Glendo Subphase located south of the Black Hills (Reeves 1983: 317). Reeves considers Pelican Lake sites in the western part of the CPE to belong to a Mortlach Phase. This Pelican Lake Phase should not be confused with the late period, ceramic-using Mortlach culture, found primarily in southern Saskatchewan, northeastern Montana and the western edge of Manitoba. The Pelican Lake Mortlach Phase sites listed by Reeves (1983: 316) include Head Smashed In, Old Women's, Mortlach, Walter Felt and Long Creek. The campsite occupations at the Vera and Kain sites could likely be added to this list.

While there is evidence for the practice of a local resource adaptation in the Pelican Lake Phase, particularly in the Larter subphase, there appears to be a greater focus on communal mass-kill technology than was the case for earlier McKean Complex hunter-foragers in the CPE. This is particularly the case in the High Plains and adjacent Foothills. Sites such as Head-Smashed-In and Old Womens' Buffalo Jump show repeated evidence for mass-kills and the associated processing of the bison. Notwithstanding the clear evidence for mass kills of bison, requiring large numbers of participants to conduct the drives and process the animals, there is no evidence for large base camps. Dyck and Morland (2001: 122) observe that "Pelican Lake campsites all seem to be of a small, transitory, or task-specific type."

The fate of the Pelican Lake people remains enigmatic (Dyck and Morlan 2001; Reeves 1983). Reeves (1970, 1983: 164–66) has suggested that in the west, mountain sub-phases of Pelican Lake could have been ancestral to the Avonlea complex. In any case, the Pelican Lake complex fades rather quickly from the archaeological record, ca. 350 AD, after a short co-existence with Sonota/Besant.

Conclusion

The archaeological record from the period between 5000 BP and 2000 BP indicates that while distinct, identifiable groups entered the CPE and developed successful adaptations, they were successively replaced by later groups whose lifeways and practices differed. An overlap between these occupations is evident and it is usually assumed that the succeeding groups were more efficient and likely had developed a superior subsistence strategy and/or social organization. In some cases the recent immigrants may simply have absorbed members of the preceding group. It is evident that technologies and subsistence practices, and social practices such as burial patterns did change. However, it is not clear what became of the earlier occupants in many cases. There is some evidence that McKean populations, coming from the southwest, displaced the Oxbow people towards the north. Pelican Lake immigrants may have pushed McKean people eastward and possibly assimilated the remaining McKean hunter-gatherers.

Throughout this time interval there is evidence for the development of an increasingly effective technology for bison procurement, especially in terms of seasonal mass kills. This trend climaxed with the advent of the succeeding Sonota/Besant people (Chapter 4, this volume).

References

Ansell, Emily. 2008. A Faunal Analysis of the Sarah Site (DiMe-28) in Southwestern Manitoba. Honour's thesis, Brandon University.

Barnosky, C.W., E.C. Grimm and H.E. Wright, Jr. 1987. Towards a Postglacial History of the Northern Great Plains: A Review of the Paleoecologic Problems. *Annals of the Carnegie Museum* 56: 259–73.

Brumley, J.H. 1975. *The Cactus Flower Site in Southeastern Alberta: 1972–1974 Excavations.* Mercury Series. Archaeological Survey of Canada, Paper No.46. National Museum of Man, Ottawa.

Boyd, Matthew. 2000. Changing Physical and Ecological Landscapes in Southwestern Manitoba in relation to Folsom (11,000–10,000 BP) and McKean (4000–3000 BP) Site Distributions. *Prairie Forum* 25, no. 1: 23–44.

Buchner, A.P., P. Carmichael, G. Dickson, I. Dyck, B. Fardoe, J. Haug, T & L Jones, D. Joyes, O. Mallory, M. Mallot, D. Meyer, D. Miller, R. Nash, L. Pettipas, C.T. Shay, E.L. Syms, M.A. Tisdale and J.P. Whelan.1983. Introducing Manitoba Prehistory. *Papers in Manitoba Archaeology*. Popular Series No. 4. Manitoba Department of Cultural Affairs and Historic Resources.

Duke, P.G. 1986. A Locational and Subsistence Analysis of Pelican Lake Phase Sites in Crowsnest Pass, Alberta. In *Eastern Slopes Prehistory: Selected Papers*, ed. Brian Ronaghan. Occasional paper No. 30, Archaeological Survey of Alberta.

Dyck, Ian.1983. The Prehistory of Southern Saskatchewan. In *Tracking Ancient Hunters*, ed. Henry T. Epp and Ian Dyck, 55–62. Regina: Saskatchewan Archaeological Society.

Dyck, Ian and Richard E. Morlan. 2001. Hunting and Gathering Tradition: Canadian Plains. In *Handbook of North American Indians*, vol. 13, part 1 of 2, ed. Raymond J. DeMallie, 115–30. Washington, DC: Smithsonian Institution.

Frison, G.C. and M. Huseas. 1968. Leigh Cave, Wyoming 48WA 304. *The Wyoming Archaeologist* 11: 20–33.

Green, D'Arcy. 2005. A Re-Evaluation of the Oxbow Dam Site (DhMn-1): Middle Holocene Cultural Continuity on the Northern Plains. *Occasional Papers of the Archaeological Society of Alberta*, Number 5. Archaeological Society of Alberta, Calgary.

Hamilton, Scott, B.A. Nicholson and Dion Wiseman. 2006. Extrapolating to a More Ancient Past: Images of Northeastern Plains Vegetation and Bison Ecology. In *Changing Opportunities and Challenges: Human-Environmental Interaction in the Canadian Prairies Ecozone*, ed. B.A. Nicholson and Dion Wiseman (eds.), Memoir 38, Plains Anthropologist 51, no. 199: 231–486.

King, D.R. 1961. The Bracken Cairn: A Prehistoric Burial. *The Blue Jay* 19: 45–53.

Kooyman, Brian P. 2000. *Understanding Stone Tools and Archaeological Sites*. Calgary: University of Calgary Press.

Morlan, R.E. 1993. A Compilation of Radiocarbon Dates in Saskatchewan. *Saskatchewan Archaeology* 13: 3–84.

Meyer, David, James S. Wilson and Olga Klimko. 1981. *Archaeological Mitigation Along the Key Lake Access Road*. Saskatchewan Research Council. Publication No. C-805-11-E-81.

CHAPTER 3: Human Ecology of the Canadian Prairie Ecozone ca. 3000 BP

Millar, J.F.V. 1978. *The Gray Site: An Early Plains Burial Ground.* Parks Canada Manuscript Report Number 304, Volume 2.

———. 1980. Introduction. Proceedings of 1980 Symposium: The Oxbow Complex in Time and Space. *Canadian Journal of Archaeology* 5: 83–88.

———. 1981. Mortuary Practices of the Oxbow Complex. *Canadian Journal of Archaeology* 5: 103–17.

Mulloy, W.B. 1958. *A Preliminary Historical Outline for the Northwestern Plains.* University of Wyoming Publications 22, nos. 1–2: 1–235.

Nicholson, B.A. 1995. Na-ha-stew-in: Where They Put Things Away. *Manitoba Archaeological Journal* 5: 67–80.

Nicholson, B.A. and Scott Hamilton. 1997. Preliminary Report on Middle Precontact Occupations at the Vera Site in the Makotchi-Ded Dontipi Locale. *Manitoba Archaeological Journal* 7, no. 2: 37–49.

Nicholson, B.A. and Dion Wiseman (eds.). 2006. Changing Opportunities and Challenges: Human-Environmental Interaction in the Canadian Prairies Ecozone. Memoir 38, *Plains Anthropologist* 51, no. 199.

———. 2007. Introduction to Building a Contextual Milieu: Interdisciplinary Modeling and Theoretical Perspectives from the SCAPE Project. In *Building a Contextual Milieu: Interdisciplinary Modeling and Theoretical Perspectives from the SCAPE Project*, ed. B.A. Nicholson and Dion Wiseman. *Canadian Journal of Archaeology* 31, no. 3 (Supplement).

Playford, Tomasin and B.A. Nicholson. 2006. Vickers Focus Subsistence: Continuity Through the Seasons. In *Changing Opportunities and Challenges: Human-Environmental Interaction in the Canadian Prairies Ecozone*, ed. B.A. Nicholson and Dion Wiseman. Memoir 38, *Plains Anthropologist* 51, no. 199.

Reeves, Brain O.K. 1983. *Culture Change in the Northern Plains: 1000 BC–AD 1000.* Occasional Paper No. 20. Edmonton: Archaeological Survey of Alberta, Alberta Culture.

Robertson, Elizabeth. 2004. Communal Hunting as a Social Model for the Paleo-Indian to Early Archaic Transition on the Plains. In *Archaeology on the Edge: New Perspectives from the Northern Plains*, ed. Brian Kooyman and Jane H. Kelly. Canadian Archaeological Association Paper No.4. Calgary: University of Calgary Press.

Spurling, B. and B. Ball. 1981. On Some Distributions of the Oxbow "Complex." *Canadian Journal of Archaeology* 5: 89–102.

Syms, E. Leigh. 1969. The McKean Complex as a Horizon Marker in Manitoba and on the Great Northern Plains. MA thesis, University of Manitoba.

———. 1970. The McKean Complex in Manitoba. In *Ten Thousand Years: Archaeology in Manitoba*, ed. Walter M. Hlady, 123–38. Winnipeg: Manitoba Archaeological Society.

Tratebas, A.M.1998. Reexamining the Plains Archaic McKean Culture. In *Explorations in American Archaeology: Essays in Honor of Wesley R. Hurt*, ed. M.G. Plew, 259–309. Lanham, MD: University Press of America Inc.

Vickers J. Rod and Trevor R. Peck. 2004. The Significance of Wood in Winter Campsite Selection on the Northern Plains. In *Archaeology on the Edge: New Perspectives from the*

Northern Plains, ed. Brian Kooyman and Jane H. Kelly. Canadian Archaeological Association Paper No. 4. Calgary: University of Calgary Press.

Van Dyke, Stan and Sally Stewart. 1985. The Hawkwood Site (EgPm-179): A Multi-component Prehistoric Campsite on Nose Hill. Archaeological Survey of Alberta, Manuscript Series No.7.

Walker, E.G. 1984. The Graham Site: A McKean Cremation from Southern Saskatchewan. *Plains Anthropologist* 29, no. 104: 139–50.

——. 1992. *The Gowen Sites: Cultural Responses to Climatic Warming on the Northern Plains (7500–5000 BP)*. Mercury Series Archaeological Survey of Canada, Paper 145. Gatineau: Canadian Museum of Civilization.

Watt, Sandra Frances. 2003. An Examination of the Middle and Late Plains Archaic Stone Tools from the Vera Site. Specialist thesis, Brandon University.

Webster, S.M. 2004. A Re-Evaluation of the McKean Series on the Northern Plains. PhD dissertation, University of Saskatchewan.

——. 2009. *A Re-Evaluation of the McKean Series on the Northern Plains*. Occasional Papers in Archaeology No. 1, Saskatchewan Archaeological Society and Dept. of Archaeology and Anthropology, University of Saskatchewan, Saskatoon.

Wedel, W.R. 1961. *Prehistoric Man on the Great Plains*. Norman: University of Oklahoma Press.

Wiseman, Dion and James Graham. 2007. Quantifying Landscape Diversity and Uniqueness in the Prairie Ecozone. In *Building a Contextual Milieu: Interdisciplinary Modeling and Theoretical Perspectives from the SCAPE Project*, ed. B.A. Nicholson and Dion Wiseman. *Canadian Journal of Archaeology* 31, no. 3 (Supplement).

Yansa, C.H. 2007. Lake Records of Northern Plains Paleo-Indian and Early Archaic Environments: The Park Oasis Hypothesis. *Plains Anthropologist* 52, no. 201: 109–44.

Chapter 4
Human Ecology of the Canadian Prairie Ecozone ca. 1500 BP: Diffusion, Migration and Technological Innovation

Scott Hamilton, Jill Taylor-Hollings, and David Norris

This chapter summarizes northern Plains cultures dating to about 1500 BP (years before present), but this is not a particularly meaningful time unless discussed in a broader context, encompassing trends and processes spanning a millennium (ca. 2000–1000 BP). The Late Pre-contact period begins about 2000 BP, and is associated with two important technological innovations: the widespread adoption of bow-and-arrow technology, and the initial appearance of pottery (Dyck 1983: 110; Peck and Hudecek-Cuffe 2003). In the northeastern Plains this time period is sometimes called the Plains Woodland Period, and is treated as a prelude to the development of sedentary horticultural village life (Plains Village) (Figure 4.1).

Bow-and-arrow technology may have originated earlier (Pyszczyk 2003), but it became the dominant means of weapon launching after about 2000 BP. Pottery originated in the Eastern Woodlands perhaps as early as 4000 BP and is associated with increased population density based on intensive foraging, and culminated with the development of sedentary horticultural societies (Jennings 1989: 225–26). Pottery appears on the northern Plains after about 2000 BP but is often minimally represented in the northwestern Plains. At issue is whether these trends reflect extra-regional diffusion and acceptance of new technology by resident Plains populations, migration of non-local groups into the Plains, or some combination.

We focus on the first half of the Late Pre-contact Period, and emphasize Eastern Woodland influences that became increasingly visible through time, particularly in the eastern Plains. This includes technological innovations (pottery), new social practices (burial mound ceremonialism), some evidence of generalized foraging, and later, sedentary horticultural village life. This begs

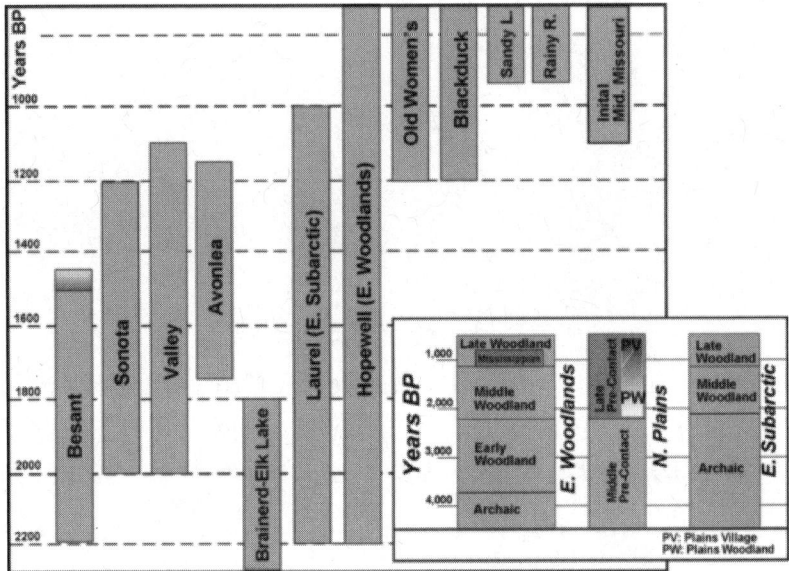

Figure 4.1. Northern Plains culture sequence compared to that of the Eastern Woodlands and Eastern Subarctic.

questions why such changes might have occurred. We propose that these trends can be usefully considered in light of socio-political, demographic and economic developments occurring in the Eastern Woodlands. While the boundaries between the Plains and Eastern Woodlands "culture areas" have always been permeable, we propose that they were particularly so after 2000 BP at a time of westward expansion of forest foragers. Since simply documenting cultural diffusion in the archaeological record does not offer a particularly compelling explanation why it might have occurred, we briefly review important cultural and historical developments in the Eastern Woodlands that might have contributed to this diffusion.

The General Climatic Context
Traditional macro-scale models of the northern Plains paleo-climate indicate trends that seldom offer better than century-level temporal resolution, and which lack uniform geographic applicability. However, these general climatic episodes are summarized following Dyck (1983), with the time of interest likely experiencing a trend from cool, wetter conditions towards warmer and more arid ones:

> 1) Sub-Atlantic (2900–1690 BP): A climatic episode representing a cooling trend, with summers moister and cloudier and with generally stormier winters.

CHAPTER 4: Human Ecology of the Canadian Prairie Ecozone ca. 1500 BP

2) Scandic (1690–1100 BP): Consistent with warmer and drier conditions of the earlier Atlantic.

3) Neo-Atlantic (1000–760 BP): Continued warm conditions with greater precipitation occurring.

It is not clear what role, if any, long-term climatic trends had on cultural transformations that occurred after ca. 2000 BP. Gregg (1994: 72–74) asserts that they had some cultural impact in the northeastern Plains, with a "peak of cultural developments" about 2000 BP when the mesic conditions of the Sub-Atlantic Period prevailed and with fewer archaeological sites dating to the drier Scandic period. However, Gregg (1994: 74) suggests that a population hiatus

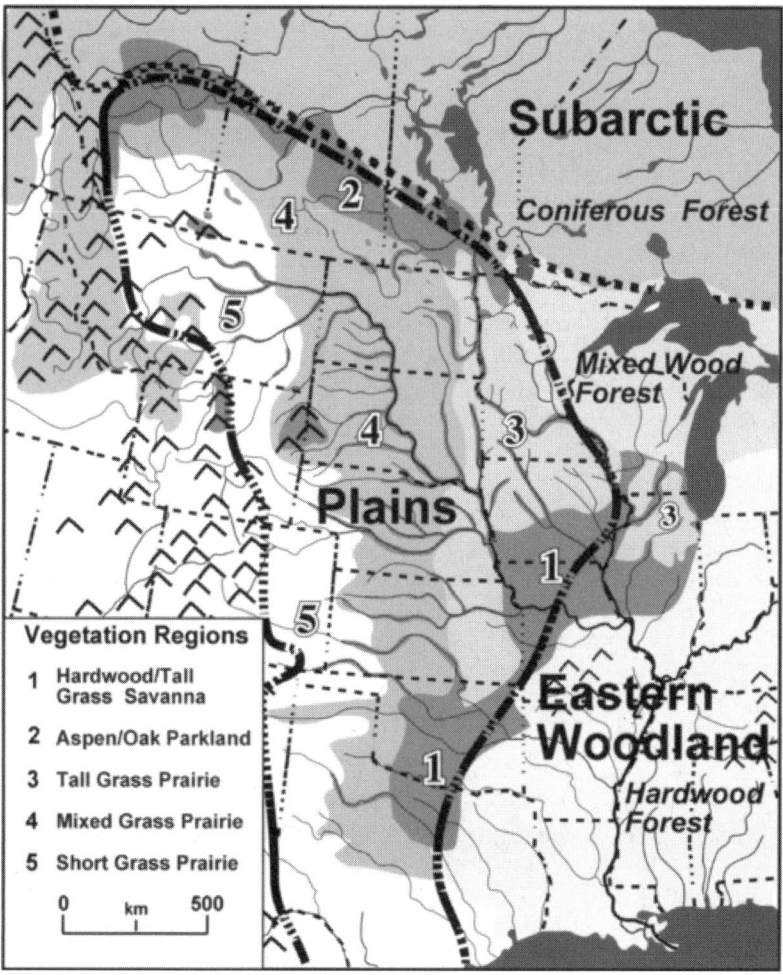

Figure 4.2. Vegetation of the Great Plains and adjacent regions.

did not occur during the Scandic. Rather, the carrying capacity was apparently reduced, thereby impacting human population density. In his view the reduced biomass of Scandic times led to "a time of transition for Northeastern Plains Woodland cultures" that involved adoption of bow-and-arrow technology, shifts in subsistence economy, increased emphasis on burial mounds to assert territoriality, and transformations in pottery wares (Gregg 1994: 74). We believe that such generalizations have limited value given year-to-year climatic variability and the considerable short-term adaptive flexibility of hunter-gatherers.

Also problematic is that biotic characterizations of the northern Plains and adjacent areas are generally coarse-grained and static, mainly due to a lack of detailed information. This is evident in Figure 4.2 that distinguishes between the short grass prairie of the west and the mixed and tall grass prairie zones of the east. Climate change, different soils, topography, and anthropogenic burning also continually altered grassland/forest borders during much of the Holocene epoch (Boyd 2002). Biotic variability within the Plains also derived from localized forest vegetation on uplands or within deeply incised river valleys. The Aspen Parklands adjacent to the eastern and northeastern Plains (Figure 4.2) offered another archaeologically important ecological mosaic. We propose that such intermingling of forest and grassland biotic communities, and particularly the forested river valleys draining the eastern Plains, were important since they provided a familiar environmental "threshold" that facilitated the spread of ideas, technology, and people from the Eastern Woodlands into the Plains region. In light of this complexity, Wood (1985: 1) observes that the relationships between people who occupied the Northern Plains and those of the prairie-forest border in Minnesota and Manitoba are one of the oldest and least understood topics in Plains anthropology.

The Broader Cultural Historical Context
The beginning of the Late Pre-contact Period is traditionally defined by material culture transformation, specifically bow-and-arrow use and pottery production, the latter likely deriving from the Eastern Woodlands.

In the Eastern Woodlands, pottery production was part of long-term trends involving population growth and sedentism, burial ceremonialism, social inequality, and technological diversification—all based upon intensive foraging and later horticulture (see Fagan 2005; Fiedel 1988; Jennings 1989). The origins of these trends date from the middle Holocene (Archaic Period) and accelerated throughout the past 3500 years of the Woodland and Mississippian Periods (Figure 4.1). These developments had implications far beyond the Eastern Woodlands. Beginning at least by 2200 BP, pottery use spread northward throughout the upper American Midwest and into the northern temperate and Boreal Forests of eastern Canada. In some regions this included the spread of burial mound ceremonialism, and the exchange of Adena and Hopewell influenced goods amongst neighbouring autonomous groups. At about the same time, some Eastern Woodlands cultural traits also became evident in the forest/grassland interface along the Mississippi River valley, and then spread further west to contribute to the Plains Woodland Tradition (e.g., Gregg 1994).

The Plains Woodland Tradition
Gregg (1994: 72) describes the Plains Woodland Tradition as a lifestyle based upon "hunting and gathering, but sometimes involved gardening and the production and use of ceramic vessels." It began as early as 2500 BP in the Prairie-Peninsula of the upper Midwest with some expressions in the eastern Plains (Figures 4.1, 4.2). While many Plains Woodland groups exploited bison, others appear to have foraged primarily in the forested river bottoms, with periodic exploitation of the surrounding grasslands. Indeed, Gregg (1994: 76) explicitly points to the Mississippi River headwaters and its connections west and north as the mode by which Eastern Woodland societies emerged in the northeastern Plains (Missouri and Red Rivers through southern Minnesota, Iowa, and the Dakotas) (Figure 4.2). Some expressions of these eastern societies also appear in southern Manitoba. While water transportation might have facilitated this interregional communication, the forested river valleys (Figure 4.2) also eased adaptation from forest foraging to one involving the forest/grassland interface, bison hunting, and eventually horticulture.

Consistent with their Eastern Woodland roots, the most distinctive Plains Woodland archaeological traits include pottery production, use of food storage pits, and burial mound and earthwork building. These traits are most strongly expressed near the forested river valleys of the eastern Plains (Figure 4.2), and as time passed, some Plains Woodland societies became increasingly sedentary and committed to horticulture mixed with foraging (e.g., Michlovic and Schneider 1993; Schneider 2002; Toom 2004). During the latter half of the Late Pre-contact Period, these trends culminated in the development of the Plains Village Tradition characterized by fortified earthlodge villages associated with maize, bean and squash horticulture (Ahler et al. 1991; Ahler and Kay 2007; Lehmer 1971). Other Plains Woodland-influenced groups were specialized bison hunters who moved widely throughout the northern Plains, but retained and reworked some Eastern Woodland cultural traits (i.e., pottery production, burial mound ceremonialism, and perhaps more frequent and sustained multi-family social groupings (see Walde 2006b).

Reflecting a Midwest perspective, Gregg (1994: 74) indicates that Plains Woodland cultures are distinctive from indigenous bison hunting specialists on a continuum that varied through time and across space (Figure 4.3):

> Archaeological complexes named for distinctive ceramic styles and other diagnostic remains of that time include Boyer, Arthur, Lake Benton, and Fox Lake in the south (Benn 1981b, 1982b, 1983, 1986, 1990; Bonney 1970), Sonota in the central and northern regions (Gregg 1987a;

Neuman 1975; Syms 1977), Besant and Avonlea in the west (Reeves 1983; Schneider and Kinney 1978), Laurel (Stoltman 1973) in the prairie-woodland ecotone to the northeast, and St. Croix in the east (Gibbon and Caine 1980: 61–62). These complexes are often referred to as late or terminal Middle Woodland cultures. If all of these complexes were contemporary and represent ethnic and social diversity, then the maintenance of group territories was likely a continual problem. Mounds may have served as territorial markers in addition to cemeteries (Lofstrom 1987: 11), a practice which may have originated in Archaic times (cf. Charles and Buikstra 1983: 130).

In our view, the clinal archaeological expression of Plains Woodland traits across the northern Plains may suggest variable commitment to this lifestyle by migrant eastern groups, or selective incorporation of non-local technology by indigenous Plains people.

Middle and Late Woodland Influences on the Plains

The Middle Woodland cultures of the Eastern Woodlands had widespread cultural and technological influence. This is most evident with the wide geographic spread of utilitarian conoidal-shaped pottery, burial mound ceremonialism, and occasionally exotic funerary objects (Mason 2002). This dispersal is often thought to reflect the influential Hopewell Culture of the American Midwest and its expansive exchange network (Mason 2002). The most northerly of the Middle Woodland archaeological cultures was Laurel, found widely throughout northern Minnesota and the Boreal Forest of Saskatchewan, Manitoba and northern Ontario (Figures 4.1, 4.3) (Meyer and Hamilton 1994). While Laurel Composite is generally characterized by broad-spectrum forest foraging, some of their sites are found along the forest/grassland transition but do not have a well-established presence in the northern Plains (Meyer and Epp 1990). However Walde et al. (1995: 22 citing Landals 1994: 130–35) note that the artifacts from the Miniota Site (Avonlea affiliation) in western Manitoba suggest "Laurel contacts and cultural influences." These linkages are addressed later in this chapter.

In the Late Woodland Period (ca. 1200–400 BP), new pottery forms and types appear widely throughout the American Midwest, eastern Subarctic, and portions of the northern Plains (Figure 4.1). The Blackduck Horizon was the most expansive of these archaeological cultures, appearing first in northern Minnesota and then much more widely to the north from eastern Saskatchewan to western Québec (Hamilton et al. 2007; Meyer and Hamilton 1994; Meyer et al. 1999; Walde et al. 1995). Blackduck sites in the Boreal Forest suggest generalized foraging by small mobile groups, with little evidence of the intensification of settlement and production generally seen in the more temperate Eastern Woodlands. A possible exception is suggested by Gibbon's (1994, 2003) general

CHAPTER 4: Human Ecology of the Canadian Prairie Ecozone ca. 1500 BP

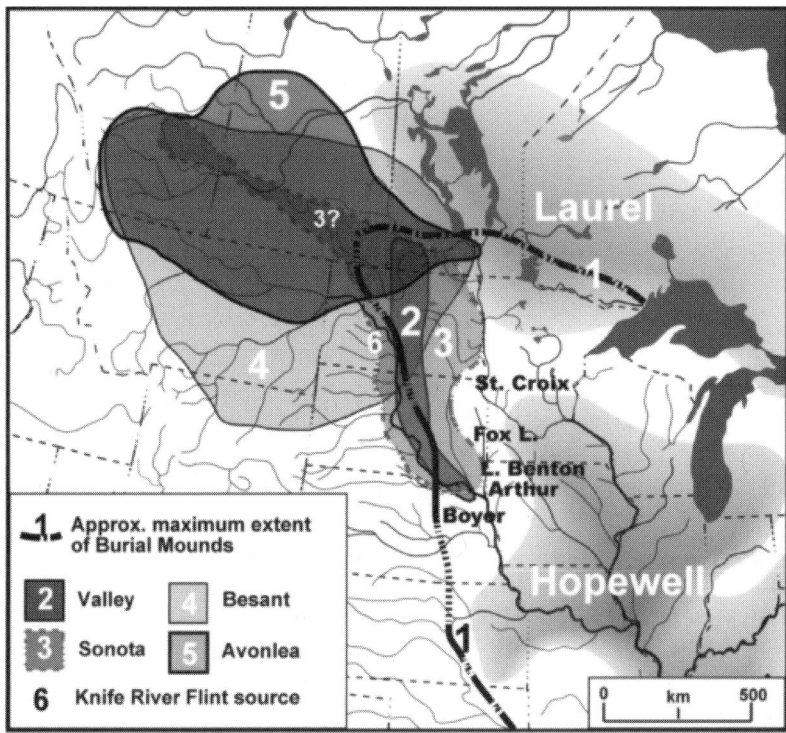

Figure 4.3. Middle Woodland Cultures and their influences on the Northern Plains (after Fagan 1995; Gregg 1994; Jennings 1989; Meyer and Hamilton 1994; Reeves 1983; Syms 1977; Walde 2006b).

comments about larger and more sustained settlement based upon some horticulture and intensive exploitation of fish and wild rice in the mixed wood forests of northern Minnesota. Similar intensification in this region based upon wild rice and fishing is also noted with the Psinomani Culture (producers of Sandy Lake Ware) (Gibbon 1994, 2003; Taylor-Hollings 1999). This culture also inhabited parts of the Boreal Forest in Manitoba and Ontario where mobile generalized foraging was the norm (Taylor-Hollings 1999). Blackduck Ware (Hamilton et al. 2007) and Sandy Lake Ware (Taylor-Hollings 1999) also are found widely throughout the Plains and Aspen Parklands of southern Manitoba, and indicate adaptive shifts from generalized foraging to specialized bison exploitation. Walde et al. (1995) used the term "Plains Blackduck," a concept continued by Hamilton et al. (2007), to reflect this bison-focused regional economy. Michlovic and Schneider 1993 report a fortified village at the Shea Site in North Dakota, with evidence of horticulture, bison hunting and a pottery assemblage dominated by Sandy Lake Ware and Northeastern Plains Village Wares. Clearly, these archaeological cultures provide evidence of both adaptive flexibility and the transfer of ideas between residents of the plains and forest ecozones.

The Middle Missouri and Northeastern Plains Village Traditions

Late in the time period considered here, the beginnings of horticultural village life are evident along the river valleys of the eastern Plains (Figure 4.1). The Plains Village Tradition is best known at fortified horticultural villages in the middle reaches of the Missouri River that culminated in the ethnographically known Mandan, Hidatsa, and Arikara villages (Ahler et al. 1991; Johnson 1998; Lehmer 1971; Winham and Calabrese 1998). Less well known are small semi-sedentary villages in the eastern Dakotas, Nebraska, Iowa and Minnesota for which there are fewer ethnographic analogues (Ahler et al. 1991: 38; Ahler and Mehrer 1984; Ahler and Kay 2007; Arzigan 1987; Gregg 1994; Johnson and Johnson 1998; Kordecki and Gregg 1986; Michlovic 1990; Michlovic and Schneider 1993; Shay 1990; Toom 2004). Southern Manitoba marks the most northerly extent of these mixed foraging and horticultural groups, with some ongoing debate about the extent of horticultural production in more northerly locales (Boyd et al. 2006, 2008; Flynn and Syms 1996; Nicholson 1990, 1991, 1994a; Nicholson et al. 2002; Schneider 2002). Even farther removed from this region is the Cluny Site (Forbis 1977) in southern Alberta, which is a unique (and Proto-contact) fortified village. Different processes contributed to diverse adaptations throughout the northeastern Plains, and while appearing after the period under consideration here, we briefly address them as a prelude to more extended discussion in the following chapter.

Northern Plains Culture History (ca. 2000–1000 BP)

Pelican Lake/Sandy Creek/Besant

Further to discussion in the previous chapter regarding the Pelican Lake Phase, we note Vickers' (1986: 80–81) comments about a possible cultural relationship between the Pelican Lake Phase and the Besant Complex based upon an inter-assemblage overlap in tool types. Vickers (1986: 81) also suggests that Sandy Creek projectile points are early versions of those made by Besant Complex people and may reflect part of the technological transition from Pelican Lake to Besant (Dyck 1983: 108; Dyck et al. 1980). We also note Reeves' (1983: 102) earlier model regarding the Napikwan versus Tunaxa Traditions that proposes a transition from Pelican Lake to Avonlea. Peck and Hudecek-Cuffe (2003: 76) offer a useful summary of these differing perspectives.

Besant Complex (ca. 2200–1500 BP)

The Besant Complex is documented over much of the northern Plains (Figure 4.3) and is defined primarily by distinctive side-notched projectile points thought to have been mounted on atlatl-launched darts (Figure 4.4). While it may be the last Plains culture to not use bow-and-arrow technology, Kehoe (1974) proposes that the small Samantha projectile points may represent gradual integration of bow and arrow technology over time by Besant peoples, and there has been general acceptance of this idea (e.g., Reeves 1983: 63; Vickers

CHAPTER 4: Human Ecology of the Canadian Prairie Ecozone ca. 1500 BP

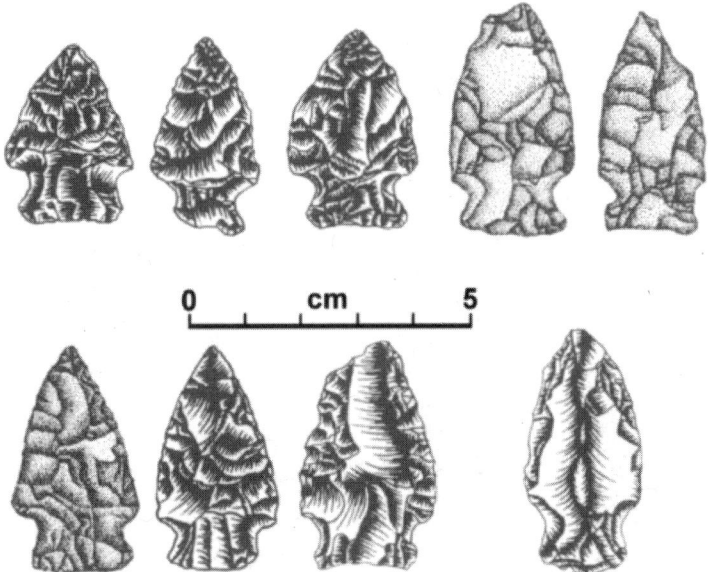

Figure 4.4. Besant Complex projectile points from the Melhagen Site (after Dyck 1983: 118). These specimens evince a "stubbier" form and less frequently are produced from Knife River Flint. Some might identify more lanceolate Knife River Flint specimens from this site as Sonota Complex.

1986: 84–85, 1994: 9). It is not agreed whether the persistence of atlatl-launched darts indicates that Besant Complex should be treated as the terminus of the Middle Pre-contact Period (Reeves 1983; Forbis 1992), or whether the sporadic appearance of Besant pottery (Scribe 1997) and Samantha projectile points indicates a technological transition marking the beginning of the Late Pre-contact Period (Walde and Meyer 2003: 137; Walde et al. 1995). We include the Besant Complex as part of the Late Pre-contact Period in light of some Besant pottery recoveries and other proposed relationships with Eastern Woodland societies.

The Besant Complex dates from as early as 2200 years BP and persisted up to between 1500 BP and 1100 BP, with some temporal overlap with the Avonlea Horizon (ca. 1700–1100 BP) (Morlan 1988: 306; Vickers 1994: 8) (Figure 4.1). Walde et al. (1995: 19) challenge this perspective, suggesting that the temporal overlap between Besant and Avonlea may not be evident in the Canadian Plains (see also Cloutier 2004). They (Walde et al. 1995: 19) assert that in Canadian stratigraphic sequences Besant materials always pre-date Avonlea deposits:

> While Avonlea succeeded Besant on most of the Canadian Plains about A.D. 500, this was clearly not the case everywhere. Besant persisted in the Dakotas (Gregg 1994: 75), in

eastern Montana, and in south central Saskatchewan (see also Greiser 1994: 44). In the latter areas there is simply no, or very little, evidence of Avonlea occupation at any time (Fraley 1988: 132). The scenario would appear to be, therefore, that there was an initial Besant occupation of the whole of the northern plains but by A.D. 500, a large portion of this region was taken over by people of Avonlea culture. By A.D. 800 Besant ended in the Dakotas as Initial Middle Missouri populations began to colonize the region and establish farming villages. (Winham and Lueck 1994)

Thus, the evidence suggests some degree of temporal overlap between Avonlea Horizon and Besant Complex, with geographic contraction of Besant from the Canadian Plains region late in its history.

Besant projectile points are the most distinctive element of the tool kit and have a side-notched form, with bases that are either straight or slightly concave with basal thinning and grinding (Peck and Hudecek-Cuffe 2003: 73; Reeves 1983: 54–57) (Figure 4.4). The side-notches are generally shallow, being twice as wide as they are deep (Peck and Hudecek-Cuffe 2003: 73), and are located close to the base. Vickers (1994: 11) notes that Besant stone tool assemblages, especially in Alberta, are generally dominated by locally available raw materials (see also Peck and Hudecek-Cuffe 2003: 75), although non-local Avon chert (Montana) or Knife River chalcedony (western North Dakota) is abundant at some sites. The latter includes the Muhlbach (Gruhn 1969) and Melhagen Sites (Phenix 1969; Ramsay 1991), whose occupants are interpreted to have either traveled far to acquire raw material or who enjoyed broad exchange connections (see also Vickers 1994: 12 and Walde et al. 1995: 19).

While not common in the northwestern Plains, Besant pottery has been recovered occasionally in Alberta (Loveseth 1983: 63; Peck and Hudecek-Cuffe 2003: 74–75; Quigg 1986: 119–23) and in Montana at the Whiskey Hill Site (Johnson 1977a, 1977b). In Saskatchewan, Besant pottery is reported somewhat more frequently at sites that include the Long Creek, Walter Felt, Garratt and Intake sites (Dyck 1983: 120; Walde et al. 1995: 17–18). Walde et al. (1995: 17 citing Scribe 1997) also report Besant pottery from the Pinew Watchi and Wapiti Sakihitaw sites in the Tigers Hills of southwestern Manitoba, and along the Souris River in southern Saskatchewan (Meyer and Rollans 1990). While more sparsely recovered than in the east, these vessels resemble contemporaneous early Plains Woodland vessels (Figure 4.5) (Dyck 1983; Johnson 1977a; Walde et al. 1995: 18). They are generally conoidal in shape with straight rim profiles and typically similar surface treatment (smooth or cord marked paddle). Decoration is minimal, confined to the lip and rim, and consists of punctates, bosses and sometimes simple dentate or other stamped impressions (Walde et al. 1995: 18) (Figure 4.5).

The eastern technological affinities evident in the pottery led Reeves (1983)

CHAPTER 4: Human Ecology of the Canadian Prairie Ecozone ca. 1500 BP

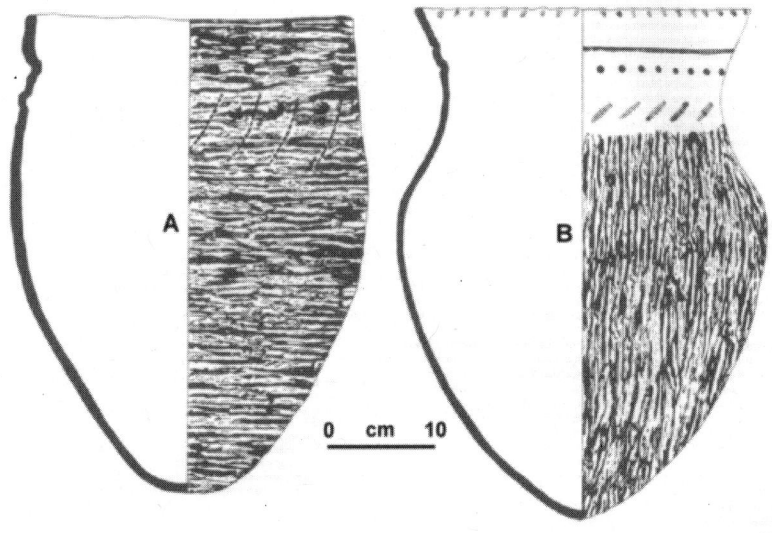

Figure 4.5. Two generic Plains Woodland pottery forms (after Gregg 1994: 77, 82). Gregg (1994: 77) describes Vessel A as dating to ca. 1400–1500 BP, and is based upon a vessel recovered from the Arpan Site (Sonota mound, Neuman 1975: 189). The general shape and finish is likely consistent with Besant, Valley and Sonota wares. Vessel B is a generic form that Gregg (1994: 82) considers to date to ca. 1100–1200 BP. While still generally conoidal, the constricted neck and outflaring rim is more consistent with some Late Woodland wares such as Blackduck.

to propose that Besant, including Sonota, emerged on the Plains through participation in the Hopewell Interaction Sphere (see also Boyd 2002: 483) (Figure 4.3). Indeed, in his 1970 PhD dissertation Reeves (1983: 190–92) proposed that the Besant Complex originated in the Eastern Woodlands, and that these more politically integrated and populous groups expanded westward up the Missouri River basin, undertook communal bison hunting (to build supplies of provisions and hides), and controlled access to favoured lithic raw material sources. He further suggested that these commodities were then redistributed eastward through the Hopewellian exchange system. While this assertion remains controversial (see Wright 1999: 789 for an alternative perspective), it is clear that the Eastern Woodlands had a significant role in the technological and cultural innovations marking the beginning of the Late Pre-contact Period. The possible role of the Hopewell Interaction Sphere in the northern Plains will be addressed more fully below in the context of Sonota Complex burial rituals.

Dyck (1983: 113) notes that the Besant Complex became prominent archaeologically at a time when the climate likely underwent a transition from cooler and wetter conditions in the Sub-Atlantic to warmer and drier circumstances in the Scandic episode. Whether such macro-scale climatic transformations contributed to the Besant Complex becoming more archaeologically visible is not yet demonstrated. In any case, Dyck (1983: 113) and Frison (1978: 223) observe that Besant is associated with increased archaeological visibility of communal bison mass procurement (see also Walde 2006b; Walde et al. 1995: 19). This involved more intensive use of communal killing methods using jumps, pounds, or corrals, and is often associated with midden deposits featuring butchered bison bone (Dyck 1983; Frison 1971, 1978; Gruhn 1969; Hjermstad 1993, 1995; Hlady 1967; Peck and Hudecek-Cuffe 2003; Phenix 1969; Ramsay 1991). Perhaps the best-known example of intensive Besant Complex communal bison hunting is the Ruby Site (Frison 1971, 1978), which is located along a dry arroyo in Wyoming's Powder River basin. The site includes a drive lane and pound complex located within the arroyo with extensive butchering and processing zones along its margins. Also discovered was a structure that Frison (1971) interprets to have served ceremonial functions. The site appears to have been repeatedly used with a significant investment in communal labour to construct, maintain, and operate the structures. Frison (1971) asserts that the design and placement of such mass kill sites demonstrates a comprehensive understanding of how to use the landscape to manipulate bison behaviour.

Dyck (1983) reports that Besant Complex sites in southern Saskatchewan are particularly visible, dense, and prominent, suggesting either climate-induced increases in bison numbers or cultural innovations favouring the development of communal bison mass-killing technology. While Dyck's (1983) perspective is consistent with Frison's (1971) Wyoming observations, Vickers (1986: 82, 1994: 13) asserts that the density of Besant sites in Alberta is not particularly noteworthy. That being said, communal bison hunting suggests a higher level of political integration, labour coordination, and greater group size than that required for more individualistic bison-hunting tactics. Walde (2006b: 299) outlines these social implications, which he proposes became more archaeologically visible after ca. 2000 BP:

> Communal bison hunting... involved entire communities in secular and sacred activities ... directed by a specialist leader with strong acquired skills and religious authority. Under the kill master's direction and prayers, drive lanes ... to jump cliffs or pounds were constructed. If pounds (wooden corrals) were necessary, the pound master supervised the erection closely to ensure that no open spaces were present ... When the facilities were ready, specialist hunters were dispatched to gather the bison and convince them to move towards the killing facility. This process could take many days and required the services of highly skilled hunters who used fire, wolf and bison calf disguises, and a variety of other means to manoeuvre a target herd, frequently over a distance of many kilometers, into the drive lines. Here they would

stampede the herd, which would be confined to the drive lines by people stationed along the lines who yelled and waved robes and blankets. Once the animals entered the pound or ran over the jump they were dispatched. Religious ceremonies concluded the hunt, which was followed by processing of the animals.

The growing importance of this mode of bison hunting suggests significant changes in the social structure and communal involvement of northern Plains people at this time. In contrast, Kehoe (1978: 79) offers the perspective that the earliest evidence for "complex, ritualized, patterned bison drives" is associated with Avonlea sites. In any case, Reeves' (1983) and Walde's (2006b) important discussions of possible motivation for such surplus-producing effort are discussed below.

In his palaeoecological analysis of a deep stratigraphic section in the Lauder Sandhills of the Glacial Lake Hind basin, southwestern Manitoba, Boyd (2002) notes a peak in the recovery rate of burned grass phytoliths (an indicator of grassland fires) after about 2500 BP. Boyd's (2002: 479) analysis indicates that throughout this timeframe the region was predominately open grassland, but gradually transformed to the historically apparent mixed grassland-forest habitat. The peak frequency of burned phytoliths is interpreted to reflect a significant increase in anthropogenic burning (Boyd 2002: 480–81), probably reflecting efforts to influence plant growth and thereby manipulate bison herd behaviour. Boyd (2002: 481–83) briefly describes the regional archaeological site inventory dating to this time, and observes a strong representation of Besant and Sonota Complex materials in the Glacial Lake Hind basin, including Sonota burial mounds. He concludes that the Plains of the Souris River valley (bisecting the Glacial Lake Hind basin) were more intensely occupied by Besant and Sonota people compared to the rest of southern Manitoba. While discussing hypothesized relationships between Hopewell and contemporaneous Besant and Sonota populations, Boyd (2002: 483) draws attention to the role of deliberate burning as part of the "Eastern Agricultural Complex" (Cowan 1985: 206). He speculates that the westward spread of Eastern Woodlands cultural traits included burning as a habitat manipulation strategy to enhance biotic productivity and to manipulate bison distribution and density. Boyd (2002) concludes that this enhanced productivity enabled denser local occupation by Besant-Sonota peoples. Walde (2006b) offers similar arguments about the westward spread of Eastern Woodland traits that are summarized later in this chapter.

Evidence consistent with the proposal that the Besant Complex represents a dramatic increase in communal bison procurement from previous times includes the discovery of larger and more substantial house structures at some sites. While commonly associated with conical tipis (Finnigan 1981, 1982; Quigg 1986; Reeves 1980; Dyck 1983: 113), the partial exposure of a Besant post-in-ground structure at the Mortlach Site in Saskatchewan is discussed in Wettlaufer (1955), and Hoffman (1968) reported a similar feature at the La Roche Site in South Dakota. The latter yielded an oval arrangement of post molds suggesting a structure about 8 by 7 m in size, with a large central fire pit and associated midden. Dyck (1983) comments on the similarity of the La Roche structure to Early Woodland bark-covered houses found in the Eastern Woodlands region. Neuman (1975: 82–84) described the La Roche site structure, and while commenting on the similarity between Besant and Sonota, suggested that it was of Sonota affiliation on the basis of similarity of pottery to that from the Stelzer Site—an important Sonota "type site." Also consistent with the notion of Besant intensification, many researchers (Dyck 1983: 113; Quigg 1986; Reeves 1980; Vickers 1994: 11) agree that Besant tipi rings are generally larger than others reported in Alberta. Indeed, Brumley and Dau (1988: 36) note that the Ross Glen Besant Site (Quigg 1986: 192) yielded tipi rings with an average inside diameter of 6.8 m (n=5) compared to the average of 4.6 m (n=651) for other reported stone rings in Alberta. Perhaps the communal work required for mass bison killing fostered the maintenance of larger groups (with larger households or tipis) than bands that engaged in smaller-scale and single bison predation. However, in a paper addressing tipi ring size variability through time in Wyoming and Alberta, Wilson (1983: 113–38) offered a cautionary note, challenging this generalization. He notes that large tipi rings have been observed in Alberta that date as far back as the "Middle Prehistoric" period, and reports that some variability in mapping and measurement methodology might be contributing to the reported variability. He also draws attention to taphonomic processes affecting ring diameter.

Beginning with the Besant Complex, Walde (2006b) argues that the trend towards more intensive communal bison procurement had significant social implications, including the development of tribally organized groups reminiscent of the intensive foragers and horticulturalists of the Eastern Woodlands. While not suggesting that the same degree of sedentism and social complexity developed on the northern Plains, he asserts that communal bison hunting required multi-family collaboration, and perhaps sodalities, to conduct large-scale bison killing and processing. Since individualistic predation methods were effective and continued to be practiced into the 19th century, Walde (2006b) suggests that some larger motivation drove the intensification of production reflected by more frequent communal mass bison killing. Perhaps more complex levels of political organization deriving from the east served to facilitate semi-sedentism, or rather, seasonal sedentism. Walde (2006b) proposes that mass bison killing and intensive provisioning generated food surpluses used to sustain larger gatherings of people in long-term camps over the balance of the winter (see Hamilton and Nicholson 2006 for a review of the ethnohistoric literature regarding this pattern). Such surplus-producing efforts may well have had impacts upon contemporary populations:

> Features of semi-sedentary tribally organized Woodland groups ... appear on the northern plains as early as Besant times and it appears that these people retained major features of their social organization. Warfare with band-level peoples on the northern plains, and resistance to migration from other Eastern Woodlands groups, may well have been a factor in the retention of tribal social organization and the force of tradition—that is, maintenance of previously existing social relations of production and reproduction—must also be recognized as another factor. Existing band societies in the northern plains faced with ... encroachments from ... tribal peoples to their southeast would have been forced to adopt the social organization of their enemies or face expulsion or extinction. The advance ... of tribally organized peoples from the Eastern Woodlands onto the plains coincides with the florescence of communal bison hunting in the area.... . (Walde 2006b: 305–6)

At issue is what other Eastern Woodland influences appear along the eastern Plains at this time and whether similar evidence of intensification is apparent.

Sonota Complex (ca. 2000–1200 BP)
The Sonota Complex has a controversial place in northern Plains archaeology since some archaeologists treat it as a discrete archaeological complex while others view it as a regional variation of the Besant Complex. Sonota Complex sites appear to be confined to the northeastern Plains (North and South Dakota and southern Manitoba), with a few possible ones reported in Saskatchewan and Alberta (Peck 2007) (Figure 4.3). Pettipas (1983: 103) proposes that Sonota sites date to between ca. 2000 BP and 1400 BP along the Missouri River valley in South Dakota, but were occupied from 1750–1200 BP to the north in the Canadian Plains. He describes bison hunting as the basis of the Sonota economy, with particular emphasis on mass killing using riverbank jumps, mires and pounds. This emphasis on bison hunting forms a sharp contrast to the generalized forest-edge foraging lifestyle of other early Plains Woodland groups who appeared in the eastern Plains at about the same time (as discussed below).

Sonota projectile points are often produced from Knife River chalcedony and are similar to those of the Besant Complex, but some researchers describe the former as more lanceolote in form and exhibiting finer, more symmetrical flaking (Figure 4.6) (Syms 1977: 88). Whether these differences reflect overt stylistic distinctions or are due to differential access to superior raw materials is not clear (see Ramsay [1991] and Scribe [1997] for more systematic discussions). Like those classified as part of the Besant Complex, these projectile points were likely mounted on atlatl-launched darts.

The relationship between Besant and Sonota assemblages is controversial

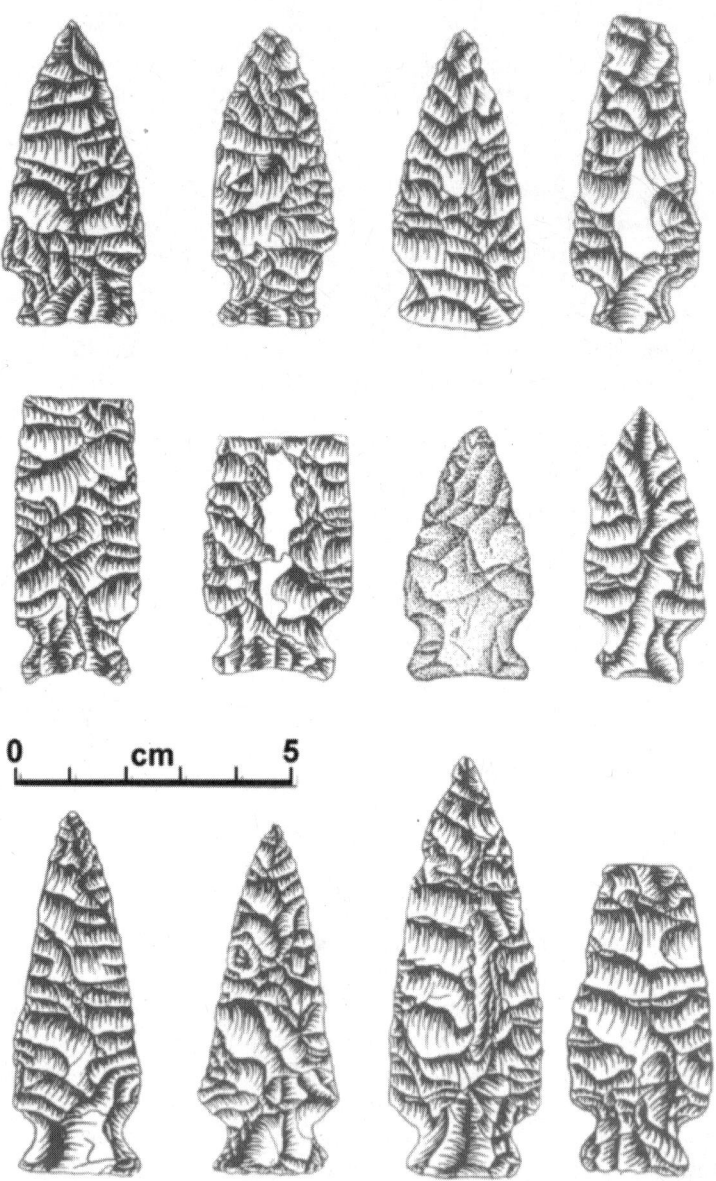

Figure 4.6. Sonota style projectile points. Dyck (1983: 117) identifies more lanceolate projectile points (mostly Knife River Flint) from the Melhagen Site as Besant. Some archaeologists in the eastern Plains might identify such objects as being Sonota Complex.

(Ramsay 1991: 87–90; Reeves 1983: 11–13; Scribe 1997; Syms 1977: 88–92). The Besant Complex is widely recognized throughout the northern Plains on the basis of hunting camps and bison kills, while the Sonota Complex is best known in the northeastern Plains for burial mound ceremonialism and heavy reliance upon Knife River chalcedony. Dyck (1983: 114–15), Gregg (1994: 76), Reeves (1983: 10–13) and others propose that the Sonota and Besant Complexes should be treated as regional variants on the basis of general similarities in the tool kit and temporal duration, and that Sonota appears regionally distinctive because of burial mound ceremonialism and ready access to Knife River chalcedony sources (Figure 4.3). Others, most notably Neuman (1975) and Syms (1977), assert that Sonota is sufficiently distinctive culturally and technologically to be treated as a discrete entity, albeit one with some relationship with Besant people.

Sonota Complex sites sometimes yield conoidal vessels with smoothed or cord-roughened surfaces consistent with general early Plains Woodland vessel forms (Figure 4.5). Pettipas (1983: 108) indicates that pottery is not common in Sonota assemblages. This rarity is also consistent with Besant, and contrasts with the relative abundance of pottery in the Eastern Woodlands at this time.

In light of Sonota Complex burial ceremonialism and the similarities discussed previously, we find it analytically most useful to think about the Sonota Complex as a regionally distinct entity, albeit one with linkages to the Besant Complex. Syms (1977: 90) as well as Johnson and Johnson (1998: 221) cite Neuman's (1975) recoveries from Sonota burial mounds (small quantities of obsidian, dentalium and olivella shells, and imitation grizzly bear teeth) as evidence of participation in the Hopewell Interaction Sphere exchange system, something not noted with the Besant Complex. This extra-regional exchange is apparent with some South Dakota sites yielding both Wyoming obsidian and Minnesota pipestone (Pettipas 1983: 108). Syms (1977: 90) observes that Hopewellian finished goods (platform pipes, copper objects, pan pipes, ear spools, fresh water pearls, etc.) are seldom found in Sonota burials, thus suggesting limited Hopewellian influence and persistence of "individually achieved status" (Syms 1977: 90). While echoing this perspective, Johnson and Johnson (1998: 221) suggest a stronger Hopewellian influence in the burial mounds that "combine Hopewellian construction, burial treatment, and distinctive artifacts with an adaptation of the ceremony to include bison carcasses in the mound fill." Ramsay (1991: 84) offers a substantive summary of Sonota Complex burial ritual and mound construction. She cites Neuman's (1975: 94) description of low dome-shaped earthen mounds that appear singly or in small clusters on the upper brink or first terrace of river valleys, presumably to afford maximum visibility to these structures. This is consistent with Gregg's (1994) general observations, cited previously, about the overt visibility of Plains Woodland burial mounds and their proposed function to validate territorial claims. Ramsay (1991) describes secondary burials interred within a single sub-floor pit below the mound, with rare cases of burials in the mound fill. All age categories and both sexes were included in the mounds, with the actual bundle burials usually consisting of articulated torsos with purposefully disarticulated skulls and limbs stacked beside them. While grave offerings are common, there does not appear to be any sex- or age-related pattern associated with them. Ramsay (1991: 84–85 citing Neuman 1975: 88–95) seems to downplay the Hopewellian connection in her description:

> Offerings included such things as pendants made from bear, beaver and human bones and teeth, and marine and freshwater shells. Beads were made of bone, marine shells, copper and fossils. Pigments such as hematite, greenstone, magnetite and yellow ochre were also found, usually in the form of powdery deposits or small lumps. Buffalo offerings sometimes included complete or almost entire carcasses. This would seem to reflect the importance of the bison to these people, in both a spiritual and a practical context. The seasonality of the bison remains also suggests that the mound was constructed between the spring and fall when the ground was not frozen.

Reeves (1983), Syms (1977), Walde (2006b) and others emphasize cultural linkage of Besant and Sonota Complexes with the Hopewell Interaction Sphere through trade and exchange, but Peck and Hudecek-Cuffe (2003: 76–77) cite Vickers' (1986: 86–87, 1994: 14) observation that Knife River chalcedony and obsidian (supposed western exchange commodities) are rare in Hopewell assemblages, and for that matter, obsidian is also rare in Besant-Sonota assemblages. Reeves (1983: 190–91 citing Griffin 1968) also tempered his perspective on extra-regional exchange by suggesting that Hopewellian access to western lithic sources was limited, and may reflect comparatively few direct procurement expeditions by Hopewell people into the northern Plains. Reeves (1983: 191) asserts that the minimal representation of obsidian in Besant sites might indicate that it was too valuable as an exchange commodity with eastern Hopewellian groups to permit common domestic use. All such discussion of extra-regional exchange must be tempered with the observation that obsidian is rarely found in Hopewellian contexts, and that such limited representation might well be overstated in the archaeological literature.

In summary, existing evidence of Sonota Complex burial mound ceremonialism suggests some level of involvement in the Hopewell Interaction Sphere, but that these non-local traits were selectively incorporated using local frames of reference. Particularly compelling are the bison carcass inclusions within some burial mounds. Despite the apparent linkages of the Besant and Sonota Complexes with Middle Woodland societies in the eastern forests, these significant and geographically widespread complexes were strongly oriented to a

Plains bison-hunting lifestyle. Echoing Frison's (1978) observations, their political economy appears to be structured around communal bison exploitation to an unprecedented degree, with significant labour and spiritual investment in mass killing, presumably to generate surplus production (Dyck 1983; Walde 2006b). An unresolved issue is whether such communal effort was designed to facilitate extra-regional exchange (Reeves 1983) or to enable maintenance of larger groups in semi-sedentary winter aggregations (Walde 2006b). In any case, we agree that this might reflect organizational patterns that diffused westward as part of the emergence of the Plains Woodland Tradition. However, not all Plains Woodland groups reflect this bison-focused economy and socially facilitated intensification of production.

Valley Complex and Other Plains Woodland Foragers
The Valley Complex is not well known in the northern Plains archaeological literature, but we include it here on the basis of Syms' (1977) and Neuman's (1975: 83–84) observations that it is found primarily in the central Plains and northwards along the Missouri River and much more sparsely into northeastern Montana and southwestern Manitoba (Figure 4.3). Reeves (1983: 106–12) offers a different geographic perspective regarding the Valley "Phase" and succeeding Loseke Creek Phase, suggesting a more limited range in the river valleys of northeastern Nebraska and adjacent South Dakota (Figure 4.3). Interestingly, Neuman (1975: 83–84) comments on the general similarity of Valley Complex pottery and other material culture to that of Sonota Complex, and also cites a personal communication from Reeves (1967) suggesting Valley Complex pottery was recovered as far west as Havre (northeastern Montana). Some of the ambiguity regarding these early Plains Woodland cultural influences reflects the early state of northern Plains archaeological research in the 1960s, whereby the Havre pottery might now be treated as wares associated with the Besant Complex. Also, generic Plains Woodland pottery appeared sporadically in several cultural entities throughout the eastern Plains at this time and it is still not well understood.

The Valley Complex dates from about 2000–1100 BP and is defined by medium-sized conical pottery (Syms 1977: 88). Reeves (1983: 108) describes it as being conoidal-shaped with vertically oriented cording and decoration consisting of bosses, punctates, some cord-wrapped object impressed designs or sometimes dentate stamping on the lip and/or rim (Figure 4.5) (see also Neuman 1975: 83–84). Kivett (1952, 1970) and Syms (1977: 88) characterize Valley Complex people as being generalized foragers of small- and medium-sized animals, aquatic birds, and turtles, with only minimal representation of bison, beaver, and canid remains in their sites. Reeves (1983: 108–9) also suggests that Valley Phase people practiced a generalized foraging lifestyle that featured use of small ungulates, shellfish, fowl and plants, all reflecting a strong focus on riverine habitats. With sites containing storage pits and trash-filled basins, greater stability of occupation and perhaps also early horticultural activity is suggested (Reeves 1983: 108–9). These Eastern Woodland influences are also indicated by burial ritual involving secondary burials in pits, sometimes with an overlying mound (Reeves 1983: 109). This persistent exploitation of woodland species within the forested river valleys is remarkable given the apparent general availability of bison at the time.

Gregg (1994: 78–79) also comments on the importance of the wooded fringes of rivers and lakes, as opposed to the open prairies, for early Plains Woodland occupations. Coupled with the warm season biotic diversity of such areas, these sheltered places also attracted bison (and also perhaps Plains-adapted bison hunters) in winter (see Hamilton and Nicholson 2006). These encampment localities are also periodically associated with conical and linear burial mounds further emphasizing their Eastern Woodland cultural influences (see Chomko and Wood 1973: 15; Snortland-Coles 1985). According to Gregg (1994: 78), Plains Woodland peoples:

> sometimes hunted big game and gathered wild plant foods including tuberous roots at sites in upland settings (cf. Deaver 1985: 262). There are indications from excavations in the southern part of the study area [Iowa, SW Minnesota] that people were gardening (Benn 1986: 28). Cucurbita pepo seeds were ubiquitous through all the Mid-America Woodland levels at the Rainbow site (Benn 1990: 199). This is not surprising since contemporary folk in the riverine Midwest were growing squash and marsh elder (Kelley et al. 1984: 125). Bison were the principal focus of attention in most subsistence economies, and they were also a focal point in religious and spiritual practices...

The last sentence refers specifically to the Sonota Complex and the central economic and spiritual role of bison to these people. We emphasize that not all early Plains Woodland people were focused on bison. Perhaps this reflects adaptive conservatism of some groups, or alternatively, temporal shifts whereby newcomers first gravitated to familiar forested habitats (i.e., Valley Complex) until they adjusted to new opportunities involving migratory bison hunting on the open grassland (i.e., Besant and Sonota Complexes).

Avonlea Horizon (ca. 1750–1150 BP)
Sites assigned to Avonlea cultural affiliation are found in the northern Plains, Aspen Parkland and edge of the Boreal Forest of British Columbia, Alberta, Saskatchewan, Manitoba, Montana and the Dakotas (Meyer and Walde 2009) (Figure 4.5). At the Avonlea type site in Saskatchewan, Kehoe and McCorquodale (1961) first named the Avonlea Horizon, with the Timber Ridge Side Notched point type as a horizon marker using the Willey and Phillips

CHAPTER 4: Human Ecology of the Canadian Prairie Ecozone ca. 1500 BP

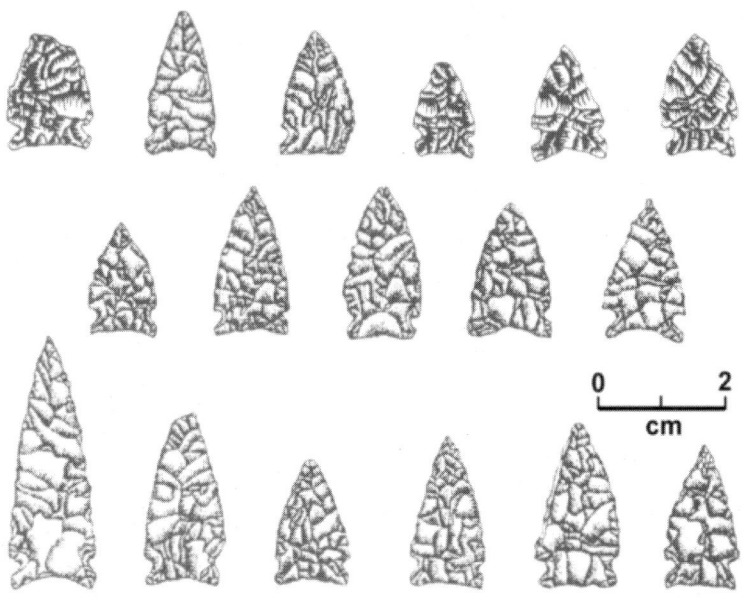

Figure 4.7. Avonlea projectile points (after Dyck 1983: 122).

(1958) taxonomic system (Figure 4.7). Reeves (1970) later proposed the Avonlea Phase with several sub-phases. After decades of research, Meyer and Walde (2009; Meyer et al. 2008; Meyer and Epp 1990; Walde and Meyer 2003; Walde et al. 1995) summarize the growing body of evidence that indicates, while Avonlea projectile points are comparatively uniform over its geographic range, there is regionally based variation in pottery form and decoration. They assert that this variability requires taxonomic reformulation involving returning to treatment of Avonlea as a Horizon with the definition of a series of regionally discrete named Phases. We summarize this recent synthesis (Meyer and Walde 2009).

Avonlea assemblages evince some degree of temporal and spatial overlap with those of the Besant Complex throughout portions of the northern Plains (Figures 4.1, 4.3), but the former used only bow-and-arrow technology. Indeed, based on the recovery of both arrow projectile points and pottery, some researchers suggest that the Avonlea Horizon marks the true beginning of the Late Pre-contact Period. Avonlea projectile points are small and thin, with a triangular outline and small, finely made side-notches located low on the lateral edges and close to the slightly concave bases (Figure 4.7) (Peck and Hudecek-Cuffe 2003: 79; Walde et al. 1995: 20). Kehoe (1966) and Davis (1966) described such projectile points as the Timber Ridge Side Notched type, and Meyer and Walde (2009) recently re-attributed this type to the Avonlea Horizon. While some Besant and many Sonota assemblages indicate intensive use of Knife

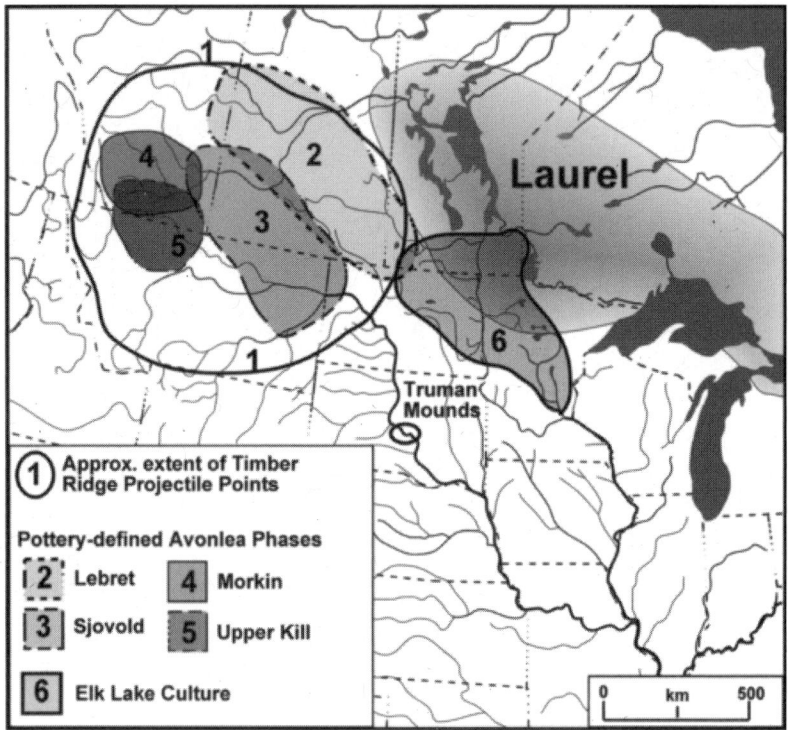

Figure 4.8. Avonlea phases and related cultures (after Meyer and Walde 2009; Norris 2007).

River chalcedony, Dyck (1983: 123) reports that Avonlea assemblages reflect heavy reliance upon a range of locally derived lithic resources.

Peck and Hudecek-Cuffe (2003: 78) observe that Avonlea sites are less frequently found in eastern Montana, the western Dakotas and southern Manitoba, and more common in the northwestern Plains (southern Alberta and Saskatchewan as well as adjacent Montana), thereby suggesting a 'cultural centre' (Figure 4.8). Avonlea sites are also reported in the foothills and montane regions of western Montana and southeast British Columbia (Roll 1988). Avonlea components in sites within the southern Boreal Forest of central Saskatchewan further indicate considerable economic flexibility in adjusting to diverse ecological conditions (Klimko 1985; Meyer et al. 1988; Meyer and Hamilton 1994: 108; Wilson-Meyer and Carlson 1985).

While Avonlea people were effective bison hunters, it is not clear whether they relied heavily upon communal mass killing or even if bison were the year-round economic focus. Walde et al. (1995: 23) describe Avonlea components at mass kill sites (bison jumps and pounds) such as Head-Smashed-In (Alberta) and Rousell (Saskatchewan) (Dyck 1972). Indeed, Kehoe (1978: 79) offered the perspective that Avonlea represents the earliest evidence of bison mass killing.

However, the Miniota Site in Manitoba (Landals 1994) and other forest fringe sites (Meyer et al. 1988) also suggest generalized winter foraging. Davis and Fisher (1988) (and again in Davis et al. 2000) report a pronghorn antelope kill in Montana at the Lost Terrace Site, and Roll (1988) describes evidence of deer hunting at an Avonlea Horizon site in the forests of southeast British Columbia. Also reflecting a seasonally diverse economy, the Lebret Site at Katepwa Lake in the Qu'Appelle River Valley of Saskatchewan indicates spring fishing activities (Smith 1986; Smith and Walker 1988). Consistent with historically reported northern Plains seasonality (Hamilton and Nicholson 2006), Peck and Hudecuk-Cuffe (2003: 82) and Walde et al. (1995: 23) propose that the Avonlea Horizon economy reflects a cycle of open Plains bison hunting in the warm seasons, with winter pursuit of the herds into sheltered and ecologically diverse forested zones where more varied subsistence choices were also available. This is further evident from the recovery of micro-botanical evidence of maize in carbonized residue from Avonlea pottery recovered from the Miniota Site (Manitoba) (Lints and Boyd 2011).

Avonlea Horizon cultural origins have been the subject of continued speculation, with some suggestion that it represents southward Athapaskan migration onto the northern Plains (Dyck 1983: 123; Kehoe 1966: 839; and see Wilcox 1988 for a more recent re-evaluation supporting this idea). Walde (2006a), along with Peck and Hudecek-Cuffe (2003: 84), summarize the Avonlea Horizon's debated origins including Reeves' early proposal of an *in situ* origin for Avonlea in the northwestern Plains as part of the Tunaxa Tradition (see also Dyck 1983: 124–25; Vickers 1994: 17). This is thought to reflect processes of diffusion whereby bow-and-arrow technology spread between discrete groups, with a consequent transformation of archaeological identity. That is, the earliest appearance of bow-and-arrow technology in the western Arctic occurred about 3750 BP, with subsequent appearance in the southern interior of British Columbia between 2950 and 2300 BP, in the northern Plains with Avonlea after about 1800 BP, and then widely throughout the Americas after about 1550 BP (Pyszczyk 2003). Finally, on the basis of pottery attributes, Morgan (1979: 209) proposed that Avonlea origins derive from the east, specifically in north-central Minnesota.

While Avonlea assemblages were initially thought to not contain pottery (Kehoe 1966), they sometimes yield sparse collections of conoidal, conical, and even bowl-shaped vessels reflecting several wares (Davis 1988; Meyer and Walde 2009; Norris 2007; Walde et al. 1995: 21) (Figure 4.9). Avonlea pottery surface finishes include net/fabric-impressed, parallel-grooved, cord-roughened or plain/smoothed versions; decoration, when present, includes encircling punctates, incising, single-cord impressions, finger pinching, and cord-wrapped object impressions upon the upper vessel (Dyck 1983: 123; Meyer and Walde 2009: 55–64; Peck and Hudecuk-Cuffe 2003: 80). In the northern Plains, net impressed (Avonlea) pottery was first described by avocational archaeologist

Chris Vickers as well as MacNeish and Capes (1958) in Manitoba. At about the same time, Kehoe (1959) named Ethridge Ware and Byrne (1973) later described the Saskatchewan Basin Early Variant (see also Dyck 1983; Vickers 1986: 90–91).

Meyer and Walde (2009) offer the most recent overview of Avonlea pottery and proposed phases, and we summarize their work here. They refine or name four wares found in Avonlea assemblages: 1) Rock Lake Net/Fabric-Impressed (MacNeish and Capes 1958), 2) Truman Parallel-Grooved (Johnson 1988; Walde and Meyer 2003), 3) Ethridge Cord-Roughened (Kehoe 1959), and 4)

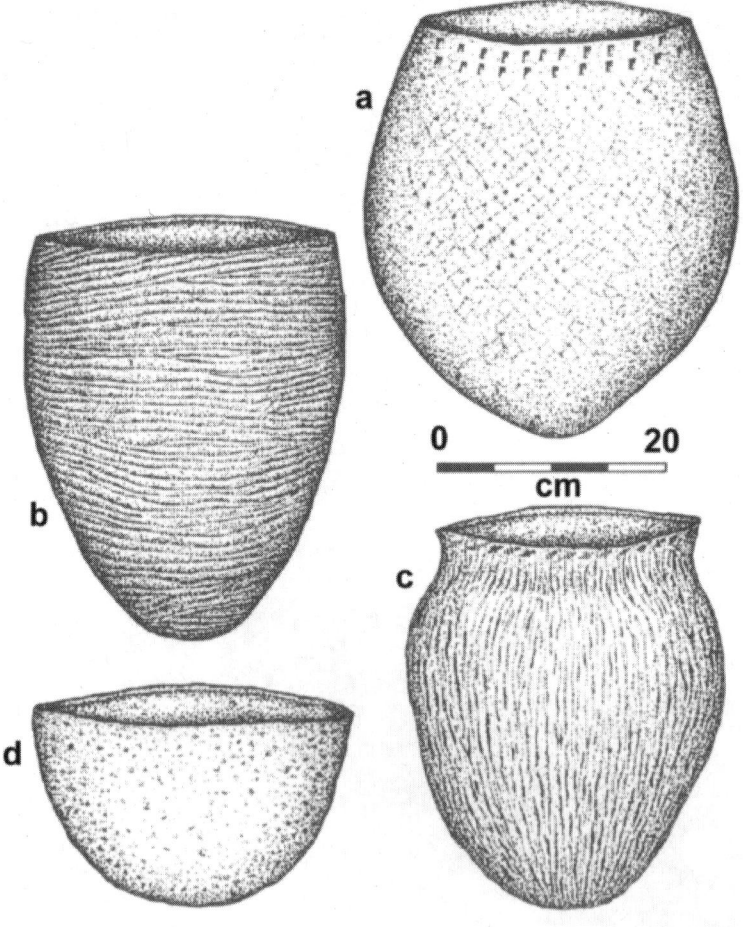

Figure 4.9. Avonlea wares (after Meyer and Walde 2009: 51) (a: Rock Lake Net/Fabric Impressed, b: Truman Parallel-Grooved, c: Ethridge Cord-Roughened, d: Plain bowl form).

Avonlea Plain Ware (Meyer and Walde 2009). The most geographically widespread, commonly found, and distinctive Avonlea pottery is Rock Lake Net/Fabric-Impressed Ware, which is defined primarily by a net/fabric-impressed surface finish (MacNeish and Capes 1958; Norris 2007). Such pottery is sparsely found in a broad arc across the northern prairies from southeastern Alberta and eastward across Saskatchewan and southern Manitoba (Walde et al. 1995) (Figure 4.8). Meyer and Walde (2009) define the Lebret Phase using components yielding sparsely decorated examples of this ware with Timber Ridge Side Notched points in central Saskatchewan (Figure 4.8). They also suggest that the Garratt and Miniota Site net-impressed pottery may warrant two separate phase designations of the same names (Meyer and Walde 2009: 65). In addition, Meyer and Walde (2009: 66) define the Morkin Phase for the most westerly occurrence of Rock Lake Net/Fabric-Impressed Ware. Along the northeastern limits of its range (Nipawin area of the Saskatchewan River valley), this fabric/net-impressed pottery is occasionally associated with the newly defined late Middle Woodland River House Complex (Meyer et al. 2008) and Middle Woodland Laurel pottery of the Boreal Forest (Figure 4.8) (Meyer et al. 1988; Walde et al. 1995: 21). A mixed Avonlea and Laurel assemblage was recovered at the Miniota Site on the upper Assiniboine River, western Manitoba (Landals 1994, 2004). Net-impressed pottery has also been reported in central Minnesota and is called Brainerd Ware (Johnson 1971, Lugenbeal 1978).

Avonlea pottery also includes Truman Parallel-Grooved Ware, which consists of conoidal vessels with encircling parallel grooves on the exterior surface that are found in southern Alberta, south-central Saskatchewan and Manitoba, as well as adjacent parts of northeastern Montana with some overlap with other wares (Meyer and Walde 2009; Norris 2007: 114; Walde and Meyer 2003; Walde et al. 1995: 22;) (Figure 4.8). Peck and Hudecek-Cuffe (2003: 80) assert that this pottery type is less common in the Canadian Plains and cite Quigg (1988a: 148) to suggest that it and Plain Wares were made during a shorter time span than the net-impressed ware. Walde and Meyer (2003) indicate that Truman Parallel-Grooved Ware and Timber Ridge Side Notched projectile point recoveries define the Sjovold Phase, but they also note that parallel grooved pottery without associated Avonlea projectile points has been found at the Forks Site in Manitoba, in Brainerd Ware assemblages in Minnesota, and from the Truman burial mound locality in the lower reaches of the Missouri River (Figure 4.8) (see also Walde 2006b). In light of the latter observation, parallel-grooved pottery from this time frame is sometimes called Truman Parallel-Grooved Ware (Walde and Meyer 2003: 139–43). In light of observations offered by Norris (2007), perhaps these more easterly recoveries of parallel-grooved pottery that are not associated with Timber Ridge Side Notched projectile points might be Brainerd Ware, and may reflect the more westerly expression of Elk Lake Culture (see below).

In northern Montana and adjacent southern Alberta, a third Avonlea ware is found named Ethridge Ware (Kehoe 1959), which is characterized by more complex vessel forms that feature shoulders and slightly constricted necks with outflaring rims (Quigg 1988a; Walde et al. 1995: 22) (Figure 4.9). Meyer and Walde (2009) describe these assemblages as part of the Upper Kill Phase. Similar pottery is also found in much the same area in assemblages of the succeeding Old Women's Phase, suggesting some sort of cultural continuity (Walde et al. 1995: 22–23). Such Old Women's Phase pottery was originally named as Saskatchewan Basin Late Variant (Byrne 1973).

The fourth variation of Avonlea pottery is termed Avonlea Plain Ware (Figure 4.9). It has a plain surface finish and has been found in southern Alberta, Saskatchewan and Manitoba with one component in Montana (Meyer and Walde 2009: 63–64). It is somewhat problematic to identify, since examples of smoothed Laurel Ware are also found in some of the same regions. Meyer and Walde (2009: 63–64) note that Avonlea pottery is not coiled, whereas there is abundant evidence that Laurel pottery was manufactured by this technique. Some of these vessels are not "plain," as the term is sometimes used, but actually have decoration that resembles that of other Avonlea Wares (Meyer and Walde 2009: 63–64). The Plain Ware is also bowl-shaped in some cases, a trait not yet noted in Laurel Ware. Although this ware has not been assigned as part of a particular phase, since the occurrences are fairly rare, Meyer and Walde (2009) discuss the validity of several other phases or subphases for further defining Avonlea assemblages.

This growing understanding and re-examination of Avonlea Ware forms, surface finishes, and decoration, particularly by Meyer and Walde (2009; Walde et al. 1995; Walde and Meyer 2003), sparked a re-examination by Norris (2007) of pottery assemblages from southern Manitoba that were originally described by Vickers (1948, 1949, 1950) and MacNeish (1958; MacNeish and Capes 1958). Completed during a time before radiocarbon dating and often from sites with compromised stratigraphic integrity, these pioneering excavations have not played a major role in recent interpretations. With an increasing understanding of the distribution and affiliation of net-impressed and horizontally corded wares, Norris (2007) re-examined these southern Manitoba materials in light of Morgan's (1979) suggestion that Avonlea pottery might have linkages to similar wares from Minnesota (Meyer and Walde 2009; Norris 2007; Walde 2006a: 191; Walde and Meyer 2003). After considering the technological attributes associated with Avonlea and the Minnesota-based Brainerd Ware, Norris (2007) addressed whether the Manitoba net-impressed pottery more closely resembled Brainerd Ware from central Minnesota or Avonlea pottery from the northern Plains. Before addressing this work in more detail, we include an overview of Brainerd Ware from the most recent summary (Norris 2007).

Elk Lake Culture/Brainerd Ware (ca. perhaps 3000–1800 BP)
Brainerd Ware was originally recovered near the Mississippi River headwaters of central Minnesota (Figure 4.8) and defined by Johnson (1971) after burial

CHAPTER 4: Human Ecology of the Canadian Prairie Ecozone ca. 1500 BP

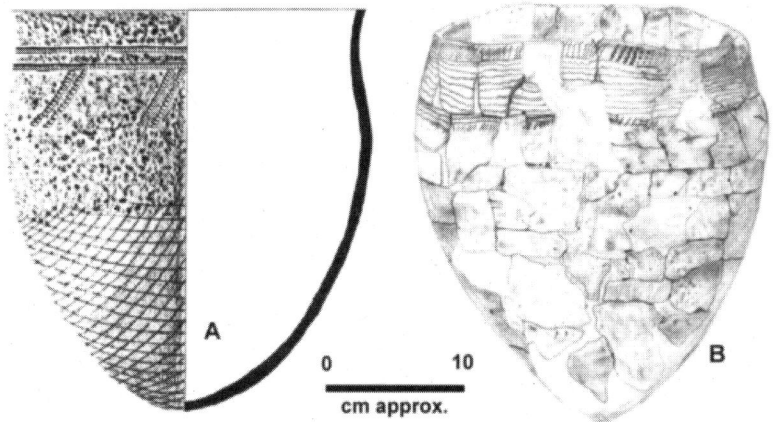

Figure 4.10. Brainerd and Laurel pottery types. Vessel A (Norris 2007: 37 citing Lugenbeal 1978) is a Brainerd Ware vessel from the Gull Lake Dam Site in Minnesota. Vessel B is Laurel from northwestern Ontario (collections of the Dept of Anthropology, Lakehead University).

mound excavations yielded fabric-impressed sherds, sometimes with superimposed coarse net-impressions. There are at least 150 sites in north-central Minnesota with Brainerd Ware identified (Norris 2007), indicating a very significant archaeological expression. Consistent with other Middle Woodland and early Plains Woodland wares, the vessels are conoidal or sub-conoidal in shape. Decoration is observed on the upper third of the vessel above the net-impressed exterior and included faint cord-wrapped object impressions (Figure 4.10). Lugenbeal (1978) also proposed that Brainerd Ware dominated what had hitherto been called "undifferentiated Woodland ware," leading to the identification of at least two wares: net-impressed and horizontally corded. Consistent with the general vessel form and pottery associations, Lugenbeal (1978, 1982: 8) judged Brainerd Ware to be contemporaneous with Middle Woodland Laurel assemblages and predated Late Woodland Blackduck as well as Sandy Lake Ware assemblages. Neumann (1978, 1984) further subdivided Brainerd Ware on the basis of subtle variation in surface treatment (single net-impressed and multiple net-impressed types).

Norris (2007: 118) notes that Brainerd Ware currently consists of four types based on surface finish: 1) net-impressed, 2) horizontally corded, 3) parallel-grooved, and 4) plain. They are similar to the Avonlea Wares and provide a cultural link between what has been identified as two cultural affiliations (Norris 2007: 119). Hohman-Caine and Goltz (1995) systematically describe the decorative variation of Brainerd Ware, defining five decorative variants: 1) plain, 2) cord-wrapped object stamped, 3) angled stamped, 4) incised, and 5) reed stamped. Norris (2007: 67) notes that these are similar to Avonlea pottery decorations.

Hohman-Caine and Goltz (1995) also address Brainerd Ware spatial distribution and non-pottery material culture associations and present a revolutionary rethinking of its antiquity. Many of the Minnesota excavations have compromised stratigraphic integrity due to bioturbation and frost action, often compounded by poor organic preservation—which are problems throughout the northern temperate and Boreal Forest regions. Thus, multi-component sites with limited organic material and suspect depositional context are often difficult to date using conventional radiocarbon sampling methods. This led Hohman-Caine and Goltz (1995: 124) and others to supplement conventional radiocarbon dates with AMS dates obtained from carbonized residues adhering to the pottery surfaces. These direct absolute dates derive from materials closely tied to the production and use of the pottery and yielded unexpectedly old dates, suggesting that Brainerd Ware might date from 3000 BP or even 3500 BP through to about 1800 BP (Early Woodland through to late Middle Woodland times).

This conclusion about the antiquity and temporal duration of Brainerd Ware has been met with some skepticism from other researchers. It suggests the development of well-fired, grit-tempered, and comparatively thin-walled conoidal pottery of general Middle Woodland form in Minnesota at the same time that seemingly experimental, poorly fired, fibre-tempered and coarse grit-tempered, thick-walled pottery of the Early Woodland Period was appearing in the southeast United States. Jennings (1989: 225–26) generalized that pottery made its initial appearance in Georgia as early as 4500 BP and spread throughout the southern parts of the Eastern Woodlands and as far as New York by about 3000 BP, then into southern Ontario and the Midwest by 2600 BP. Even this more recent of the Early Woodland pottery (i.e., Vinnette I, Marion Thick) appears much thicker and more experimental than Brainerd Wares.

The direct dating of Brainerd Ware suggests its development long before other pottery in the Midwest. If these AMS dates are accepted, it requires significant revision of Eastern Woodlands cultural history to account for the appearance of comparatively well-made conoidal pottery in Minnesota long before it appeared elsewhere in the eastern United States. Alternatively, perhaps some presently unknown "reservoir effect" is contributing to artificially old direct AMS dates from the cooking residues. By way of example, we cite observations by Leigh Syms (2004) of a "fresh water reservoir effect" whereby heavy dietary reliance upon aquatic food resources (fish) may be resulting in "older" absolute dates from human bone than those deriving from associated terrestrial sources. This may be due to complex fractionation effects altering the relative abundance of various carbon isotopes in aquatic food webs. In this way meals containing high concentrations of aquatic food sources might yield carbonized pottery residue that appears older (in radiocarbon years) than its actual calendrical age. While this observation of dating discrepancies due to fractionation effects is disquieting, we do note that Syms (2004) suggests a divergence between aquatic and terrestrial samples of only between 220 and 370 years, a discrepancy that is insufficient to account for the unexpectedly old Brainerd residue dates. Skeptics of the interpretations offered by Hohman-Caine and Goltz (1995) must also account for a few old terrestrial charcoal dates that are associated with Brainerd Ware that would not be affected by any freshwater reservoir effect. This issue is beyond the scope of this chapter, but demonstrates that Brainerd Ware is critically important for understanding Aboriginal history of the upper Midwest and beyond.

Hohman-Caine and Goltz (1995) formally defined Elk Lake Culture to subsume Brainerd Ware and other associated material culture. They note a range of projectile point associations commonly considered to be from Late Archaic and Early-Middle Woodland timeframes, albeit some of these associations may be spurious due to complex depositional issues. These projectile points also differ from the small Timber Ridge Side Notched type associated with the Avonlea Horizon Wares. In sum, Hohman-Caine and Goltz (1995) assert that Elk Lake Culture appeared in the Late Archaic/Early Woodland Period, as early as 3500 BP, within the prairie-woodland ecotone of central Minnesota. With post-Altithermal stabilization of the climate, hydrology, and ecology, this region would have offered a diverse array of resources that sustained the Elk Lake Culture for at least 1500 years (Hohman-Caine and Goltz 1995).

After close examination of the net-impressed and horizontally corded pottery from southern Manitoba, Norris (2007) concluded that three of the four types of Brainerd Ware are present at the four sites he examined (Avery, United Church, Lockport and Cemetery Point). Since Avonlea projectile points are not found in the Avery and United Church Site assemblages, and since the Manitoba pottery shows strong similarity to Brainerd Ware, Norris (2007) concluded that the Manitoba materials should be treated as the most northwesterly expression of Elk Lake Culture (Figure 4.8). Given the apparent antiquity of Brainerd Ware, Elk Lake Culture may significantly predate most Avonlea assemblages. Neumann (1978, 1982) also defined surface finish admixtures on Brainerd Ware vessels (net-impressed lower body treatment with parallel-grooved upper body surface treatment) and reported other Avonlea-like pottery in Minnesota (see Figures 4.9 and 4.10) (Gonsior 2003). This led Norris (2007) to propose that technological admixture and influence occurred between Avonlea and the late Elk Lake Culture.

In light of the temporal and stylistic overlap between late Elk Lake Culture and early Avonlea Horizon, we return to Morgan's (1979) suggestion that Avonlea origins might lie in central Minnesota. Norris (2007) asserts that the net-impressed and horizontally corded pottery from south-central Manitoba has Elk Lake Culture affiliations, and he agrees with others (Hohman-Caine and Goltz 1995; Walde and Meyer 2003) that a migratory expansion occurred from the Eastern Woodlands following the prairie border to eventually occupy the Plains of Saskatchewan, Alberta and Montana. Perhaps elements of such an expansion occurred from the prairie-woodlands of the Mississippi River headwaters, to the ecologically similar Pembina Trench of southern Manitoba. With an expansion of Elk Lake Culture, these people could have readily come in contact with Avonlea people, also noted for their seasonally-based economic flexibility and technological linkages with Laurel Culture. Walde (2006: 300–301) comments more definitively on these broad-based cultural influences:

> The [Avonlea] projectile point form appears first in southern Saskatchewan and Alberta and seems to be an indigenous development there. As the use of the point style spread easterly, however, it met and merged with at least two northwesterly diffusions of ceramics from the Eastern Woodlands in Minnesota (Walde and Meyer 2003). Rock Lake net/fabric impressed ware (Walde and Meyer 2003) originated in Minnesota as a manifestation of the Elk Lake culture (Fig. 4) some three thousand years ago (Hohman-Caine and Goltz 1995) and had spread onto the northern plains area via the parklands by about AD 400 to be found initially in both Avonlea and non-Avonlea Horizon contexts (Walde and Meyer 2003). Although Morgan (1979) suggests this diffusion was the result of migration from the Eastern Woodlands, it is entirely possible that the idea for this particular ware could have spread along existing trade and exchange networks… Similarly, Truman mounds parallel grooved ware (Walde and Meyer 2003) also originated in Minnesota (Gonsior 2003) and spread west to the Missouri River system and then onto the northern plains to be recovered in Avonlea Horizon contexts.

Avonlea, while clearly Plains-oriented, owes much of its archaeological distinctiveness to diffused technology: the bow and arrow as well as pottery. On the basis of on-going research by Lints (Lints and Boyd 2011), it appears that access to maize represents yet another element of this cultural diffusion. However, distinctive Avonlea projectile points may have been an indigenous development since they only appear in Saskatchewan and Alberta (Walde 2006a). While largely reflecting a bison-focused migratory lifestyle, a number of sites located along the north and northeastern margins of its range illustrate seasonally-based subsistence flexibility and continued contact or exchange with Middle Woodland Boreal Forest foragers.

Old Women's Phase (ca. 1200–400 BP)

The Old Women's Phase represents people who were primarily migratory bison hunters. It is defined by the production of pottery originally named Saskatchewan Basin Complex Late Variant (Byrne 1973: 356), and associated with a range of small arrow points consistent with the Prairie and Plains side-

CHAPTER 4: Human Ecology of the Canadian Prairie Ecozone ca. 1500 BP

notched types (Vickers 1986: 95) (Figure 4.11). This circumstance is somewhat problematic as these projectile points also appear widely throughout the northern Plains either in contexts without pottery (originally called Saddle Butte Phase by Brumley and Dau [1988: 56]) or with a variety of pottery wares that suggest diverse cultural affiliations. Superficially similar small, side-notched and triangular points are also found in the southern Boreal Forest of Saskatchewan, Manitoba and northwestern Ontario, but no Boreal Forest archaeological assemblages of sufficient size and depositional integrity are currently available to address the issue taxonomically. When considering the northern Plains, Peck

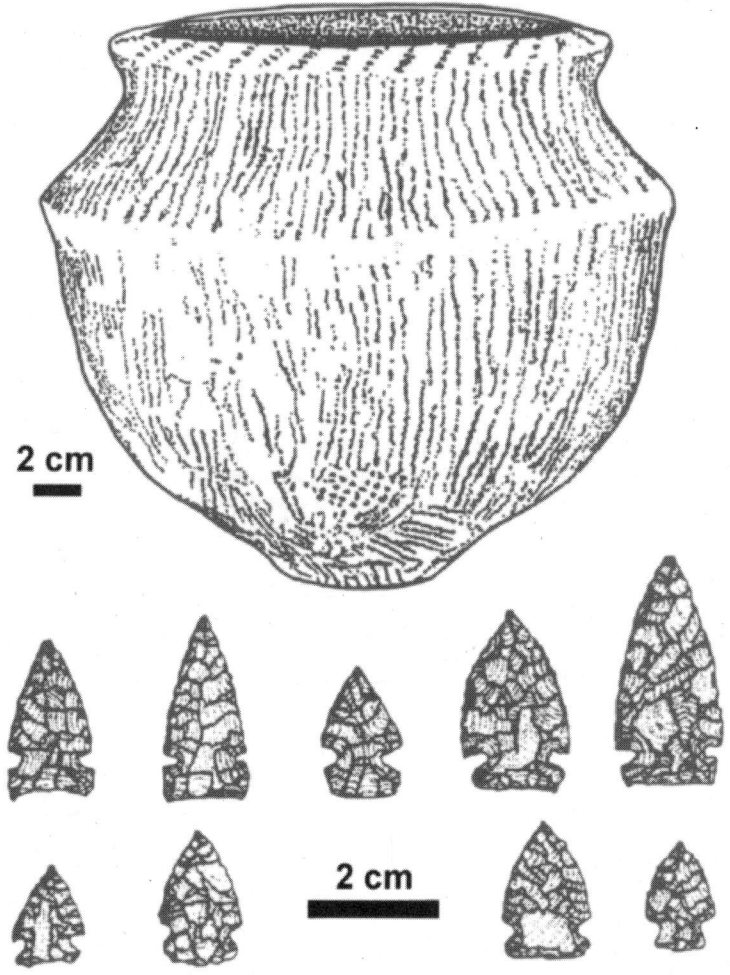

Figure 4.11. Old Women's Phase pot and projectile points (after Walde et al. 1995: 27).

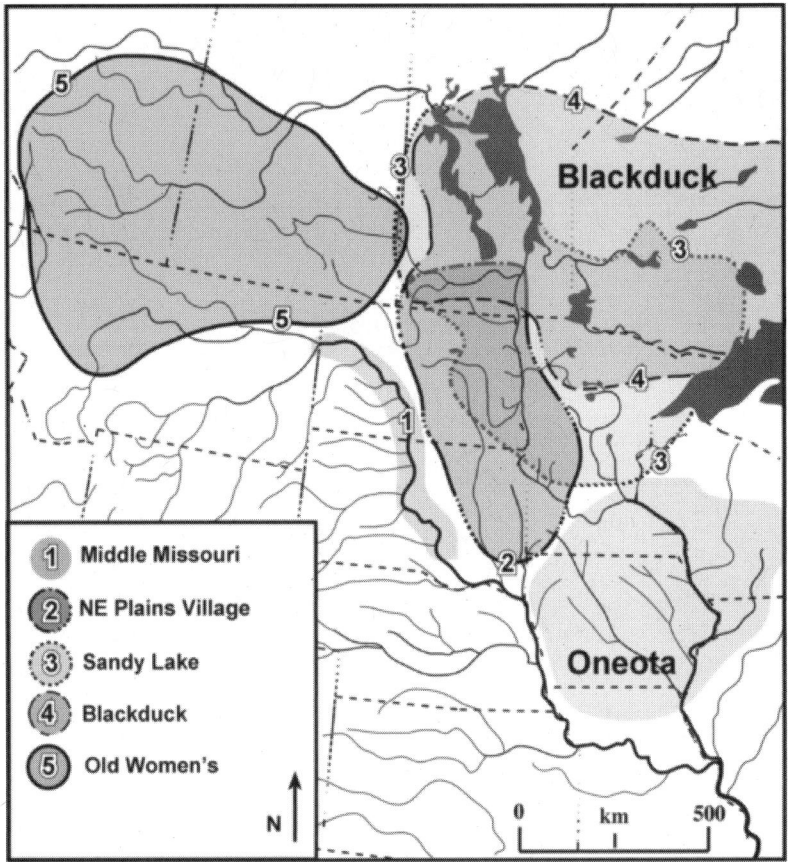

Figure 4.12. Geographic distribution of cultures contemporaneous with Late Woodland (after Nicholson et al. 2002b; Vickers 1994; Meyer and Hamilton 1994; Gregg 1994; Henning 1998; Schneider 2002; Taylor-Hollings 1999; Toom 2004; Walde et al. 1995).

(1996) and Peck and Ives (2001) address this problem by proposing a new classification scheme that reorders the diversity of late side-notched arrow tips to reflect "the continuity of projectile point stylistic change through time on the Alberta and Saskatchewan Plains" (Peck and Hudecek-Cuffe 2003: 86). This led them to propose that Cayley Series projectile points more commonly appear with Saskatchewan Basin Late Variant pottery and are the diagnostic artifacts for the Old Women's Phase (Peck and Hudecek-Cuffe 2003: 86–87).

The Old Women's Phase, based mainly on pottery finds, is thought to appear earliest in northern Montana and adjacent southern Alberta but has also been recovered widely in southern Saskatchewan (Meyer 1988) (Figure 4.12). Following Byrne's (1973) characterizations, these vessels are generally globular in form, with occasional flat bottom varieties (Figure 4.11). They differ from earlier northern Plains conoidal pottery types, having thick-walled shoulders and short straight necks (Peck and Hudecek-Cuffe 2003: 87). Overall, this pottery typically has very thick walls (typically over 10 mm thick), as observed by the second author on many examples in Saskatchewan. The exterior surfaces exhibit obliterated fabric or vertically oriented fabric impressions but some are smoothed. Decoration consists of punctates, cord-wrapped tool impressions or incisions generally on the exterior lip, neck and upper shoulder (Byrne 1973: 334–35; Meyer 1988: 56).

We reiterate suggestions offered earlier that this pottery resembles that of the Upper Kill Phase of the Avonlea Horizon that may represent the cultural antecedent for Old Women's Phase (Brumley and Dau 1988: 51; Walde et al. 1995). Peck and Hudecek-Cuffe (2003: 90) assert that Old Women's Phase represents an *in situ* cultural development in northern Montana and southern Alberta, with minimal evidence of cultural influence from elsewhere. While Alberta researchers generally agree that Old Women's Phase dates from about 1200 BP (perhaps as early as 1500 BP) and persisted into the Proto-contact Period, Meyer (1988) proposed that it disappeared from southern Saskatchewan after about 700 BP as the Mortlach Phase appeared. These processes are addressed more fully in the next chapter.

Blackduck Horizon (ca. 1200–400 BP)

Emerging perhaps as early as 1200 BP and persisting to as late as 400 BP, the Blackduck Horizon represents one of several Late Woodland forager societies that are found widely throughout the eastern Subarctic, but which also appeared in the Aspen Parkland and northeastern Plains (Figure 4.12) (Hamilton et al. 2007). It is primarily associated with a generalized forest hunting-and-gathering lifestyle, however throughout much of southern Manitoba a number of early Blackduck sites reveal a strong emphasis on bison exploitation (Hamilton et al. 2007), and we follow Walde (et al. 1995) in the identification of this regional variant as "Plains Blackduck." Plains Blackduck is currently limited to the Plains and Aspen Parkland zones of southern Manitoba (Figure 4.12), with minimal representation in east-central Saskatchewan, and no sites reported in the Dakotas. Lenius and Olinyk (1990) propose that the Blackduck Horizon ends much earlier than discussed above and is replaced by the Rainy River Composite in Ontario and adjacent regions. Cooper and Johnson (1964) also suggest that Blackduck Horizon was replaced in Minnesota by makers of Sandy Lake Ware. In that area, Arzigian (2008) discusses the Blackduck-Kathio Complex, including the related Clam River Ware, as providing more evidence of related Late Pre-contact wares.

Blackduck assemblages are readily identifiable by their distinctive Late Woodland pottery: relatively thin-walled globular vessels with constricted necks, wedge-shaped lips and outflaring rims (Figure 4.13). They have textile impressed globular bodies with the neck, rim and lip areas often decorated with

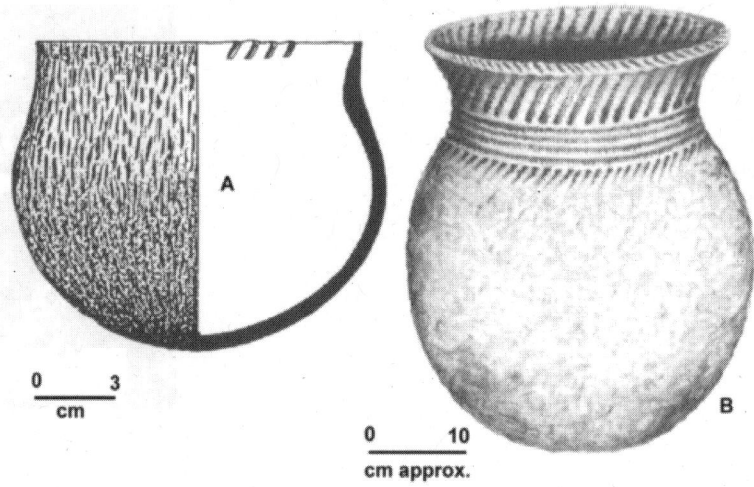

Figure 4.13. Blackduck and Sandy Lake Wares. A: Artist's rendering of a Sandy Lake Ware vessel from north-central Minnesota (after Birk 1977a: 43). B: Artist's rendering of a Blackduck vessel based upon recoveries from a site in southeastern Manitoba (Pettipas 1983: 129).

complex and highly variable patterns of cord-wrapped object impressions, punctates and/or bosses that may be found on the exterior, on the lip and sometimes on the interior of the vessel. Some vessels also have vertically oriented combing as the surface finish. Blackduck sites also often yield a range of small side-notched and triangular projectile points that conform to the general parameters of the Late Plains and Prairie side-notched series (Figure 4.14) (but see refinement of this typology by Peck and Ives 2001 as well as Belsham and Richards 2004).

While Plains Blackduck sites evince a strong orientation towards bison exploitation, the expression of this bison-oriented economy varies significantly. Some sites demonstrate mastery of communal mass-killing techniques using steep valley walls such as the Stott (Badertscher et al. 1987; Hamilton 1982; Hamilton et al. 1981; Tisdale 1978) and Gompf Sites (Hamilton et al. 2007: 117) or slough-edge mass killing at the Hokanson Site (Norris and Hamilton 2004; Hamilton et al. 2007), while other sites suggest smaller scale and individualistic bison hunting (Gosselin and Heron Sites in the Tiger Hills) (Belsham 1996; Hamilton et al. 2007). Still others, such as the Oak Lake Island and Bell Sites, are found along lakeshores and suggest generalized woodland/lake-edge foraging economies (Graham 2005; Hamilton et al. 2007). Again, it is not clear

CHAPTER 4: Human Ecology of the Canadian Prairie Ecozone ca. 1500 BP

whether this economic variability reflects adaptation over time by migrant woodland foragers to new ecological circumstances, or seasonal shifts in habitat and economy by Plains Blackduck groups.

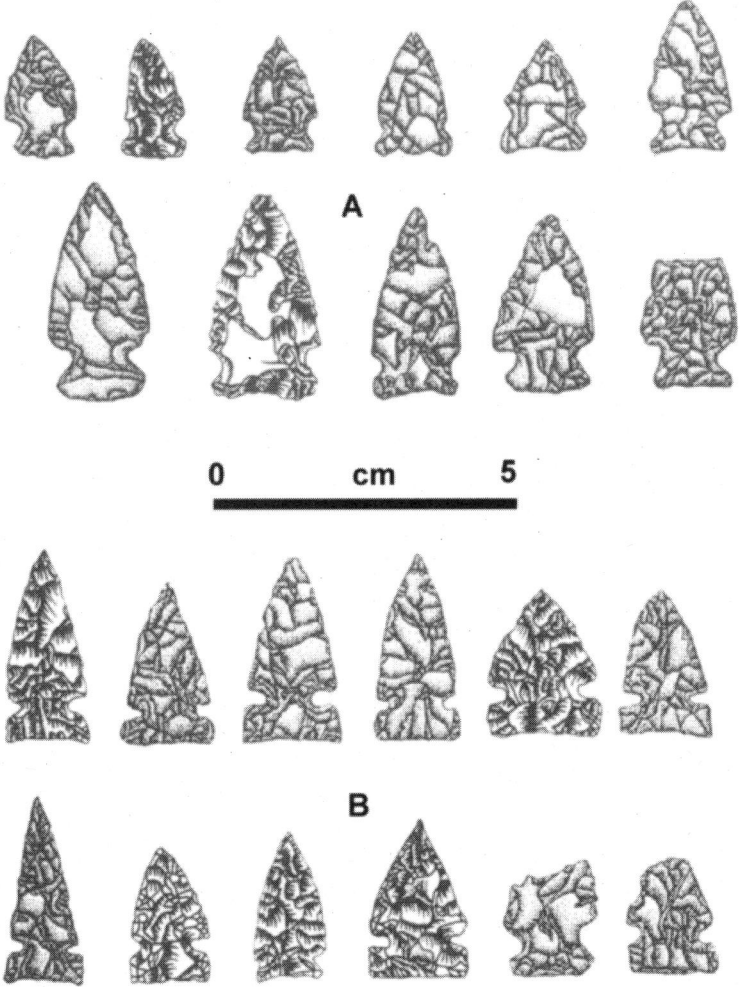

Figure 4.14. Late Plains and Prairie side-notched projectile points. A: Plains Side-notched Type from the Gull Lake and Tschetter Sites (Saskatchewan) (after Dyck 1983: 130). Note the low position of the side notches that leave a 'corner notched' appearance. B: Prairie Side-notched Type from the Gull Lake Site (Saskatchewan) (after Dyck 1983: 131). Note the side notches positioned higher on the lateral edges, with squarer shoulders and bases.

Sandy Lake Ware/Psinomani Culture (ca. 950–200 BP)

While occurring at the end of the 2000–1000 BP timeframe, we include the Psinomani Culture (Gibbon 1994) because associated evidence is consistent with some of the key themes addressed here. Sandy Lake Ware, the most diagnostic artifact class associated with the Psinomani Culture, was first described by Cooper and Johnson (1964) in the mixed wood forest of Minnesota and Wisconsin. Most sites of this affiliation are found in this region, but more recent work reveals a wider distribution (Taylor-Hollings 1999) (Figure 4.12). In a workshop dedicated to Sandy Lake Ware research, Participants of the Lake Superior Basin Workshop (1987) noted sites in adjacent parts of Ontario, a few in Manitoba, and several in North Dakota. Taylor-Hollings (1999) further defined the Canadian distribution, attributes, site dating, and other information associated with Sandy Lake Ware.

Sandy Lake Ware is characterized generally by the following attributes: straight rim profile, flat or scalloped lip, thickened neck, grit and/or shell tempered, somewhat squat globular shape, and is thin walled (Figure 4.13). The ware is divided into several types based on surface finish: 1) Corded (vertical textile impressed), 2) Smooth (obliterated to smoothed), and more rarely 3) Stamped (checked and simple stamped as proposed by Birk 1979: 178) (Taylor-Hollings 1999). Peterson's (1986) study of Minnesota Sandy Lake Ware introduced two alternate types based on temper—Sandy Lake Grit tempered and Sandy Lake Shell tempered. In addition, Notched Lip and Plain variants of the above types have been identified, based on decoration (Cooper and Johnson 1964), although most researchers just refer generally to the ware (Birk 1979; Peterson 1986; Taylor-Hollings 1999). Decoration, when present, usually consists of interior lip notches or notched lip corners made with various tools or cord-wrapped tool impressions. One unusual attribute is the placement of decoration on the inner neck or shoulder portion of some vessels (Birk 1977). Arthurs (1978) first described regional variation in Ontario of Sandy Lake Ware that includes only grit tempered, Corded Type vessels that sometimes have a row of punctates/bosses on the exterior. Sandy Lake Ware is often associated with other wares in archaeological assemblages, with single component Psinomani Culture assemblages being somewhat rare (Taylor-Hollings 1999). As is typical of most Late Woodland pottery, Sandy Lake Ware from Canadian sites is associated with small triangular and also side-notched projectile points. Several burial mounds in Minnesota and North Dakota are attributed to the Psinomani Culture due to the recovery of complete or nearly complete Sandy Lake Ware vessels (Birk 1977b).

Gibbon (1994) introduced the Siouan term Psinomani "Culture," meaning "wild rice gatherer," to replace the Ojibwe word Wanikan Culture (denoting 'hole in the ground' for threshing pits) first used by Birk (1977b) to describe Late Woodland assemblages with mainly Sandy Lake Ware. Arzigian (2008: 126–27) presents an alternate definition of the Psinomani Complex for northern and central Minnesota during the Late Woodland, Proto-contact and Post-contact times, which includes sites (n=275) with Sandy Lake Ware and/or Ogechie pottery as well as some sites without pottery. Participants of the Lake Superior Basin Workshop (1987) agreed that the producers of this ware were likely Siouan, as opposed to the Algonquians also found in the region; this is largely due to some Proto-contact sites in Minnesota. Johnson (1985) proposed the Proto-contact Bradbury Phase (Birk 1992: 8; Birk and Johnson 1992) to explain the activities of the Eastern Dakota, or Mdewakanton, at the time of French contact. These sites are identified by the association of French trade goods and Late Woodland artifacts such as Sandy Lake Ware, Ogechie, and Orr Wares in the Mille Lacs lake region of east-central Minnesota (Birk and Johnson 1992: 209). The general subsistence economy of people associated with this archaeological phase indicates a dependence on large animals (mainly bison) and wild rice (Birk and Johnson 1992: 209).

While Gregg (1994: 88–89) comments that "there was no indication until recently that the Sandy Lake complex was ever anything but Woodland," Taylor-Hollings (1999) noted that Psinomani Culture exhibits notable adaptability in subsistence economy. Johnson (1985: 162) explains that the producers of Sandy Lake Ware used a Woodland-Plains edge adaptation that dates from at least the beginning of the Late Pre-contact. Peterson (1986: 173) argues that these people were involved in resource utilization from multiple environments throughout an annual cycle. These adaptations included bison hunting, fishing, wild-rice harvesting, hunting woodland mammals, and gathering activities in both the prairie and forest (Gibbon 1994: 147). There are strong associations between sites with Sandy Lake Ware and wild rice harvesting in Minnesota and Wisconsin, but other sites also indicate bison hunting was very important. This economic and subsistence complexity is evident at the Shea Site located in southeastern North Dakota (Figure 4.12). While this site was fortified and yields evidence of maize production, it is not a conventional Middle Missouri Village. Instead, Sandy Lake and Northeastern Plains Village Wares dominate the assemblage (Michlovic and Schneider 1993). Sandy Lake Ware has also been identified in the Boreal Forest of northwestern Ontario (Arthurs 1978; Taylor-Hollings 1999) and in the Plains/Aspen Parkland of Manitoba (Nicholson 1990; Taylor-Hollings 1999). In the northern forest sites, generalized foraging of typical Boreal Forest plant and animal species is inferred from assemblages with Sandy Lake Ware, while the plains-edge sites in Manitoba often reflect a bison-centred economy similar to those in North Dakota (Taylor-Hollings 1999). Thus, the Psinomani Culture was particularly adept at utilizing many different ecozones, rather than strictly occupying the Eastern Woodlands.

Taylor-Hollings (1999) proposes that Psinomani Culture moved north and westward from the Eastern Woodlands, on the basis of both pottery attribute studies and dating of components. Absolute and relative dating of Psinomani Culture components indicate that the oldest sites appear to be on the Plains of

North Dakota and adjacent Minnesota and Wisconsin, while the most recent components appear to be in the Bradbury Phase and southern Canadian sites (Taylor-Hollings 1999), with late persistence in Minnesota indicated by some proto-contact sites (Birk and Johnson 1992).

Rainy River Coalescent (ca. 950–600 BP) and Composite (ca. 600–300 BP)

Lenius and Olinyk (1990) revised, somewhat controversially, Late Woodland taxonomy using Syms' (1977) archaeological taxonomic system after extensive examination of recoveries from many sites in the Rainy River and adjacent regions, including some from the northeastern Plains. Their proposed changes are particularly relevant to this paper since there is temporal and geographical overlap with the archaeological cultures described previously. Their revisions include discussions about late Laurel, early Blackduck, and Late Woodland manifestations. Although Ontario's Rainy River region is adjacent to the northeastern Plains, some of the people inhabiting this region evidently moved to the Plains and Aspen Parklands of Manitoba (Lenius and Olinyk 1990: 92, 98).

Lenius and Olinyk (1990) define the Western Woodland Algonkian Configuration, which is subdivided into the Selkirk and Rainy River Composites; these, in turn are subdivided into several complexes that were already described by researchers for the Selkirk Composite (see Meyer and Russell 1987) but were newly defined for the Rainy River Composite by Lenius and Olinyk (1990). They also refined the Blackduck Horizon (Early Blackduck), suggesting that it emerged by about 1250 BP, possibly as early as 1450 BP, and that it is not found in sites dating beyond 950 BP (Lenius and Olinyk 1990: 82). Lenius and Olinyk (1990) describe the Rainy River Coalescent archaeological entity as resulting from the "coalescence" or blending between the Laurel and Blackduck Cultures from about 950–600 BP. Following this cultural change, the Rainy River Composite appears in the archaeological record and continues until about 600 BP to a maximum of 300 BP (Lenius and Olinyk 1990: 84). Lenius and Olinyk (1990) propose three regionally and temporally defined complexes of this composite, which had to share common pottery traits and perceived social, political, and religious activities including the Winnipeg River, Bird Lake, and Duck Bay Complexes (Lenius and Olinyk 1990: 82). According to their criteria, significant numbers of vessels of at least one definitive type must be represented in the smaller burial mounds (as opposed to older, larger Laurel mounds) and at least one habitation site had to be present for a proposed complex to have been part of the Rainy River Composite (Lenius and Olinyk 1990: 82–83). Winnipeg River and Duck Bay Complexes have been identified at a few sites in southern Manitoba (Lenius and Olinyk 1990) indicating that the people represented by this material culture had likely lived on the Plains seasonally or for short durations. Hanna (1984) uses examples of Duck Bay Ware to trace possible marriage connections through Pre-contact sites, which is another possible explanation for the sparse number of Rainy River Composite sites on the Plains. Lenius and Olinyk (1990: 84) observe that, in "the northwest the Duck Bay Complex is likely replaced by Plains-related groups" which, if true, suggests that Plains groups were also moving into the Parkland and Boreal Forest during earlier parts of the Late Woodland period. Thus, the people who were part of the Rainy River Composite archaeological entity were also moving back and forth between the northern Plains, Parklands and Eastern Woodlands.

Horticulturalists on the Northeastern Plains
Beginning at about 1150 BP, horticultural village life gradually spread onto the eastern Plains. This began with small village groups in the Mississippi and lower Missouri River valleys and developed into the Central Plains Village as well as the Initial Middle Missouri Traditions (Anfinson 1979; Gregg 1994; Henning 1998; Nicholson 1990, 1991; Pettipas 1996; Syms 1977). Given the recovery of Mississippian Culture goods in some eastern Plains burial mounds, regional influence from these chiefdoms is also indicated (see Pettipas 1996; Syms 1977: 110–24, 1979, 1982). The evidence implies westward migration of Woodland- and Mississippian-influenced people into the western Mississippi River drainage basin, where a mixed horticultural and foraging economy was used. While bison hunting was important, some groups also relied upon horticulture.

While often presented as a cultural evolutionary succession (Figure 4.1), Late Plains Woodland and Plains Village societies were often contemporaneous, particularly in the northeastern Plains (see Winham and Lueck 1994). In fact, the distinctions reflect variation in degree rather than in kind. Plains Village societies are defined by: multi-family houses with sub-floor storage pits; comparatively permanent settlements, often fortified with moats and stockades; stone and bone agricultural implements; small projectile points and distinctive pottery wares (Fagan 1995: 151). In contrast, late Plains Woodland societies are generally viewed as foragers for whom horticulture played a supplemental economic role and who are not associated with fortified villages, large numbers of agricultural tools or food storage facilities.

In the northeastern Plains, such distinctions have limited analytic value. For example, the Shea Site (32CS101) is a fortified village in southeastern North Dakota that dates to about 600 BP. It yielded mixed pottery assemblages dominated by Sandy Lake Ware but with some northeastern Plains Village and Oneota vessels (Michlovic and Schneider 1993: 128–29; Toom 2004). The site is fortified but has not yielded evidence of semi-subterranean or communal houses. However the recovery of scapula hoes, storage pits, and maize kernels and phytoliths demonstrates that horticulture was important (Michlovic and Schneider 1993). This blend of Plains Village and Plains Woodland traits sporadically appears across northern North Dakota, and is associated with mixed pottery assemblages, storage pits and short-lived village occupations (the Scattered Village Complex [Ahler and Mehrer 1984; Ahler et al. 1991] or the Northeastern Plains Village Complex [Toom 2004]) (Figure 4.12).

This pattern is also evident at the multi-component Lockport Site (EaLf-1), located along the Red River in southern Manitoba (Figure 4.12). The brief horticultural occupation has yielded mixed pottery wares, storage pits, scapula hoes, maize kernels and cupules, but no evidence of fortifications or semi-subterranean houses (Buchner 1985, 1986, 1989; Deck and Shay 1992; Flynn 1993; Flynn and Kogan 1991; Flynn and Syms 1996; Hems n.d.; Roberts 1991). The recoveries suggest a mixed economy involving horticulture, bison hunting, and the Lockport Rapids fishery (Roberts 1992).

Throughout the northeastern Plains, horticulture was employed along with foraging and bison hunting (Gregg 1994: 86, citing Schneider 1988). This economic flexibility appears to be common with many groups, and Henning's (1998) overview of the Oneota Tradition economy offers a useful interpretative model. While not yet systematically documented, many of these Plains Woodland sites yield mixed pottery assemblages and other cultural traits reflecting Woodland, Plains Village, Middle Missouri and Mississippian affiliations (Michlovic and Schneider 1993; Nicholson 1991: 169–70, 1994a, 1994b; Nicholson et al. 2002). It implies a widespread migration of autonomous horticultural/forager village populations into the eastern Plains, and Nicholson (1994a) asserts that some groups coalesced to form more socially complex co-residence groups. This northeastern Plains forager/horticulture way of life is addressed more fully in the next chapter.

Summary and Conclusion

During the period from 2000–1000 BP, northern Plains Aboriginal cultures underwent significant changes in part through technological innovations deriving from extra-regional sources. This involved the spread of bow-and-arrow technology throughout the Plains, along with the appearance of pottery in the eastern Plains, but with a sparser representation of pottery in the northwestern Plains. Pottery production is one of several cultural traits that either diffused westward from the Eastern Woodlands, or reflects a pattern of sustained migration. Recently there has been a growing body of work that indicates that maize consumption was more important among northern Plains hunter-gatherers than ever formerly thought (Boyd et al. 2006; Boyd et al. 2008; Boyd and Surette 2010). Whether this reflects extra-regional exchange of food produce or local food production by hunter-gatherers remains to be resolved. In this chapter we have focused discussion on the influence of the Eastern Woodlands upon the culture history of the northern Plains. This effect extends beyond the geographic spread of earthenware cooking containers. It includes integration by some western groups of important ceremonial and funerary rites that involved construction of earthen burial mounds and exchange of exotic raw materials or finished goods. Woodland cultural influence also included the appearance of some generalized foragers in the forested river valleys of the eastern Plains, and eventually, the spread of horticultural production and settled village life. These cultural traits do not have uniform expression, but rather, exhibit considerable variability through time and across space. We also note that some archaeologically defined cultures originally deriving from woodland habitats chose to become mobile bison-hunting specialists. Indeed, some even engaged in large-scale communal bison hunting.

The last 2000 years of northern Plains Aboriginal history reveals a sustained pattern of east-west exchange of ideas, technology and people. This evokes questions about why such diffusion and/or migration occurred. The northern Plains was profoundly affected by the transformations occurring in the Eastern Woodlands that began as early as 6000 BP with a long trend involving intensive foraging, semi-sedentism and population growth. As these long-term trends were amplified in the Woodland Period, there was a widespread increase in population density and commitment to sedentary life, that was sustained first by intensive foraging and later by horticultural production. In some cases these changes were associated with new forms of political integration that involved multi-family co-residence, territorial circumscription, and the emergence of status inequality. In the context of population growth in the Eastern Woodlands of the United States and adjacent parts of southeastern Canada, we can imagine situations of growing competition for strategic resources that likely contributed to the socio-economic and ecological implications of the Woodland and Mississippian Traditions. We speculate that the sustained expression of the Plains Woodland (and later the Plains Village) Traditions reflects a kind of cultural ripple effect, whereby some populations were pressed to move westward in search of new lands in face of population pressure, and declining resource productivity (especially in situations of semi-sedentary horticulture or intensive foraging).

Other important manifestations of extra-regional cultural influence include the early Plains Woodland societies, appearing first along the forested river valleys of the eastern Plains, and then with greater visibility throughout the northern Plains. Likely originally reflecting westward migrations of Woodland foragers into the forest-grasslands of western Minnesota, Iowa, and the eastern Dakotas, these people brought innovations beyond earthenware cooking vessels. Burial mound ceremonialism appeared throughout much of the eastern Plains and as far as eastern Saskatchewan (e.g., Moose Bay burial mound [Hanna 1976]), coupled with some of the exotic ritual goods associated with Middle Woodland and later Mississippian societies (Capes 1963; Syms 1977, 1979). These east-west linkages appear to have facilitated an expanded level of exchange between the eco-regions. This was coupled with a transplantation and persistence of broad-spectrum woodland foraging by some groups, and gradually led to the diffusion westward of small-scale village horticultural life after ca. 1000 BP.

While bison hunting is a common theme among most groups in the northern Plains at this time, there is considerable variability in how bison predation was conducted. Indeed, it is widely suggested that communal mass killing of bison became increasingly important during the Late Pre-contact, with Besant and Sonota Complexes reflecting a height in expertise of such efforts (see Dyck 1983; Frison 1971, 1978; Walde 2006b). This reflects a sophisticated understanding of bison behaviour and how to manipulate them using the landscape. It also required a large and coordinated labour force to affect such communal mass killing, and implies multi-family effort (Walde 2006b). Indeed, Walde (2006b) considers it to represent tribal organization, something he believes to reflect organizational prototypes indicating yet more influence from the Eastern Woodlands. This is particularly noteworthy since individuals or small families could effectively conduct small-scale bison predation, and did so into the late 19th century. We share the perspective that such mass bison killing implies larger social motivations centred on a desire for production of a food surplus. Whether it reflects efforts to generate preserved commodities valued in an extra-regional exchange system (Reeves 1983), or to facilitate seasonal winter aggregation in large groups (Walde 2006b), it indicates the development of larger and more enduring social units. We share Walde's (2006b) perspective that this forms part of the larger pattern of cultural and demographic influences deriving ultimately from the Eastern Woodlands. It also provides the foundations for new innovations involving the development of horticultural village life throughout much of the Eastern Plains after ca. 1000 BP. While most strongly expressed in the Central Plains and the Middle Missouri regions, such communities appear in the northeastern Plains (eastern Dakotas, western Minnesota and southern Manitoba) and exerted widespread influence throughout much of the rest of the northern Plains. These processes form an important part of the discussion of the following chapter.

Acknowledgements

This chapter reflects a synthesis of work conducted by a large number of scholars in both Canada and the USA over many years. The authors acknowledge the role of I. Dyck, D. Meyer, B. Nicholson, B. Reeves, L. Syms and D. Walde in refining our understanding of northern Plains culture history. We owe a particular debt of gratitude to Bev Nicholson and David Meyer. Bev's sustained archaeological field program allowed the senior author an opportunity to return to Manitoba archaeology, and the other authors gained much of their early field training under his supervision. David Meyer was also the primary MA thesis supervisor for both Jill and David. Thanks also to our families for enabling periodic absences to conduct field work and enduring our preoccupations in preparing this manuscript.

References

Ahler, Stanley A., and Marvin Kay (eds.). 2007. Plains Village Archaeology: *Bison-hunting Farmers in the Central and Northern Plains*. Salt Lake City: The University of Utah Press.

Ahler, S.A. and E.L. Mehrer. 1984. *The KNRI Small Sites Report: Test Excavations at Eight Plains Village Archaeological Sites in the Knife River Indian Villages National Historic Site*. Report submitted to the Midwest Archaeological Center, U.S. National Park Service.

CHAPTER 4: Human Ecology of the Canadian Prairie Ecozone ca. 1500 BP

Ahler, S.A., T.D. Thiessen and M.K. Trimble. 1991. *People of the Willows: The Prehistory and Early History of the Hidatsa Indians*. Grand Forks: University of North Dakota Press.

Anfinson, S.F. (ed.). 1979. *A Handbook of Minnesota Prehistoric Ceramics*. Occasional Publications in Minnesota Anthropology, No. 5, Minnesota Archaeological Society, Fort Snelling.

Arthurs, David. 1978. Sandy Lake Ware in Northwestern Ontario: A Distributional Study. *Archae-facts: Journal of the Archaeological Society of South-western Manitoba* 5, nos. 2 and 3: 57–64. Also in Manitoba Archaeological Quarterly 2, nos. 1–2: 57–64.

Arzigan, Constance. 1987. The Emergence of Horticultural Economies in Southwestern Wisconsin. In *Emergent Horticultural Economies of the Eastern Woodlands*, ed. William F. Keegan, 217–42. Centre for Archaeological Investigation, Occasional Paper No. 7. Carbondale: Southern Illinois University at Carbondale.

———. 2008. *Minnesota Statewide Multiple Property Documentation Form for the Woodland Tradition*. Mississippi Valley Archaeology Center at the University of Wisconsin-La Crosse, MVAC Report No. 735. Submitted to the Minnesota Department of Transportation, Contract No. 89964.

Badertscher, P.M., L.J. Roberts and S.L. Zoltai. 1987. *Hill of the Buffalo Chase: 1982 Excavations at the Stott Site, DlMa-1*. Final Report No 18, Papers in Manitoba Archaeology, Manitoba Culture, Heritage and Recreation, Historic Resources, Winnipeg.

Belsham, Leanne. 1996. A Descriptive Analysis of the Heron Site. BA Specialist thesis, Brandon University.

Belsham, Leanne and Andrea Richards. 2004. A Re-Analysis of the Late Side-Notched Projectile Point Typology for the Northeastern Plains. Paper presented at the 2004 Annual Conference of the Canadian Archaeological Association, Winnipeg.

Benn, David W. 1981. Ceramics from the MAD Sites and Other Prairie Peninsula and Plains Complexes. In *Archaeology of the MAD Sites at Denison, Iowa*, ed. David W. Benn. Iowa City: Iowa State Historical Department, Division of Historic Preservation.

———. 1982. Woodland Cultures of the Western Prairie Peninsula: An Abstract, In *Interrelations of Cultural and Fluvial Deposits in Northwest Iowa*, ed. E.A. Bettis and D.M. Thompson, 37–52. Iowa City: Association of Iowa Archaeologists.

———. 1983. Diffusion and Acculturation in Woodland Cultures on the Western Prairie Peninsula. In *Prairie Archaeology*, ed. Guy E. Gibbon, 75–85. Publications in Anthropology 3. Minneapolis: University of Minnesota.

———. 1986. *The Western Iowa Rivers Basin: An Archaeological Overview*. Iowa River Basin Report Series, Vol. 3. Springfield, MO: Center for Archaeological Research, Southwest Missouri State University.

Benn, David W. (ed.). 1990. *Woodland Culture on the Western Prairies: The Rainbow Site Investigations*. Iowa City: University of Iowa, Office of the State Archaeologist Report 18.

Birk, Douglas A. 1977a. The Norway Lake Site: A Multicomponent Woodland Complex North Central Minnesota. *Minnesota Archaeologist* 36, no. 1: 16–45.

———. 1977b. Two Sandy Lake Ware Vessels from Onigum Point, Cass County, Minnesota. *Minnesota Archaeologist* 36, no. 1: 9–15.

———: 1979. Sandy Lake Ware. In *A Handbook of Minnesota Prehistoric Ceramics*, ed. Scott F. Anfinson, 175–82. Occasional Publications in Minnesota Anthropology No. 5. Fort Snelling: Minnesota Archaeological Society.

———. 1992. Putting Minnesota on the Map: Early French Presence in the Folle Avoine Region Southwest of Lake Superior. *Minnesota Archaeologist* 51: 7–26, Omnibus Edition, vols. 51–54 (1992–1995), issued in 1997.

Birk, Douglas A. and Eldon Johnson. 1992. The Mdewakanton Dakota and Initial French Contact. In *Calumet and Fleur-De-Lys: Archaeology of Indian and French Contact in the Midcontinent*, ed. John A. Walthall and Thomas E. Emerson, 203–40. Washington and London: Smithsonian Institution Press.

Bonney, Rachel A. 1970. Early Woodland in Minnesota. *Plains Anthropologist* 15: 302–4.

Boyd, Matthew. 2002 Identification of Anthropogenic Burning in the Paleoecological Record of the Northern Prairies: A New Approach. *Annals of the Association of American Geographers* 92, no. 3: 471–87.

Boyd, M., C. Surette. and B.A. Nicholson. 2006. Archaeobotanical Evidence of Prehistoric Maize (*Zea mays*) Consumption at the Northern Edge of the Great Plains. *Journal of Archaeological Science* 33: 1129–1140.

Boyd, M., T. Varney, C. Surette and J. Surette. 2008. Reassessing the Northern Limit of Maize Consumption in North America: Stable Isotope, Plant Microfossil, and Trace Element Content of Carbonized Food Residue. *Journal of Archaeological Science* 35: 2545–56.

Brumley J.H. and B.J. Dau. 1988. *Historical Resource Investigations within the Fort Mile Coulee Reservoir*. Archaeology Survey of Alberta, Manuscript Series No. 13, Edmonton, Alberta.

Buchner, A.P. 1985. *Archaeological Research at the Lockport Site: 1866–1985*. Report on file with the Historic Resources Branch, Manitoba Culture, Heritage and Recreation, Winnipeg.

———. 1986. A Brief Note on the Lockport Radiocarbon Dates. *Manitoba Archaeological Quarterly* 10, no. 1: 72–73.

———. 1989 The Geochronology of the Lockport Site. *Manitoba Archaeological Quarterly* 12: 2.

Byrne, William J. 1973. *The Archaeology and Prehistory of Southern Alberta as Reflected by Ceramics*. National Museum of Man, Mercury Series, Paper No. 14. Ottawa: Archaeological Survey of Canada.

Capes, Katherine H. 1963. *The W.B. Nickerson Survey and Excavations, 1912–1915, of the Southern Manitoba Mounds Region*. Anthropology Papers Number 4. Ottawa: National Museum of Canada, Dept. of Northern Affairs and Natural Resources.

Charles, Douglass K. and Jane E. Buikstra. 1983 Archaic Mortuary Sites in the Central Mississippi Drainage: Distribution, Structure, and Behavioral Implications. In *Archaic Hunters and Gatherers in the American Midwest*, ed. James L. Phillips and James A. Brown, 117–45. New York: Academic Press.

Chomko, Steven A. and W. Raymond Wood. 1973 Linear Mounds in the Northeastern Plains. *Archaeology of Montana* 14, no. 2: 1–19.

Cloutier, Riel. 2004. Testing Contemporaneity: The Avonlea and Besant Complexes on the Northern Plains. MA thesis, University of Saskatchewan.

Cooper, Leland R. and Elden Johnson. 1964. Sandy Lake Ware and Its Distribution. *American Antiquity* 29, no. 4: 474–79.

Cowan, C.W. 1985. Understand the Evolution of Plant Husbandry in Eastern North America: Lessons from Botany, Ethnography, and Archaeology. In *Prehistoric Food Production in North America*, ed. R.I. Ford, 205–44. Anthropological Papers No. 75. Ann Arbor: Museum of Anthropology, University of Michigan.

Davis, Leslie B. (ed.). 1988. *Avonlea Yesterday and Today: Archaeology and Prehistory.* Saskatoon: Saskatchewan Archaeological Society.

Davis, Leslie. 1966 Avonlea Point Occurrence in Northern Montana and Canada. *Plains Anthropologist* 11: 100–116.

Davis L. B. and J.W. Fisher. 1988. Avonlea Predation on Wintering Plains Pronghorns. In *Avonlea Yesterday and Today: Archaeology and Prehistory*, ed. L.B. Davis, 101–18. Saskatoon: Saskatchewan Archaeological Society.

Davis, L.B, J.W. Fisher Jr., M.C. Wilson, S.A. Chomko and R.E. Morlan. 2000 Avonlea Phase Winter Fare at Lost Terrace, Upper Missouri River Valley of Montana: The Vertebrate Fauna. *Plains Anthropologist*, Memoir 32: 53–69.

Deaver, Ken (ed.). 1985. *Mitigation of the Anderson Tipi Ring Site (32Ml111), McLean County, North Dakota.* Report on file, Ethnoscience, Billings, Montana.

Deck, D.M., and C.T. Shay. 1992 A Preliminary Report on the Plant Remains from the Lockport Site (EaLf-1). *Manitoba Archaeological Journal* 2, no. 2: 36–49.

Dyck, Ian G. 1972. *1971 Excavations at Four Sites in the Dunfermline Sand Hills, Saskatchewan.* Report submitted to the National Museum of Man, Ottawa.

———. 1983. The Prehistory of Southern Saskatchewan. In *Tracking Ancient Hunters: Prehistoric Archaeology in Saskatchewan*, ed. H.T. Epp and I. Dyck, 63–139. Regina: Saskatchewan Archaeological Society.

Dyck, I.G., K. Elliott and I.G. Brace. 1980. Saskatchewan Museum of Natural History 1980 Summer Projects. *Saskatchewan Archaeological Society Newsletter* 1, no. 5: 9–10.

Epp, H.T. and I. Dyck (eds.). 1983. *Tracking Ancient Hunters: Prehistoric Archaeology in Saskatchewan.* Regina: Saskatchewan Archaeological Society.

Fagan, Brian M. 2005. *Ancient North America: The Archaeology of a Continent.* New York: Thames and Hudson.

Fiedel, Stuart J. 1988. *Prehistory of the Americas.* Cambridge: Cambridge University Press.

Finnigan, James T. 1981. The Elma Thompson Site: A Preliminary Report. *Saskatchewan Archaeological Society Newsletter* 2, no. 4: 72–73.

———. 1982 *Tipi Rings and Plains Prehistory: A Reassessment of Their Archaeological Potential.* National Museum of Man, Mercury Series, Paper No. 108. Ottawa: Archaeological Survey of Canada.

Flynn, Catherine M. 1993. The Horticultural Component at the Lockport site (EaLf-1): An Overview of Ceramic and Cultural Affiliations. Paper presented at the 51st Annual Meeting of Plains Anthropology Society, Saskatoon, Sask.

Flynn, Catherine M. and A. Zoe Kogan. 1991. A Compositional Analysis of the Late Prehistoric Ceramics From the Lockport Site (EaLf-1), Manitoba. *Journal of the Manitoba Anthropology Student's Association* 11, no. 1: 36–73.

Flynn, Catherine and E. Leigh Syms. 1996. Manitoba's First Farmers. *Manitoba History* 31: 4–11.

Forbis, Richard G. 1977. *Cluny: An Ancient Fortified Village in Alberta*. Occasional Papers No. 4. Calgary: Department of Archaeology, University of Calgary.

———. 1992. The Mesoindian (Archaic) Period in the Northern Plains. *Journal of American Archaeology* 5: 27–70.

Fraley, David C. 1988. Avonlea and Besant in Eastern Montana: Archaeological Distributions in the Lower Yellowstone Region. In *Avonlea Yesterday and Today: Archaeology and Prehistory*, ed. L.B. Davis, 129–36. Saskatoon: Saskatchewan Archaeological Society.

Frison, George C. 1971. The Buffalo Pound in Northwestern Plains Prehistory: Site 48CA302, Wyoming. *American Antiquity* 36: 77–91.

———. 1978. *Prehistoric Hunters of the High Plains*. New York: Academic Press.

Gibbon, Guy. 1994. Cultures of the Upper Mississippi River Valley and Adjacent Prairies of Iowa and Minnesota. In *Plains Indians, A.D. 500–1500: The Archaeological Past of Historic Groups*, ed. K. Schlesier, 128–48. Norman: University of Oklahoma Press.

———. 2003 *The Sioux: The Dakota and Lakota Nations*. Malden: Blackwell Publishing.

Gibbon, Guy and Christy A.H. Caine. 1980. The Middle to Late Woodland Transition in Eastern Minnesota. *Midcontinental Journal of Archaeology* 5: 57–72.

Gonsior, L. 2003. Terminal Brainerd Ware from the Lake Carlos State Park Beach Site (21DL2). *The Minnesota Archaeologist* 62: 17–26.

Graham, James. 2005. Blackduck Settlement in South-western Manitoba. MA thesis, University of Manitoba.

Gregg, Michael L. 1985. Archaeological Classification and Chronology for Western and Central North Dakota. In *An Overview of the Prehistory of Central and Western North Dakota*, ed. Michael L. Gregg and Dale Davidson, 67–78. Montana: Bureau of Land Management, Billings.

———. 1987a. *Archaeological Excavation at the Naze Site (32SN246)*. Grand Forks: Department of Anthropology, University of North Dakota.

———. 1987b. Knife River Flint in the Northeastern Plains. *Plains Anthropologist* 32: 367–77.

———. 1994. Archaeological Complexes of the Northeastern Plains and Prairie-Woodland Border. In *Plains Indians, A.D. 500–1500: The Archaeological Past of Historic Groups*, ed. K. Schlesier, 71–95. Norman: University of Oklahoma Press.

Gregg, Michael L. and Paul R. Picha. 1989. Early Plains Woodland and Middle Plains Woodland Occupation of the James River Region in Southeastern North Dakota. *Midcontinental Journal of Archaeology* 14, no. 1: 38–61.

Greiser, Sally T. 1994. Late Prehistoric Cultures on the Montana Plains. In *Plains Indians, A.D. 500–1500: The Archaeological Past of Historic Groups*, ed. K. Schlesier, 34–55. Norman: University of Oklahoma Press.

Griffin, James B. 1968. Hopewellian Obsidian in the Middle West. *Bulletin of the American Anthropological Association* 1, no. 3.

Gruhn, Ruth. 1969. *Preliminary Report on the Muhlbach Site: A Besant Bison Trap in Central Alberta*. National Museum of Canada Bulletin 232: 128–56.

Hamilton, Scott. 1982. The Blackduck Culture: Plains Periphery Influences. In *Approaches to Algonquian Archaeology*, ed. M.G. Hanna and B. Kooyman, 97–117. Proceedings of the 13th Annual Conference of the Archaeological Association of University of Calgary, Calgary.

Hamilton, S., W. Ferris, S. Hallgrimson, G. McNeely, K. Sammons, E. Simonds, and K. Topinka. 1981. *1979 Excavations at the Stott Site (DlMa-1), with Interpretations of Cultural Stratigraphy*. Papers in Manitoba Archaeology, Miscellaneous Paper No. 12. Winnipeg: Manitoba Dept. of Cultural Affairs and Historical Resources.

Hamilton, Scott, James Graham and B.A. Nicholson. 2007. Archaeological Site Distributions and Contents: Modeling Late Precontact Blackduck Land Use in the Northeastern Plains. In *Building a Contextual Milieu: Interdisciplinary Modeling and Theoretical Perspectives from the SCAPE Project*, ed. B.A. Nicholson and Dion Wiseman, 93–136. Canadian Journal of Archaeology 31, no. 3.

Hamilton, Scott, and B.A. Nicholson. 2006. Aboriginal Seasonal Subsistence and Land Use on the Northeastern Plains: Insight from Ethnohistoric Sources. *Plains Anthropologist* Memoir 38, no. 199: 253–80.

Hanna, Margaret G. 1976. *The Moose Bay Burial Mound: EdMq-1*. Regina: Saskatchewan Department of Tourism.

———. 1984. Do You Take This Woman? Economics and Marriage in a Prehistoric Band. *Plains Anthropologist* 29, no. 104: 115–30.

Hems, David. N.d. Final Report of the 1987 and 1988 Field Seasons at EaLf-1. Report submitted to the Historic Resources Branch, Manitoba Culture Heritage and Recreation, Winnipeg.

Henning, Dale R. 1998. The Oneota Tradition. In *Archaeology of the Great Plains*, ed. W. Raymond Wood, 345–414. University Press of Kansas, Lawrence.

Hjermstad, Benjamin. 1993. The Fitzgerald Site: A Besant Phase Kill and Processing Site in Southern Saskatchewan. Paper presented at the 26th Annual Conference of the Canadian Archaeological Association.

———. 1995 The Fitzgerald Site: A Besant Pound and Processing Area on the Northern Plains. MA thesis, University of Saskatchewan.

Hlady, W.M. 1967. A Besant Phase Bison Kill Site in Southwestern Manitoba. *Manitoba Archaeological Society Newsletter* 4, no. 2: 3–10.

Hoffman, J.J. 1968 *The La Roche Site*. River Basin Surveys Publications in Salvage Archaeology No. 11. Lincoln, NE: Smithsonian Institution.

Hohman-Caine, C.A. and G.E. Goltz. 1995. Brainerd Ware and the Early Woodland Dilemma. *The Minnesota Archaeologist* 54: 109–29.

Jennings, Jesse D. 1989. *Prehistory of North America*. Mountain View: Mayfield Publishing.

Johnson, Ann M. 1977a. Woodland and Besant in the Northern Plains: A Perspective. *Archaeology in Montana* 18, no. 1: 27–41.

———. 1977b. The Dune Buggy Site. 24RV1, and Northwestern Plains Ceramics. *Plains Anthropologist* 22: 37–49.

———. 1988. Parallel Grooved Ceramics: An Addition to Avonlea Material Culture. In *Avonlea Yesterday and Today: Archaeology and Prehistory*, ed. L. Davis, 137–43. Saskatoon: Saskatchewan Archaeological Society.

Johnson, Ann Mary and Alfred E. Johnson. 1998. The Plains Woodland. In *Archaeology on the Great Plains*, ed. W. Raymond Wood, 201–34. Lawrence: University Press of Kansas.

Johnson, Craig M. 1998 The Coalescent Tradition. In *Archaeology on the Great Plains*, ed. W. Raymond Wood, 308–44. Lawrence: University Press of Kansas.

Johnson, E. 1971. Excavations at the Gull Lake Dam (21CA27). *The Minnesota Archaeologist* 31, no. 2: 44–69.

———. 1985. The 17th Century Mdewakanton Dakota Subsistence Mode. In *Archaeology, Ecology and Ethnohistory of the Prairie-Forest Border Zone of Minnesota and Manitoba*, ed. Janet Spector and Elden Johnson, 154–66. Reprints in Anthropology, Vol. 31. Lincoln, NE: J&L Reprint Company.

Joyes, Dennis. 1970. The Cultural Sequence at the Avery Site at Rock Lake. In *Ten Thousand Years: Archaeology in Manitoba*, ed. W.M. Hlady, 209–22. Winnipeg: Manitoba Archaeological Society.

———. 1973 The Shippee Canyon Site. *Archaeology in Montana* 14, no. 2: 49–85.

———. 1988 A Summary and Evaluation of Avonlea in Manitoba. In *Avonlea Yesterday and Today: Archaeology and Prehistory*, ed. L. Davis, 227–36. Saskatoon: Saskatchewan Archaeological Society.

Kehoe, Alice B. 1959. Ceramic Affiliations in the Northwestern Plains. *American Antiquity* 25: 237–46.

Kehoe, Thomas F. 1964. Middle Woodland Pottery from Saskatchewan. *Plains Anthropologist* 9: 51–52.

———. 1966 The Small Side-notched Point System of the Northern Plains. *American Antiquity* 31, no. 6: 827–41.

———. 1974 The Large Corner-notched Point System of the Northern Plains. In *Aspects of Upper Great Lakes Anthropology: Papers in Honor of Lloyd A. Wilford*, ed. E. Johnson, 103–14. St. Paul: Minnesota Historical Society.

———. 1978 Paleo-Indian Bison Drives: Feasibility Studies. In *Bison Procurement and Utilization: A Symposium*, ed. Leslie B. Davis and Michael Wilson Plains Anthropologist Memoir 14: 23–82, pt. 2: 79–83.

Kehoe, Thomas F., and Bruce A. McCorquodale. 1961. The Avonlea Point: A Horizon Marker for the Northwestern Plains. *Plains Anthropologist* 6: 179–88.

Kelly, John E., Fred A. Finney, Dale L. McElrath and Steven J. Ozuk. 1984. Late Woodland Period. In *American Bottom Archaeology*, ed. Charles J. Bareis and James W. Porter, 215–32. Urbana: University of Illinois Press.

Kivett, M.F. 1952. *Woodland Sites in Nebraska*. Publications in Anthropology 1. Lincoln: Nebraska State Historical Society.

———. 1970. Early Ceramic Environmental Adaptations. In *Pleistocene and Recent*

Environments of the Central Great Plains, ed. W. Dort, Jr. and J.K Jones, Jr., 93–102. Department of Geology Special Publications No. 3. Lawrence: University of Kansas.

Klimko, Olga. 1985. *The Gravel Pit and Eastcott Flat Sites: Final Excavation Reports*. Nipawin Reservoir Heritage Study, Vol. 7. Ed. David Meyer, Saskatchewan Research Council Publication No. E-903-8-E-85, Saskatoon.

Kordecki, Cynthia, and Michael Gregg. 1986. James River Valley Archaeological Site Survey, 1985. Contribution No. 231. Department of Anthropology, University of North Dakota, Grand Forks. Report prepared for the U.S. Department of the Interior, Bureau of Land Management, Upper Missouri Region, Billings.

Landals, Alison J. 1994. *The Miniota Site, An Avonlea Component in Southwestern Manitoba*. Calgary: Fedirchuk, McCullough and Associates Ltd.

———. 2004. *The Miniota Site, An Avonlea Component in Southwestern Manitoba*. Occasional Papers of the Archaeological Society of Alberta No. 3. Calgary: Archaeological Society of Alberta.

Lehmer, Donald J. 1971. *Introduction to Middle Missouri Archeology*. Anthropological Papers 1. Washington: National Park Service, Department of the Interior.

Linius, Brian J., and Dave M. Olinyk. 1990. *The Rainy River Composite: Revisions to Late Woodland Taxonomy*. In *The Woodland Tradition in the Western Great Lakes: Papers Presented to Elden Johnson*, ed. Guy E. Gibbon, 77-112. Publications in Anthropology No. 4. Minneapolis: University of Minnesota.

Lints, Andrew and M. Boyd. 2011. Starch and Phytolith Analysis of Avonlea Vessels from the Miniota Site (EaMg-12), Western Manitoba. Paper presented at the 2011 Annual Conference of the Canadian Archaeological Association, Halifax.

Lofstrom, Ted. 1987. The Rise of Wild Rice Exploitation and Its Implications for Populations Size and Social Organization in Minnesota Woodland Period Cultures. *The Minnesota Archaeologist* 46, no. 2: 3–15.

Loveseth, Beatrice. 1983. The Crowsnest Lake Dancehall Site (DjPp-3): Interpretation Based on Lithic Artifact and Type Analysis. MA thesis, University of Calgary.

Lugenbeal, Edward. 1978. Brainerd Ware and Chronological Relationships. In *Some Studies of Minnesota Prehistoric Ceramics: Papers Presented at the First Council for Minnesota Archaeological Symposium—1976*, ed. A.R. Woolworth and M.A. Hall, 35–46. Occasional Publications in Minnesota Anthropology No. 2. St. Paul: Minnesota Archaeological Society.

———. 1982. Ceramics at the White Oak Point Site. *The Minnesota Archaeologist* 41, no. 2: 5–33.

Mason, Ronald J. 2002. *Great Lakes Archaeology*. Caldwell, NJ: Blackburn Press.

MacNeish, R.S. 1958. *An Introduction to the Archaeology of Southeast Manitoba*. Bulletin 157. Ottawa: National Museum of Canada.

MacNeish, R.S. and K.H. Capes. 1958. The United Church Site Near Rock Lake in Manitoba. *Anthropologica* 6: 119–56.

McKern, William C. 1939. The Midwestern Taxonomic Method as an Aid to Archaeological Culture Study. *American Antiquity* 4, no. 4: 301–13.

Meyer, David. 1988 The Old Women's Phase on Saskatchewan Plains: Some Ideas. In

Archaeology in Alberta 1987, ed. M. Magne, 55-64. Archaeological Survey of Alberta Occasional Paper No. 32. Edmonton: Alberta Culture.

Meyer, David and H.T. Epp. 1990. North-south Interaction in the Late Prehistory of Central Saskatchewan. *Plains Anthropologist* 35: 321–42.

Meyer, David and Scott Hamilton. 1994. Neighbors to the North: Peoples of the Boreal Forest. In *Plains Indians, A.D. 500–1500: The Archaeological Past of Historic Groups*, ed. K. Schlesier, 96–127. Norman: University of Oklahoma Press, Norman.

Meyer, David, Margaret Hanna and Doug Frey. 1999. The Enigma of Saskatchewan Blackduck: Pottery from the Hanson (FgNi-50) and Hokness (FgNi-51) Sites. *Midcontinental Journal of Archaeology* 24, no. 2 (Fall): 43–80.

Meyer, David, Olga Klimko, and James Finnigan. 1988. Northernmost Avonlea in Saskatchewan. In *Avonlea Yesterday and Today: Archaeology and Prehistory*, ed. L. Davis, 33–42. Saskatoon: Saskatchewan Archaeological Society.

Meyer, David, Peggy McKeand, J. Michael Quigg and Gary Wowchuk. 2008. The River House Complex: Middle Woodland on the Northwestern Periphery. *Canadian Journal of Archaeology* 32, no. 1: 43–76.

Meyer, David and M. Rollans. 1990. The Case for (Canadian) Besant Pottery. Paper presented at the 31st Annual Conference of the Western Association of Sociology and Anthropology.

Meyer, David, and Dale Russell. 1987. The Selkirk Composite of Central Canada: A Reconsideration. *Arctic Anthropology* 24, no. 2: 1–31.

Meyer, David and Dale Walde. 2009. Rethinking Avonlea: Pottery Wares and Cultural Phases. *Plains Anthropologist* 54, no. 209: 49–73.

Michlovic, Michael. 1990. Northern Plains-Woodland Interaction in Prehistory. In *The Woodland Tradition in the Western Great Lakes: Papers Presented to Elden Johnson*, ed. Guy E. Gibbon, 45–54. Minneapolis: University of Minnesota Publications in Anthropology No. 4.

Michlovic, M. and F. Schneider. 1993. The Shea Site: A Prehistoric Fortified Village on the Northeastern Plains. *Plains Anthropologist* 38, no. 143: 117–37.

Morgan, Grace R. 1979. *An Ecological Study of the Northern Plains as seen through the Garratt Site*. Occasional Papers in Anthropology No. 1. Regina: Department of Anthropology, University of Regina.

Morlan, Richard E. 1988. Avonlea and Radiocarbon Dating. In *Avonlea Yesterday and Today: Archaeology and Prehistory*, ed. L. Davis, 291–309. Saskatoon: Saskatchewan Archaeological Society.

Neuman, Robert W. 1975. *The Sonota Complex and Associated Sites on the Northern Great Plains*. Lincoln: Nebraska State Historical Society Publications in Anthropology No. 6.

Neumann, T.W. 1978. Classification of Net-Impressed Pottery from Central Minnesota. In *Some Studies of Minnesota Prehistoric Ceramics: Papers Presented at the First Council for Minnesota Archaeological Symposium—1976*, ed. A.R. Woolworth and M.A. Hall, 56–65. Occasional Publications in Minnesota Anthropology, No. 2. St. Paul: Minnesota Archaeological Society.

———. 1983. An Examination of the Difference Between Gull Lake Net-Impressed and Brainerd Net-Impressed. *The Minnesota Archaeologist* 43, no. 1: 38–60.

Nicholson, B.A. 1990. Ceramic Affiliations and the Case for Incipient Horticulture in Southwestern Manitoba. *Canadian Journal of Archaeology* 14: 33–60.

———. 1991. Modeling a Horticultural Complex in South-central Manitoba During the Late Prehistoric Period—The Vickers Focus. Midcontinental Journal of Archaeology 16: 163–88.

———. 1994a. Interactive Dynamics of Intrusive Horticultural Groups Coalescing in South-central Manitoba During the Late Prehistoric Period—The Vickers Focus. *North American Archaeologist* 15: 103–28.

———. 1994b. Orientation of Burials and Pattering in the Selection of Sites for Late Prehistoric Burial Mounds in South-Central Manitoba. *Plains Anthropologist* 39, no. 148: 161–72.

Nicholson, B.A., Sylvia Nicholson, Garry L. Running IV and Scott Hamilton. 2002. Vickers Focus Environmental Choices and Site Location in the Parklands of Southwestern Manitoba. *Géographie physique et Quaternaire* 56, nos. 2–3: 315–24.

Norris, David Stewart. 2007. The Presence of Net-impressed and Horizontally Corded Ware in Southern Manitoba: The Relationship between Rock Lake and Brainerd Ware. MA thesis, University of Saskatchewan.

Norris, D. and S. Hamilton. 2004. The Hokanson Site (DiLv-29): Preliminary Insight into Late Pre-Contact Communal Bison Hunting. *Manitoba Archaeological Journal* 14, no. 2: 16–40.

Participants of the Lake Superior Basin Workshop. 1987. Desperately Seeking Siouans: The Distribution of Sandy Lake Ware. Compiled by Grace Rajnovich. *The Western Canadian Anthropologist* 4: 57–64. Also in *Manitoba Archaeological Quarterly* 12, no. 1: 49–56; Ontario Archaeological Society Arch Notes 88, no. 3: 9–13; The Wisconsin Archaeologist 69, no. 4: 337–53; and The Minnesota Archaeologist 47, no. 1: 43–48.

Peck, Trevor R. 1996. Late Side-notched Projectile Points on the Northwestern Plains. MA thesis, University of Alberta.

———. 2007 The Besant-Sonota Debate: A Perspective from the Alberta Plains. Paper presented at the 40th annual Canadian Archaeological Association Conference, St. John's, Newfoundland.

Peck, Trevor R. and Caroline R. Hudecek-Cuffe. 2003. Archaeology on the Alberta Plains: The Last Two Thousand Years. In *Archaeology in Alberta: A View from the New Millennium*, ed. Jack W. Brink and John F. Dormaar, 72–102. Medicine Hat: Archaeological Society of Alberta.

Peck, Trevor R. and J.W. Ives. 2001 Late Side-notched Projectile Points on the Northwestern Plains. *Plains Anthropologist* 46, no. 176: 163–93.

Peterson, Lynelle A. 1986. An Attribute Analysis of Sandy Lake Ware from Norman County and North Central Minnesota. MA thesis, University of Nebraska, Lincoln.

Pettipas, Leo F. 1983 *Introducing Manitoba Prehistory*. Papers in Manitoba Archaeology Popular Series No. 4. Winnipeg: Department of Culture, Heritage and Recreation.

———. 1996. *Aboriginal Migrations A History of Movements in Southern Manitoba*. Manitoba Museum of Man and Nature, Winnipeg.

Phenix, T.S. 1969. The Alberta Point in Time and Space. *Saskatchewan Archaeology Newsletter* 17: 2–3.

Pyszczyk, Heinz. 2003. Aboriginal Bows and Arrows and Other Weapons in Alberta: The Last 2,000 years or Longer?. In *Archaeology in Alberta: A View from the New Millennium*, ed. Jack W. Brink and John F. Dormaar, 46–71. Medicine Hat: The Archaeological Society of Alberta.

Quigg, J. Michael. 1986. Ross Glen: *A Besant Stone Circle Site in Southeastern Alberta*. Archaeological Survey of Alberta Manuscript Series No. 10. Edmonton: Alberta Culture, Historical Resources Division, Edmonton.

———. 1988a. A New Avonlea Ceramic Style from North-Central Montana In *Avonlea Yesterday and Today: Archaeology and Prehistory*, ed. L. Davis, 145–54. Saskatoon: Saskatchewan Archaeological Society.

———. 1988b. A Ceramic Bearing Avonlea Component in Southwestern Alberta. In *Avonlea Yesterday and Today: Archaeology and Prehistory*, ed. L. Davis, 67–80. Saskatoon: Saskatchewan Archaeological Society.

Ramsay, Allyson M. 1991. The Melhagen Site: A Besant Bison Kill in South Central Saskatchewan. MA thesis, University of Saskatchewan.

Reeves, B.O.K. 1970. Culture Change in the Northern Plains 1000 BC–AD 1000. PhD dissertation, University of Calgary.

———. 1980. DgPl-10: Awinger Base Campsite, Waterton Lakes National Park. Unpublished report on file, Parks Canada.

———. 1983. *Culture Change in the Northern Plains: 1000 BC–AD 1000*. Archaeological Survey of Alberta, Occasional Paper 20. Edmonton (published version of 1970 PhD dissertation).

Roberts, Linda J. 1991. Bison Scapula Hoes from the Lockport Site, EaLf-1. *Manitoba Archaeological Journal* 1, no. 2: 1–22.

———. 1992. Faunal Analysis of the 1984–1986 Excavations at the Lockport Site, EaLf-1. *Manitoba Archaeological Journal* 2, no. 1: 1–13.

Roll, Tom E. 1988. Focus on a Phase: Expanded Geographical Distributions and Resultant Taxonomic Implications for Avonlea. In *Avonlea Yesterday and Today: Archaeology and Prehistory*, ed. L. Davis, 291–309. Saskatoon: Saskatchewan Archaeological Society.

Schlesier, Karl (ed.). 1994. *Plains Indians, AD 500–1500: The Archaeological Past of Historic Groups*. Norman: University of Oklahoma Press.

Schneider, Fred. 1988. Prehistoric Plant Use in Eastern North Dakota: Evidence and Interpretation Paper presented at the 46th Annual Plains Anthropological Conference, Wichita, Kansas.

———. 2002. Prehistoric Horticulture in the Northeastern Plains. *Plains Anthropologist* 47, no. 180: 33–50.

Schneider, F. and J. Kinney. 1978. Evans: A Multi-Component Site in Northwestern North Dakota. *Archaeology in Montana* 19, no. 1–2: 1–39.

Scribe, Brian. 1997. Nistam Ka-ke Askihkokechik Puskwaw-askihk: An Assessment of Besant-Sonata Pottery on the Canadian Plains. MA thesis, University of Saskatchewan.

Shay, C. Thomas. 1990. Perspectives on the Late Prehistory of the Northern Plains. In *The Woodland Tradition on the Western Great Lakes: Papers Presented in Honor of Elden Johnson*, ed. Guy E. Gibbon, 113–33. University of Minnesota Publications in Anthropology No. 4, Minneapolis.

Smith, Brian J. 1986. The Lebret Site. MA thesis, University of Saskatchewan.

Smith, Brian J. and Ernest G. Walker. 1988. Evidence for Diverse Subsistence Strategies in an Avonlea Component. In *Avonlea Yesterday and Today: Archaeology and Prehistory*, ed. L. Davis, 81–87. Saskatoon: Saskatchewan Archaeological Society.

Snortland-Coles, J. Signe. 1985. *The Jamestown Mounds Project*. Bismark: State Historical Society of North Dakota.

Stoltman, James B. 1973. *The Laurel Culture in Minnesota*. Minnesota Prehistoric Archaeology Series No. 8. St. Paul: Minnesota Historical Society.

Syms, E.L. 1977. Cultural Ecology and Ecological Dynamics of the Ceramic Period in Southwestern Manitoba. *Plains Anthropologist* Memoir 12: 22, no. 76, pt. 2: 1–160.

———. 1979. The Devils Lake-Sourisford Burial Complex on the Northern Plains. *Plains Anthropologist* 24: 283–308.

———. 1982. The Arvilla Burial Complex: A Re-assessment. *Journal of the North Dakota Archaeological Association* 1: 135–66.

———. 2004. Discovering the Fresh Water Reservoir Effect in the Boreal Forest of Northern Manitoba: A New Ripple in the Time Continuum. Manuscript, The Manitoba Museum, Winnipeg. Version entitled *The Fresh Water Reservoir Effect: Watch out for those Fish Easters* was submitted for publication to the CHACMOOL conference proceedings.

Taylor-Hollings, Jill. 1999. The Northwestern Extent of Sandy Lake Ware: A Canadian Perspective. MA thesis, University of Saskatchewan.

Tisdale, M.A. 1978. *Investigations at the Stott Site: A Review of Research from 1947 to 1977*. Papers in Manitoba Archaeology, Final Report, No. 5. Winnipeg: Dept. of Cultural Affairs and Historical Resources.

Toom, Dennis L. 2004. Northeastern Plains Village Complex Timelines and Relations. *Plains Anthropologist* 49, no. 191: 281–97.

Vickers, Chris. 1948. *Archaeological Report 1947*. Projects of the Historical and Scientific Society of Manitoba, Winnipeg.

———. 1949. *Archaeological Report 1948*. Projects of the Historical and Scientific Society of Manitoba, Winnipeg.

———. 1950. *Archaeological Report 1949*. Projects of the Historical and Scientific Society of Manitoba, Winnipeg.

Vickers, J. Roderick. 1986. *Alberta Plains Prehistory: A Review*. Archaeological Survey of Alberta Occasional Papers Nos. 27 & 28. Edmonton: Alberta Culture, Historical Resources Division.

———. 1994. Cultures of the Northwestern Plains: From the Boreal Forest Edge to Milk

River. In *Plains Indians, A.D. 500-1500: The Archaeological Past of Historic Groups*, ed. K. Schlesier, 3–33. Norman: University of Oklahoma Press.

Walde, Dale Allen. 2006a. Avonlea and Athabaskan Migrations: A Reconsideration. *Plains Anthropologist* 51, no. 198: 185–97.

———. 2006b. Sedentism and PreContact Tribal Organization on the Northern Plains: Colonial Imposition or Indigenous Development? *World Archaeology* 38, no. 2: 291–310.

Walde, Dale, and David Meyer. 2003. Pre-contact Pottery in Alberta: An Overview. In *Archaeology in Alberta: A View from the New Millennium*, ed. Jack W. Brink and John F. Dormaar, 132–52. Medicine Hat, AB: The Archaeological Society of Alberta.

Walde, Dale, David Meyer and Wendy Unfreed. 1995. The Late Period on the Canadian and Adjacent Plains. *Journal of American Archaeology (Revista de Arquelogia Americana)* 9: 7–66.

Wettlaufer, B.N. 1955. *The Mortlach Site in the Besant Valley of Central Saskatchewan.* Anthropological Series 1. Regina: Department of Natural Resources.

Wilcox, David R. 1998. Avonlea and Southern Athapascan Migrations. In *Avonlea Yesterday and Today: Archaeology and Prehistory*, ed. L. Davis, 273–80. Saskatoon: Saskatchewan Archaeological Society.

Willey, Gordon R. and Phillip Phillips. 1958. *Method and Theory in American Archaeology*. Chicago: University of Chicago.

Wilson, Michael Clayton. 1983. A Test of the Stone Circle Size-Age Hypothesis; Alberta and Wyoming. In *From Microcosm to Macrocosm: Advances in Tipi Ring Investigation and Interpretation*, ed. Leslie B. Davis. *Plains Anthropologist Memoir* 19: 28–102, pt. 2: 113–38.

Wilson-Meyer, Dianne and M. Carlson. 1985. The Yellowsky Site (FjOd-2): An Avonlea Component in West-central Saskatchewan. *Saskatchewan Archaeology* 6: 19–32.

Winham, R. Peter and Frances A. Calabrese. 1998. The Middle Missouri Tradition. In *Archaeology on the Great Plains*, ed. W. Raymond Wood, 269–307. Lawrence: University Press of Kansas.

Winham, R.P. and E.J. Lueck. 1994. Cultures of the Middle Missouri. In *Plains Indians, A.D. 500–1500: The Archaeological Past of Historic Groups*, ed. K. Schlesier, 149–75. Norman: University of Oklahoma Press.

Wood, W. Raymond. 1985. The Plains-Lakes Connection: Reflections from a Western Perspective. In *Archaeology, Ecology and Ethnohistory of the Prairie-Forest Border Zone of Minnesota and Manitoba*, ed. Janet Spector and Elden Johnson, 1-8. Reprints in Anthropology Vol, 31. Lincoln, NE: J & L Reprint Company.

Wood, W. Raymond and A.M. Johnson. 1973. High Butte, 32ME13: A Missouri Valley Woodland-Besant Site. *Archaeology in Montana* 14, no. 3: 35–83.

Wright, J.V. 1999. *A History of the Native People of Canada Vol. II (1000 BC–AD 500)*. Archaeological Survey of Canada, Mercury Series Paper 152. Gatineau: Canadian Museum of Civilization.

Chapter 5
Human Ecology of the Canadian Prairie Ecozone ca. 500 BP: Plains Woodland Influences and Horticultural Practice

B.A. Nicholson, David Meyer, Gerry Oetelaar and Scott Hamilton

KEYWORDS: Vickers Focus, horticulture, Mortlach, One Gun, ethnicity

An ongoing flow of immigration into the eastern section of the Canadian Prairie Ecozone (CPE) from Paleo-Indian to Middle Period bison hunters is displayed in the archaeological record in surface collections and in excavated sites as well. In Manitoba, the surface recoveries included a few Clovis points (5), Folsom, Agate Basin, Cody Complex and other unassigned lanceolate specimens. Excavated diagnostics included Gowen (see chapter 2, this volume), Oxbow, McKean Complex and Pelican Lake (see chapter 3, this volume). This pattern shifted from a west to east flow of peoples, accompanied by their distinctive projectile points, to a flow of ceramic-using people from the Eastern Woodlands and the Middle Missouri area beginning with Sonota/Besant ca. 200 BCE (Mokelki 2001). The dominant occupations from ca. AD 800 until AD 1300, across the CPE, were those of the Old Women's Phase, extending from the foothills into the western margin of modern Manitoba (Meyer 1988: 61), and Black Duck/Duck Bay people (Hamilton et al. this volume; Nicholson 1987: 179, 205–6) whose territory served as an eastern boundary for the Old Women's Phase. The northern boundary of Old Women's Phase materials extended from modern Edmonton to Prince Albert. The area occupied by Blackduck/Duck Bay people extended well beyond the CPE into the northern and eastern boreal forests of Manitoba and Ontario (Figure 5.1) and both groups relied heavily on bison for their subsistence in the CPE. In the boreal forest, the Blackduck/Duck Bay people, as might be expected, relied primarily upon moose, woodland caribou, aquatic rodents, fish and waterfowl (Hamilton et al. this volume; Nicholson 1987). Along the southern margins of the CPE

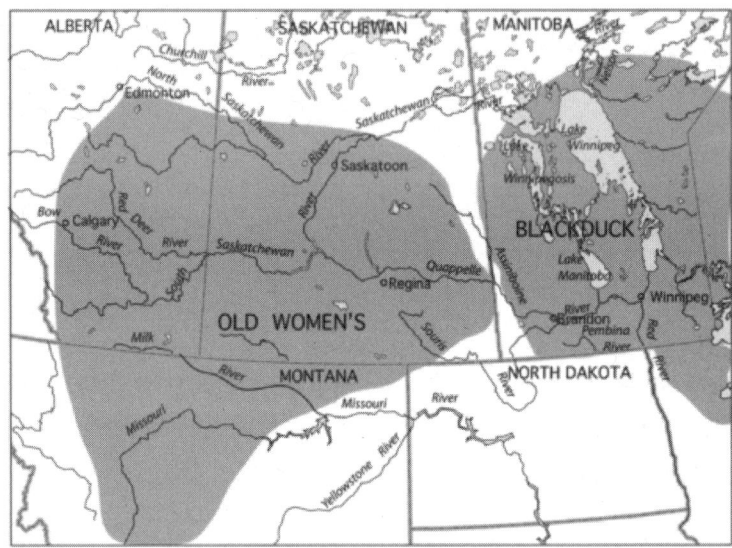

Figure 5.1. Old Women's and Blackduck c. AD 1200.

there were occasional incursions of Initial Middle Missouri groups ca. AD 1000 (Taylor 1994) but there is no evidence for long-term occupations by these groups in the CPE.

An apparent rapid replacement of Blackduck/Duck Bay people in southern Manitoba commenced ca. AD 1300 following an influx of forager horticulturists from the Eastern Woodlands (Nicholson 1991, 1994, 1996; Nicholson et al. 2008). While the Blackduck/Duck Bay people appear to have retreated from Manitoba ca. AD 1300 (Nicholson 1996), these people persisted in the boreal forest biome of northern Ontario and Manitoba until ca. AD 1600. There is ceramic evidence that there was significant contact between these immigrants and Plains Village people from the Middle Missouri area (Nicholson et al. 2007). These immigrant groups included the Vickers Focus (Figure 5.1) in southwestern Manitoba (Nicholson 1991, 1994), the Lockport site north of Winnipeg (Buchner 1986; Hems 1997) and possibly some sites in the Melita area (Syms 1977: 120–21). There are similarities between Vickers Focus and the Scattered Village Complex in North Dakota, and it has been suggested that Vickers Focus may be a northern expansion of the Scattered Village people (Nicholson 1994: 104) and consequently a part of the Northeastern Plains Village Aggregate (Figure 5.2). The Shea Phase, which shows similarities to the Initial Middle Missouri variant and Cambria, has also been subsumed into the Northeastern Plains Village Aggregate (Michlovic 2008: 35–36). The term aggregate has been used by the authors to indicate that all of these groups show some degree of similarity in their lifeways and in artifact styles—particularly in their ceramics.

CHAPTER 5: Human Ecology of the Canadian Prairie Ecozone ca. 500 BP

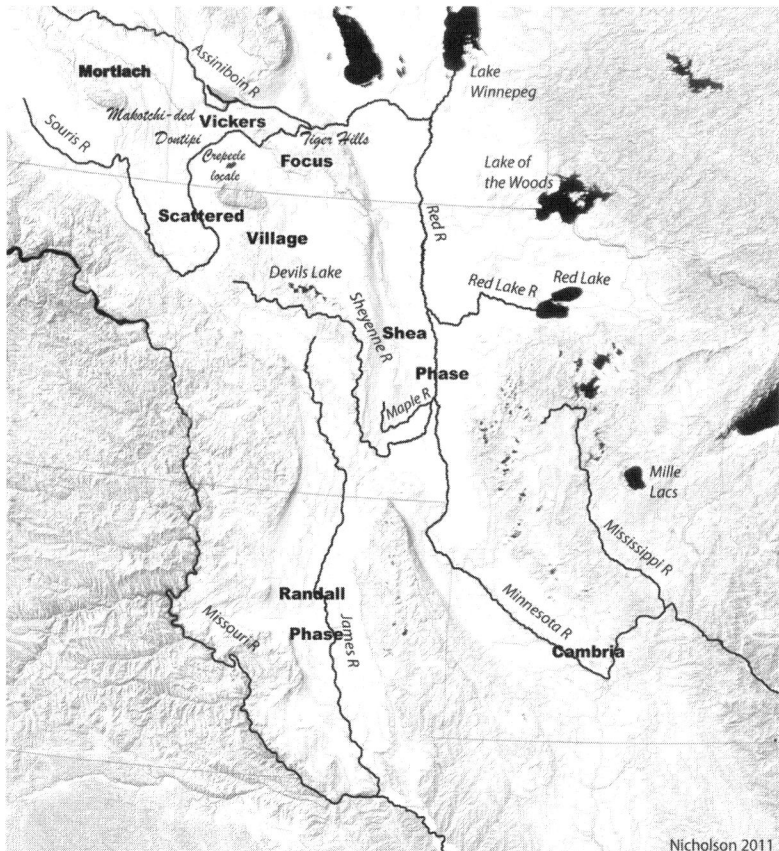

Figure 5.2. Northeastern Plains Village.

However, at the present time, they have been defined in the literature as distinct cultural entities.

It is this late precontact period, ca. 500 BP, that presents the best opportunity to assign an historic ethnic identity to the archaeological assemblages that have been identified throughout the CPE. However, this being said, several authors have published cautionary statements concerning any such exercise. Krause (1998: 73) notes that "the isomorphism between ethnic groups, and their material remains was far from exact. Distinct ethnic groups often shared elements of subsistence technology and lifestyle—a troublesome circumstance at best." Wood (2000: 42) notes the dramatic effect of European diseases on precontact and contact period populations. Many of these diseases appear to have been on a pandemic scale and severely reduced or even exterminated ethnic groups. The Mandan, after experiencing two epidemics in the early protocontact period ca. 1780 and later in 1837, declined from an estimated 12,000 people to a surviving population of around 125 individuals (Wood 2000: 42). A tiny historic remnant such as this will not supply an adequate or even a highly credible ethnographic model of the earlier precontact lifeways of the Mandan. As a consequence, the Direct Historical approach to inferring ethnicity in the recent prehistoric past is much more tenuous than has been imagined. However, the early accounts by explorers, missionaries and fur traders can be useful, when combined with archaeological data, to trace the movement of people in times past and, while still uncertain in many cases, to indicate a possible ethnic identity. With these cautionary indicators firmly in mind, some tentative ethnic assignments are made for some of the archaeological assemblages in this time period in the CPE.

The Scattered Village phase, ca. AD 1400–50, is considered to be a late arrival of the *Awaxawi* Hidatsa (Ahler et al. 1991: 28, 38–39). This is also supported by pottery recovered from excavations at the Horner-Kane Site on Graham's Island in Devil's Lake (Gregg 1992) that closely resembles Vickers Focus materials in the Tiger Hills (Figure 5.2). This recovery is particularly significant because an *Awaxawi* tradition states that they came originally from the east and the Devil's Lake area (Ahler et al. 1991: 46–47; Nicholson 1991).

At about the same time, the Old Women's phase in southern Saskatchewan, was replaced by the Mortlach Complex (Meyer 1988: 59–60). These people may have been Hidatsa since early reports of European explorers note that the *Naywatame Poets* (Hidatsa) were present in southeastern Saskatchewan (Russell 1993: 84). Malainey (1991: 359–60) believes that the northern Mortlach pottery (Wascana ware/Moose Jaw Culture) users were Atsina (Gros Ventre) and that the southern Mortlach users were Hidatsa (Figure 5.3). Fowler and Flannery (2001: 677) indicate that the Gros Ventre were a part of the Blackfoot confederacy at this time, although they spoke an Algonquian language closely related to Arapaho. This scenario is further complicated by the fact that French fur traders referred to Middle Missouri Hidatsa as Gros Ventre (Fowler and Flannery 2001: 693). Other authors, however, suggest that the makers of Mortlach pottery were Assiniboine (Walde 1994), Atsina (Forbis 1961; Kehoe and Kehoe 1968: 34) or Gros Ventre (Hidatsa group) (Wettlaufer 1960: 106–7). Meyer and Russell (2006: 318–19) have presented evidence for peaceful interaction between Gros Ventre, Assiniboine and Cree in central Saskatchewan between the North and South Saskatchewan rivers during the 18th century. It may be that all of these groups were users of Mortlach wares. However, details of the nature of this co-occupation are uncertain and any firm evidence for a common ceramic ware is lacking.

The distribution of Mortlach Aggregate pottery, however, does not support an Assiniboine assignment. The late historic range of the Assiniboine extends from northwestern Ontario to the Battlefords where "Eagle Eyed Indians" (Assiniboine group) have been recorded (Belyea 2000; Burpee 1973; Nicholson 1987: 113) and La Vérendrye encountered Assiniboine in the Lake of the

CHAPTER 5: Human Ecology of the Canadian Prairie Ecozone ca. 500 BP

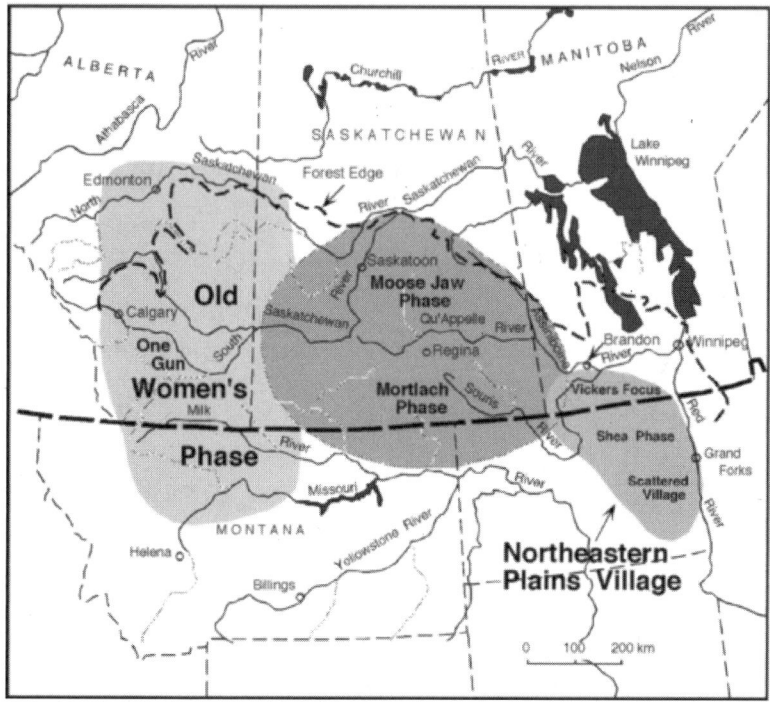

Figure 5.3. Old Women's, Mortlach, Northeastern Plains Village.

Woods area. In the event that the claim were to be made that the Assiniboine also used Selkirk pottery as well as Vickers Focus and Scattered Village wares, then the Assiniboine ethnic assignment could be pursued. This scenario seems unlikely.

Taylor-Hollings (1999: 268) has identified Sandy Lake (SL) wares, closely associated with the *Psinomani* (wild rice gatherer) culture centered in Minnesota, as widely distributed across parts of Wisconsin, northwestern Ontario, southern Manitoba and Saskatchewan, North Dakota and northeastern Montana. Dates ranging from 940 ± 100 BP to 200 ± 90 BP are listed for sites containing SL wares across this area, with the earliest dates from Minnesota and southwestern Manitoba, and the most recent dates from Minnesota and northwestern Ontario (Taylor-Hollings 1999: 112–13). She also notes that, "Typically, it [SL] occurs in small numbers with materials of other phases or complexes in this northwestern study area" (Taylor-Hollings 1999: 85). Many of the vessels that have been recovered in these mixed assemblages are more Sandy Lake-like than fitting to the classic definitions of Sandy Lake wares (Gibbon 1998: 746). It is likely that a wide range of Siouan-speaking ethnic groups deriving from the northeastern woodlands, including both Hidatsa and Nakota peoples, used these wares (Figure 5.4: Lowton site).

Figure 5.4. Vickers Focus Plain wares.

The Vickers Focus groups in the Tiger Hills appear to have arrived ca. AD 1350 and brought a forager/horticultural adaptation to this area (Nicholson 1991,1994; Nicholson et al. 2006a, 2007). Further west, Mokelki (2007) found evidence for a progressive blending of Vickers Focus and Mortlach traits in the ceramics in the *Makotchi-Ded Dontipi* locale, ca. AD 1600, with a dominance of Mortlach traits by the Protohistoric period, ca. AD 1700. She (Mokelki 2007: 119) has suggested that these later sites, "be considered a variant of the Lake Midden subphase of the Lake Midden phase." It may be that Assiniboine people moved into eastern Manitoba following the withdrawal of Vickers Focus to the west. Subsequently they may have moved into the uplands of the Manitoba escarpment, where the "Mountain Poets" (Nakota) were noted by Kelsey ca. 1691 (Meyer and Russell 2007: 169; Russell 1993: 79), and then westward into central Saskatchewan. If this speculative scenario should prove to be correct, the northern Mortlach (Moose Jaw or Wascana ware) could indeed be a footprint of the westward migration of the northern Assiniboine. This debate is far from over and is likely to continue for some time. The senior author, however, supports the assignment of the Scattered Village phase, Vickers Focus and the southern Mortlach (Lake Midden phase) to various Hidatsa-related groups.

In Alberta (Figure 5.3), the Old Women's phase continued until the proto-contact period (Walde 2004) with a late incursion of One Gun ca. AD 1740 (Forbis 1977: 1). The general consensus is that the Old Women's phase emerged in Alberta from the preceding Besant and Avonlea complexes in the region (Duke 1991: 98–101). The details of this transformation are not well understood but the early lithics indicate similarities with Besant and the later specimens—

which show greater refinement in manufacture—are consistent with an Avonlea influence (Duke 1991: 99). Byrne (1973) suggests that the early variant Saskatchewan Basin pottery, sometimes associated with old Women's assemblages, has its roots to the east and that the late variant, ca. AD 1200, ultimately was derived through stimulus diffusion from the Selkirk and Blackduck ceramics in Manitoba (Duke 1991: 96).

Beginning ca. AD 1740, the One Gun phase had a limited lifespan and small areal impact in southwestern Alberta (Forbis 1977: 1). It is generally agreed that the ceramics at the Cluny site and at the Morkin site show marked similarities with Middle Missouri wares from the Dakotas and the probable fortifications at Cluny would also fit well with Coalescent period patterns in that region as well. In general, the vessel shapes and decorations are similar to Mortlach but not as well executed, and the Middle Missouri assignment is more similar to Scattered Village wares than later Plains Village specimens. Increasingly, researchers on the ground in Alberta would agree that there was a direct, but short-lived, movement of people from the Middle Missouri area into southern Alberta, and a Middle Missouri influence is generally conceded. While the pottery and the Cluny village structures indicate a probable Middle Missouri connection, the evidence from the sites suggests a heavy reliance on bison, consistent with a bison-hunting subsistence strategy (Duke 1991: 102). A few artifacts from the Morkin site suggest a possible horticultural interest (Byrne 1973: 476), but no other recorded site lends strong support for this kind of activity. Duke (1991: 102) notes that, "If the One Gun phase does represent an actual movement of Middle Missouri villagers to north of the Missouri Coteau, it can only be presumed that they quickly abandoned agriculture in the face of the harsher Alberta climate."

Almost all of the ceramic-using late period groups in the CPE, ca. AD 1350–1750, show evidence of cultural connections to the Middle Missouri area and the Vickers Focus, in particular, indicates strong linkages to the Eastern Woodlands of Minnesota and Iowa.

Vickers Focus
The Vickers Focus people (Figure 5.2), based upon the available evidence, first appeared in the Tiger Hills area in southwestern Manitoba ca. AD 1350. At this point, the Medieval Warming Period was giving way to the Little Ice Age (Fagan 2000). They quickly replaced the bison-hunting Blackduck culture in this region and implemented a forager-horticultural subsistence strategy (Nicholson et al. 2006a). Their principal village, the Lowton site, was located on fertile silt outwash soil with a southern exposure, flanked by glacial moraine deposits to the north and west. The site is situated well away from any major stream or lake water sources and relied upon local potholes within the site area (Nicholson et al. 2002: 316). Smaller satellite villages in the Tiger Hills, including the Lovstrom, and Randall sites, and a possible Vickers occupation on the Big Tiger

Figure 5.5. Lowton site Fort Yates Ware.

geoform, were located in similar landscape situations (Nicholson et al. 2002: 319). The Vickers Focus is characterized by highly variable ceramics which range from simple decoration plain wares—often resembling Sandy Lake ware derived from the Eastern Woodlands (Figure 5.4)—to Middle Missouri derived Fort Yates and Knife River Fine wares (Figures 5.5 and 5.6) and more exotic wares, including rims with effigy tabs, that suggest Mississippian influences (Figure 5.6).

The appearance of the Vickers Focus in southwestern Manitoba brought about a significant change in the prevailing adaptive strategy in the region. Previously, Blackduck and Duck Bay groups in this region had followed a hunting-gathering strategy dominated by bison procurement. In summer this would have involved small-scale strategies such as stalking, frequently at watering holes or along well-used trails to water sources, and along the margins of the herds. In the fall and winter, communal mass kills were employed to generate a storable surplus (Hamilton et al. 2007: 129). The advent of Vickers Focus people, who followed a forager/horticultural adaptation, led to a rapid replacement of the more specialized bison hunters. Over the 300–350 years of their sojourn in the southern parklands and prairies of Manitoba, three successive patterns of subsistence appear to have been followed. Initially, the Vickers people in the Tiger Hills appear to have created a central-place settlement pattern with the large village at the Lowton site being supported, at least in part, by smaller dependencies including the Lovstrom and Randall sites (Nicholson and Hamilton 1997: 39). The rich assemblage of luxury goods in this central site

CHAPTER 5: Human Ecology of the Canadian Prairie Ecozone ca. 500 BP

Figure 5.6. Knife River Fine ware and Mississippian vessels.

suggests that there may have been some stratification or ranking of prominent individuals at this site.

The Lowton site is without precedent in southern Manitoba. Its size, estimated at 35 hectares, and the abundance of exotic ceramic vessels and the wide range of lithic materials clearly place this site in a class by itself in this region (Nicholson et al. 2006a: 343–44). The Vickers ceramics clearly identify the relationship between the Lowton site and the satellite sites but the exotic vessels and most of the exotic lithic materials are absent from the smaller satellites. There is also evidence to suggest that all of these sites shared in the forager horticultural subsistence strategy. The consumption of cultigens at all of these sites has been demonstrated by the presence of corn phytoliths and starch grains in ceramic residues and corn phytoliths in hearths. In addition, bean (*Phaseolus*) starch grains have also been identified in a few cases (Boyd et al. 2006). Similarly, agricultural implements and oral traditions support the horticultural hypothesis (Nicholson et al. 2006a: 350; Nicholson et al. 2007).

The Vickers Focus people appear to have abandoned their homeland in the Tiger Hills ca. AD 1450 with the same alacrity as the preceding Blackduck people (Figure 5.7). They reappear in the *Makotchi-Ded Dontipi* locale in the Lauder sand hills some 50–100 years later (Nicholson and Hamilton 2001). It may be that this abandonment was triggered by a drastic climatic event within the Little Ice Age, triggered by a catastrophic volcanic explosion in the South Pacific ca. 1453–54 (Mann et al. 1998, 1999; Nicholson et al. 2006b). Here a different settlement pattern and subsistence strategy emerged. The relocated Vickers

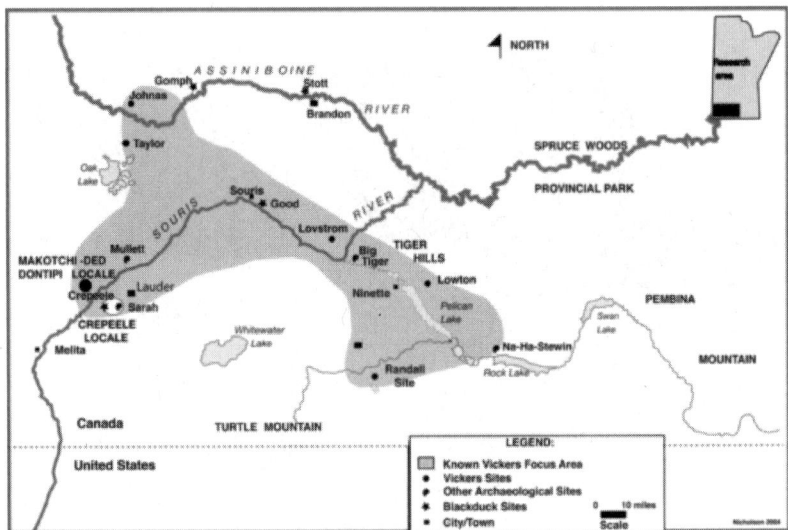

Figure 5.7. Vickers Focus sites.

Focus settlements are smaller, in the range of 5–10 hectares, and are clearly seasonal occupations with sites such as Jackson being winter occupations and the Vera site being a warm season occupation based upon recent analysis of bison foetal remains (Nicholson et al. 2006b: 332; Playford and Nicholson 2006). At *Makotchi-Ded Dontipi* the Vickers Focus people appear to have shifted their settlement pattern from a central place settlement pattern to a centre-based system with seasonal villages replacing the more permanent central place configuration. These contrasting settlement patterns have been described as follows:

> The term *center based* refers to a settlement strategy where a large, extended occupation village was established to serve as "headquarters" for more short term, satellite, or task-specific resource extraction settlements. The term *central place* refers to a settlement strategy where a seasonal village was strategically placed and from which short-term, resource extraction task groups were dispatched into the surrounding area. A *center base* would typically be occupied for more than a year and a central place would typically be chosen for seasonal extraction, although it might be reoccupied within a relatively short span of years, depending upon local availability of such materials as firewood, fresh water, plants, etc. Both systems allow for larger population aggregations than are typically represented in sites left by earlier hunter-gatherers. The earlier sites are consistent with microband or extended family social groupings. This strategy is supported by large

> macroband sites, where these smaller groups come together for communal resource extraction, determined by the seasonal abundance of a particular resource. Examples would be boreal forest seasonal fishing sites, related to spawning runs, or communal bison hunts in the late fall and early winter on the plains. (Nicholson and Hamilton 1997: 39)

In addition, some sites—such as the Bradshaw site—while quite large, have a thin discontinuous scatter of site debris. These sites may indicate a third strategy, which may have been followed either contemporaneously with the second strategy, or may represent a final phase of the Vickers forager-horticultural strategy in the region. These sites may indicate reoccupation by smaller groups on a seasonal basis with pregnant women, women with small children, and elders, being left behind to tend gardens while the hunters and the young, unencumbered women traveled further afield to hunt bison. Other sites that were found through shovel testing, but appeared to be quite small and having limited material remains, may also reflect this diminution in the size and duration of occupations, in an increasingly "bison procurement" oriented society that still retained an important gardening component. It is unlikely that small gardens were left totally unattended, particularly from July onwards when cobs were formed on the corn. Where gardens were planted by traditional horticulturists, as well as in modern times, it was necessary to provide some level of protection from wildlife. In Buffalo Bird woman's account (Wilson 1917: 26–27) she states that:

> Our fields had many enemies. Magpies, and especially crows, pulled up much of the young corn, so that we had to replant many hills. Crows were fond of pulling up the green shoots when they were a half-inch or an inch high. Spotted gophers would dig up the seed from the roots of young plants. When the corn had eared, and the grains were still soft, Blackbirds and crows were destructive.

She further notes that platforms were built where young women and girls watched over the field to prevent scavengers from damaging the crops and that "scarecrows" were also built in the fields (Will and Hyde 1917: 94; Wilson 1917: 27).

In modern times, white tail deer and raccoons are among the most destructive garden scavengers. However, neither of these species was present in southwestern Manitoba during the period that Vickers people occupied the area. Archaeological remains in the region have not contained their bones and they appear to have followed European settlement into the region. Tanner, ca. 1820, remarks on the first occurrence that he observed of "Virginia" deer in the region (James 1956: 115). No doubt traveling bison herds would have posed a threat to small fields that might have been encountered. It can reasonably be assumed that horticulturists would choose field sites that were unlikely routes to water sources, or that were known to provide usual travel ways for bison herds passing through an area. As a further remedy, normal hunting activity could be employed to discourage the approach of bison herds to their fields.

All of the known Vickers Focus sites are located in sheltered situations on warm silt/sand soils in places that are characterized by high levels of ecological complexity (Nicholson and Hamilton 2001: 55–56); areas that in the earlier literature were often referred to as ecotones (Nicholson 1987: 46–54). Similarly, with the exception of the small Vickers occupation at the Atkinson-east site, located adjacent to the Souris River, all of the Vickers sites are situated in out-of-the-way locations at a considerable distance from lakes or rivers (Figure 5.7) (Nicholson and Hamilton 2001: 54). It has also been suggested that the selection of these "off the beaten track" sites may reflect a concern for security by the people (Nicholson 1994: 118). This idea is supported by the oral tradition offered by Elder Dave Daniels, who noted that

> In that area there, years ago, my father talk [*sic*] about a different type of Indian that lived there. It wasn't the Ojibwa, it wasn't the Dakota, he called them *Ichininewuk*. I gathered from what he was trying to tell me was that these were an agrarian people, an agricultural society. They lived in along south facing banks of large hills. This was because that's where the sun was the warmest and that is where they would be protected from the north winds. He called them a special name because they were a peaceful people. Other people also picked on them a lot. He did talk about them living in the Tiger Hills area. (Scribe 2001–03)

The subsistence strategy of the Vickers Focus people in the *Makotchi-Ded Dontipi* locale appears to have changed significantly from that in the Tiger Hills. In both areas there is a wider range of faunal species that were harvested than was the case in the earlier Blackduck sites, although bison clearly dominate. However, at the north end of the Jackson site there is a small kill site that can be tied to the Jackson site processing area by a refitted projectile point (Nicholson et al. 2006: 331). This likely indicates that the Vickers Focus people were acquiring the skills and lore for communal mass kills—a trait that is noticeably absent in the Tiger Hills occupations. The presence of corn phytoliths and starch grains indicates that cultigens remained a part of their subsistence strategy in the *Makotchi-Ded Dontipi* locale, as well as in the Tiger Hills. The Vera site has been interpreted as a warm season site that may have been composed of less mobile members of the community (i.e. the elderly, pregnant women, and women with small children) who may have remained behind to care for small fields of corn or other cultigens while the hunters and young unencumbered women departed on more extended bison hunts away from the seasonal villages

(Nicholson 2006b: 332). As noted above, the Bradshaw site seasonality is uncertain but may represent multiple reoccupations by small groups during the warm season. This would be consistent with a continued progression towards the intensification of bison hunting where smaller groups remained behind to service and protect small fields while the young and able were absent on extended bison hunts.

Evidence for burial practices are absent from Vickers focus sites. It is likely that the deceased were given platform or tree burials and that no physical remains have survived the perthotaxic vectors of a surface environment following collapse of these structures.

Several later sites in the *Makotchi-Ded Dontipi* locale have been attributed to Mortlach people moving into the area from adjacent Saskatchewan in the early 18th century ca. AD 1700–50. The ceramics show a mixture of Vickers Focus and Mortlach traits. This has led Mokelki (2007) to propose that these sites clearly indicate interaction between the Vickers Focus and Mortlach people. She notes that:

> As previously discussed in detail, the pottery recovered from the Jackson and Vera sites, while still considered to be Vickers Focus pottery, has some differences from assemblages recovered in the eastern cluster of Vickers sites [Tiger Hills]. The most noticeable difference is the presence of a number of vessels at both Jackson and Vera with rim profiles that are uncharacteristic of eastern Vickers Focus sites. The vessels with wedge, square wedge and angular rim profiles recovered from Jackson and Vera are much more characteristic of Mortlach assemblages than they are of Vickers Focus. The short rim, excurvate profile vessel does not appear to be common in Saskatchewan Mortlach assemblages but accounts for a number of vessels in the Schuddemat and Twin Fawns assemblages. (Mokelki 2007: 104–5)

This interaction may account for the beginnings of communal mass kill events among the Vickers people at sites such as Jackson, and an increasing reliance upon the bison with horticulture possibly playing a lesser role. Mokelki (2007: 128) concludes that Vickers people may have "amalgamated with their Mortlach neighbors," thus accounting for the disappearance of Vickers.

Mortlach Aggregate

The classificatory term, Mortlach Aggregate, has been proposed by Schneider and Kinney (1978: 35) to subsume the wide range of ceramic variability found in sites that have been variously described in the literature of the day as components, sites and collections. This appellation has also been used by Meyer and

Epp (1990: 335). While earlier researchers tended to lump all of these assemblages into a single Mortlach entity (Byrne 1973; Meyer 1988; Syms 1977). Malainey (1991) differentiated between sites with woodland influenced Wascana Ware (also referred to as Moose Jaw) north of the Qu'appelle valley and a Mortlach Ware found to the south (Figure 5.3). Walde (1994), while recognizing differences between the northern Lozinsky subphase and the southern Lake Midden subphase, chooses to see these differences as being largely a function of differing trade and exchange networks of northern and southern Assiniboine ethnic groups, and to contact between the Lozinsky people and Selkirk people. Consequently, he retains the term Mortlach phase to subsume all pottery in southern Saskatchewan and their attendant cultures. To provide a more neutral taxonomic terminology, the designation Mortlach Aggregate will be used in this chapter whenever a collective appellation is appropriate.

In her Master's thesis, Mokelki (2007) conducted a detailed vessel-by-vessel analysis of ceramic wares from the Jackson, Vera, Shuddematt and Twin Fawns sites in the *Makotchi-Ded Dontipi* locale northwest of Lauder, Manitoba (Figure 5.3). All of these sites produced vessels that shared characteristics with Vickers Focus and Mortlach phase vessels. Her conclusions were that the Jackson and Vera vessels were sufficiently like vessels from the Lowton site (Vickers Focus type site) to be identified as Vickers Focus sites (Mokelki 2007: 124). The Shuddematt and Twin Fawns sites, however, demonstrated a greater divergence and displayed a greater number of traits that were characteristic of southern Mortlach (Mokelki 2007: 128), and should be considered a Vickers Focus variant of the Lake Midden subphase as defined by Walde (1994). The *Makotchi-Ded Dontipi* locale clearly demonstrates an extended interaction between the forager-horticulturist Vickers Focus people and the Plains-oriented bison-hunting Mortlach Aggregate in southwestern Manitoba. Further, recent work on ceramic residues (Surette 2005) indicate the presence of corn phytoliths and bean (*Phaseolus*) starch grains at the Initial Middle Missouri Duthie site and in most Vickers Focus sites in the region as well as in the Vickers Variant Mortlach sites in the *Makotchi-Ded Dontipi* locale (Boyd et al. 2006: 1,138). The Duthie site ceramics bear some resemblance to materials from the Randall phase component at the Dirt Lodge Village site in the James River Valley (Haberman 1993) as well as Blue Earth material (Taylor 1994: 112; see also Anfinson 1979: 42).

The radiocarbon dates from the Vickers Focus occupations indicate an initial presence in the *Makotchi-Ded Dontipi* locale ca. AD 1600. The dates for the nearby Mortlach-related sites fall within the atomic bomb era and are all too recent. The presence of a slot knife with a brass blade, the single historic artifact in the Twin Fawns assemblage, suggests a protocontact date as well (Hamilton and Nicholson 2007). The blending of ceramic decorative traits, together with a change in subsistence practices, with Vickers moving towards greater reliance on specialized bison procurement and Mortlach people utilizing cultigens, would logically suggest that these groups were in a collaborative relationship and may,

CHAPTER 5: Human Ecology of the Canadian Prairie Ecozone ca. 500 BP

in fact, have ultimately amalgamated in this region. It should be noted that there is, at the present time, no indication that the Mortlach Aggregate people in Saskatchewan were practicing horticulture. However, Meyer and Russell (2007: 74) have noted that some groups, including the Gros Ventre and Blackfoot in the southern part of the CPE, did practice tobacco gardening.

It has been generally conceded that the Mortlach Aggregate subsistence strategy in Saskatchewan, Montana and North Dakota was a specialized bison-hunting adaptation to the plains environment and resources. Meyer and Epp (1990) have examined this pattern in the northern area of the Mortlach Aggregate occupation in Saskatchewan. They have concluded that while interaction between boreal forest-based Selkirk people and Mortlach people did occur, as the ceramic assemblages in the adjacent parklands indicate, this did not necessarily indicate that the two groups co-inhabited the parklands (Meyer and Epp 1990: 337–38) and they note that, "[o]n the whole, Selkirk and Mortlach core areas do not overlap" (Meyer and Epp 1990: 336). Meyer and Epp (1990) have concluded that the more complex social organization that characterized plains bison hunters would have enabled them to exclude the northern hunter-gatherers from the parklands and that interaction would have been on a more casual basis with individuals from both sides occasionally coming in contact at the forest/parkland interface (Meyer and Epp 1990: 339). The plains and parklands are seen as forming a single grasslands ecosystem with the true ecotone being the narrow interface of the parklands edge with the boreal forest edge (Meyer and Epp 1990: 338–39). It is proposed that Selkirk people wintered in the forest and returned to the edge of the parklands in spring. Mortlach hunters wintered in the parklands and returned to the more open plains in the summer (Meyer and Epp 1990: 227).

While Morgan (1979) treated the upper level ceramic occupations at the Garratt site as small side-notched point traditions, an examination of the photo plates and general description of these ceramics strongly suggests Old Women's wares (Meyer 1987: 59). However, Morgan (1979: 198) subsumed these sherds into the Late Variant of the Saskatchewan Basin complex (Byrne 1973). Morgan (1979: 175–76) has proposed a seasonal settlement pattern tied to the generally predictable movement of bison herds in the north-central plains area. She sees this as a longstanding adaptation and found that "[a]lthough three cultural traditions were recognized in the excavation, their diagnostic features did not evidence sufficient variation to merit a separate analysis of their interactions with the environment" (Morgan 1979: 174). In her scheme, the occupants of the Garratt site retreated from the plains to the river valleys in the fall, to await the arrival of the bison that drifted in from the open plains to these sheltered locations to escape the cold. Similarly in spring, with the emergence of new grass on the open plains, the bison drifted away from the valleys and the people followed (Morgan 1979: 175). She also notes that the practice of prescribed burning of grassland could have been used to influence the timing and direction of bison movements and that bison pounds may have been used to harvest the bison in fall and winter (Morgan 1979: 176).

While this scenario is plausible and supported by the historic accounts of Mandelbaum (1940: 189) and Harmon (Lamb 1957), more recent studies have questioned the reliability of seasonal bison migrations and argued that bison were available at all seasons across the plains area (Hanson 1984; Malainey and Sherriff 1996). Epp (1988) convincingly argues, from both ethnographic and biological standpoints, that large ungulates, including bison, typically follow a dual strategy, with some herds migrating between parklands and open plains regularly and others remaining within the same general area throughout the year.

In contrast, it is likely that while bison were an essential resource and that availability was essential to human survival, critical resources (Vickers and Peck 2004) were likely the underlying cause for human occupation of river valleys, wooded uplands and sand dune areas, where the critical winter resources of fuel and shelter were present.

In a recent article, Vickers and Peck (2004: 98) argued that there were certain *critical resources* that were of overriding importance to hunter/gatherers living in the prairies. They argued that "the settlement pattern of the Late Prehistoric period is better understood in terms of critical resources—resources with relatively limited spatial distributions, that assume primacy in settlement decisions, even taking precedence over the essential requirements of securing bison." In addressing the determinants of winter settlement decision making, they noted the importance of shelter and the critical importance of fuel—specifically wood. In the warm season, buffalo chips were ubiquitous across the prairies and readily served as a fuel source. It should be noted that even in summer, kindling—grass or wood—was required to start the buffalo chips burning. However, due to an insulating feature of ash accumulation, as the chips burned, coupled with snow cover that hid the chips in winter, buffalo chips were not a viable winter fuel. In winter, only the hot, relatively smokeless radiant heat from a wood fire would suffice. Consequently, wintering sites had to be located in areas with forest cover, with the proximity of bison being a necessary but secondary consideration. An example of this has been provided in the account of the Reverend John McDougall. As cited in Vickers and Peck (2004: 101), McDougall noted that he had encountered a band of Cree camped near a poplar bluff, south of the Battle River in late January or early February 1865, and noted: "We were discouraged to find that these people were living from hand to mouth—that while the buffalo were within from sixty to one hundred and fifty miles distant, they [bison] had not yet attempted to come north. The camp was still waiting for this." The reason for this reluctance to move camp McDougall ascribed to "the rigor of the winter and the conditions of the grass and wood forbidding the camp moving any nearer to them." When a disjunction between the bison herd and a campsite with available wood occurred, the critical variable—wood—precluded any relocation nearer the herd. Further, a concern for grass in the late 1800s was for horse feed. Prior to introduction of the horse, which speeded mobility, any such move would have presented an even greater danger. Landals (2004) gives an excellent portrayal of the high level of management necessary for the maintenance of horses through a prairie winter.

At the Creepele locale near Lauder in southwestern Manitoba the presence of foetal bison, in almost all of the areas that have been tested, indicates cold season occupation of the area. This sand dune area is a mosaic of mesic grasses and aspen poplar bluffs and lacks any permanent water source. This is an ideal wintering area that offers wood for fuel and stands of aspen and elevated dunes that offer shelter. The site locale contains abundant bison bone and, at the Sarah site, two bone beds dated to AD 1335 (cal) *TO 13363* and 970 BCE (cal) *TO 13364*, demonstrate the use of communal mass kills—likely bison pounds—over a considerable period of time. There is also a small cold season Mortlach occupation at this locale. The model, offered by Morgan (1979), is supported by the Manitoba evidence, although it seems more likely that the critical fuel requirement was the imperative that determined winter settlement patterns. However, it is noted that the proximity of bison herds was an essential requirement for extended site viability.

The seasonal parkland/plains model offered by Meyer and Epp (1990) is functionally the same as the Morgan (1979) wooded valley/plains model, in that during the warm season the bison could be hunted from camps on the open plains and in the winter season the critical requirement for wood fuel determined where the hunting camps would be located.

Old Women's Phase
The Old Women's phase takes its name from the Old Women's Buffalo Jump, south of Calgary, that was excavated by Forbis (1962) in the 1950s. Vickers (1986: 97) notes that "[i]t is one of the few archaeological sites which is identified in Blackfoot mythology. It was to the Women's Buffalo Jump that Napi brought the men and instituted the custom of cohabitation of the sexes (Forbis 1962: 61)." Reeves (1983: 20) states that Old Women's develops ca. AD 750–800, following Besant and Avonlea, and it continues into the Protohistoric period in Alberta when small amounts of European trade goods begin to appear in sites ca. AD 1800. Peck and Hudechek-Cuffe (2003: 84) note that, "The Old Women's phase may have commenced as early as AD 500 (Reeves 1978; Morlan 1988)—its earliest radiocarbon dates overlapping with both terminal Avonlea and Besant dates (Brumley and Rushworth 1983; Morlan 1988; Vickers 1983, 1986) and continued into the Protohistoric period."

The origins of Old Women's phase lithics and ceramics are uncertain, although both Besant and Avonlea have been suggested (Vickers 1986: 100). Reeves (1983: 18) saw a role for both in the emergence of the Old Women's phase and states: "I suggested that Old Woman's developed out of both Avonlea and Besant. Various writers have further discussed this relationship, favouring one or the other, or alternate concepts (e.g. Byrne 1973; Morgan 1979)." Peck and Hudechek-Cuffe (2003: 86) argue that the Old Women's phase projectile points should not be subsumed into Kehoe's (1966: 830–34) "small side-notched system for the northwestern plains," but show sufficient variability to be identified as Cayley points (Peck and Ives 2001). Similarly, ethnicity has been discussed and Vickers (1986: 101–2) states: "While most local archaeologists would probably not dispute a Blackfoot-Old Women's phase correlation (cf. McCullough 1982: 41ff), demonstration of that correlation has remained frustratingly elusive." Brumley and Dau (1988: 56) have suggested that aceramic sites previously designated as Old Women's sites showed sufficient differentiation in lithic technology to be defined as the Saddle Butte phase. Subsequent work (Brumley and Rennie 1993: 46; cited in Peck and Hudechek-Cuffe 2003: 98) identified ceramics in the Saddle Butte occupation at the Wahkpa Chu'gn site. Consequently, Peck and Hudechek-Cuffe (2003: 91) conclude that "since the attributes defining Saddle Butte appear little different from those defining Old Women's, a separate phase may not be justified."

As has been noted earlier, the Old Women's phase people occupied the plains and parklands from the foothills in Alberta to the western margins of Manitoba until ca. AD 1300, when these people were displaced westward by incursions of Mortlach groups from the south (Figure 5.3). In this chapter we will be concerned primarily with the Old Women's phase that persisted post-AD 1300 in Alberta (Figure 5.3). Their sites are concentrated on the plains and northern parklands of Alberta during this time period (Vickers 1986: 96, 104) and Duke (1991: 97) noted that "[h]abitation sites are found on terraces and flats overlooking streams and rivers. Stone circles are especially common in this period, and these also aggregate into larger encampments." Oetelaar (2004: 139140) noted that, "[i]n essence, the largest and densest concentrations of stone circles occur in the vicinity of major rivers, streams and coulees. ... By contrast, the flat to gentle rolling prairie contains the lowest density of sites, the smallest number of rings per site, and the lowest density of artifacts within individual rings." Oetelaar (2004: 140) suggests that these categories represent longer occupation wintering sites and ephemeral summer camps respectively.

The Old Women's phase people were specialized bison hunters who used bison jumps along river valleys and escarpments, such as those at the Type site near Cayley and at Head-Smashed-In, near Fort Macleod, for the purpose of seasonal mass kills. While the use of pounds has not been demonstrated for the Old Women's phase (Duke 1991: 97), the presence of bone uprights in several sites such as Morkin (Byrne 1973) and the Boarding School Bison Drive (Kehoe 1967) may well indicate the presence of posts associated with a bison pound. This is particularly likely to be the case, since the use of pounds is well demonstrated in sites in the preceding Besant phase such as the Ruby site (Frison 1978) and Muhlbach (Gruhn 1969), as well as in the contemporary and spatially adjacent Blackduck occupation in southwestern Manitoba (Nicholson et al. 2006a). It is probable that in spring, when cows with calves were not amenable to being driven, and during the fall rut, when bison bulls were combative and likewise not drivable, small-scale stalking and ambush techniques would have been employed as well. The subsistence pattern for Old Women's people in Saskatchewan indicates that bison traps were commonly found in areas of high biodiversity such as dune complexes, hilly uplands and river valleys (Walde et al. 1995: 32). It is also noted that these sites have been identified as winter sites, suggesting winter aggregations of several bands that likely spent the warm season on the open grasslands.

The One Gun Phase
The One Gun phase appears in the late precontact/protohistoric period in south-central Alberta during the mid-to-late 18th century (Figure 5.3). The major site was the "fortified village" near Cluny, Alberta on the Siksika Blackfoot reserve, which accounts for most of the distinctive Cluny Complex pottery, although it was present in small amounts in some late Old Women's sites and in small amounts at the Morkin site together with modified scapula fragments that could have been Middle Missouri-style squash knives (Byrne 1973: 476). Duke (1991: 101) states that "Cluny Complex pottery, named after the site that has produced most of the material assigned to the complex (Byrne 1973), is entirely distinct from that of the Saskatchewan Basin Complex." The most likely cultural affiliation for Cluny Complex pottery would appear to be with wares from the Mortlach Aggregate or the Scattered Village sites in the Middle Missouri area. Walde (2004: 46), however, believes that the differences between Mortlach and One Gun ceramics are substantial, and that "[d]ifferences in the pottery and lithic raw material used to manufacture projectile points suggest that there is no close relationship between One Gun and Mortlach although it is clear that both incorporate certain aspects of Woodland approaches to ceramic decoration."

Subsistence at the Cluny site and other One Gun occupations appears to be almost totally based upon bison hunting and Duke (1991: 102) goes on to state: "If the One Gun phase does represent an actual movement of Middle Missouri villagers to north of the Missouri Coteau, it can only be presumed that they quickly abandoned agriculture in the face of the harsher Alberta climate." Zarillo and Kooyman (2006: 492) have identified starch grains consistent with maize on grinding paraphernalia from the Cluny site. They interpret this as an indication of trade with groups to the southeast.

The ditch and elevated earthen ring, together with a series of shallow pits, have led to the assumption that the site was a fortified village and the faunal remains indicate an indeterminate period of occupation of the site. Blackfoot tribal historian One Gun stated that the Cluny occupants were some earthlodge people from the southeast or southwest and that their relations with the Blackfoot were amicable (Brooks 1995: 158; Forbis 1977: 12). One Gun goes on to state that the earthlodge people remained in the area for six years, living at a different location each year. Recent work by Walde (2008: 22) indicates that the Cluny village site, while likely a single component assemblage, probably represents at least three successive occupations by these people.

Brooks (1995: 148–59) has interpreted the Cluny site as a stop-along-the-way of a dissident Hidatsa group, the *Kixa'ica*, following the vision of their leader *No Vitals* in his quest for a promised land that lay to the west. He points out that the structure of the Cluny village is not conducive to defense, but rather represents, in some way, the restructuring of the group's "new ideational world" (Brooks 1995: 156). He has identified two additional sites as possibly also being stops for this group as they head westward in their quest for meaning. These are the Hagen site on the Yellowstone (Mulloy 1942) and the White Earth Creek site on the White Earth Creek (Muller 1968). None of these sites are functional as long-term dwelling sites but they all required a significant amount of labor to construct. The case for this interpretation is interesting but at the present time cannot be uncritically accepted.

Discussion and Summary by Province
Manitoba
Following the withdrawal of Blackduck/Duck Bay people from southwestern Manitoba, ca. AD 1300, Vickers Focus people, whose antecedents were in the eastern woodlands of the present US, occupied the area (Figure 5.2). These people maintained a connection with groups in the Middle Missouri region, particularly with the Scattered Village people who have been identified with the *Awaxawi* Hidatsa (Ahler et al. 1991). There is conclusive evidence of consumption of cultivated crops by Vickers Focus people, including corn and beans (Boyd et al. 2006; Nicholson et al. 2008). It is reasonable to believe that these crops were grown locally, possibly supplemented, on occasion, by foods that were imported from the south (Nicholson et al. 2008). The larger size of the sites in the Tiger Hills, and at *Makotchi-Ded Dontipi*, indicate larger group size and possibly a more complex local social structure (Nicholson 1991, 1994). The faunal remains are strongly dominated by bison, although numerous other species are represented—more so than in the earlier Blackduck/Duck Bay assemblages. When these people left the Tiger Hills there is no ceramic evidence for replacement. Numerous small, undated lithic sites have been noted. These contain the ubiquitous small side-notched points found throughout the region that resemble those of earlier groups as well as Vickers Focus. In the early historic period fur traders noted that, while a wide range of groups hunted in the Hair Hills [Tiger Hills], including Saulteaux, Sioux, Métis and occasionally Cree, no group was able or willing to try and claim this rich hunting area for their own (Gough 1992; Nicholson et al. 2006a). It may be that this contested,

but unoccupied area was created following the withdrawal of the Vickers Focus people ca. AD 1450. The short-term logistical camps of the neighbouring but hostile groups would leave scant evidence for modern archaeological recovery. Prior to the fur trade era, it may be that the Assiniboine were a part of this sporadic utilization pattern. The Tiger Hills area may be an unusual occurrence of a hostile overlapping tertiary resource area, otherwise consistent with Syms (1977) co-influence sphere model.

Ca. AD 1450–1500 Vickers Focus people abandoned the Tiger Hills and reappeared ca. AD 1600 in the *Makotchi-Ded Dontipi* locale in the Lauder Sandhills (Nicholson and Hamilton 2001; Nicholson et al. 2006b). Here, they appear to have adopted a more "forager oriented" adaptive strategy with seasonal villages, rather than the centre-based large village with dependencies that characterized the Tiger Hills pattern (Figure5.7). The evidence from phytoliths and starch grains in the residue on pots indicates that corn and beans were still a part of their diet and likely were grown locally. While some of these groups may have migrated south into the Middle Missouri area (Nicholson 1994: 122–23) others may have amalgamated with other groups that remained in the region. In the Makotchi-Ded Dontipi locale, over time, there appears to have been a syncretization of Mortlach and Vickers Focus people to create an identifiable ceramic assemblage and a more bison-focused economy. Mokelki (2007: 119) has suggested that this new configuration might be considered a variant of the Lake Midden subphase of the Mortlach phase.

Saskatchewan

Following the withdrawal of Old Women's phase from Saskatchewan ca. AD 1300—perhaps under pressure from immigrants from the south and east—the Mortlach Aggregate became firmly established (Figure 5.3). The published evidence indicates that the Mortlach Aggregate subsistence strategy was based upon bison procurement. Bison pounds, buffalo jumps, small-scale surrounds, as well as ambush and stalking techniques were employed, depending upon animal abundance, seasonality and human resources (Duke 1991: 97, 102; Morgan 1979; Peck and Hudecek-Cuffe 2003). A well-polished scapula hoe in the Royal Saskatchewan Museum in Regina, from the Lake Midden site, would indicate horticultural activity, possibly the growing of tobacco (Myer and Russell 2007: 74). However, its within-site provenience is uncertain. To date, no residue analysis on Mortlach ceramic wares has been published to identify phytoliths or starch grains indicating the presence of domesticated food cultigens.

The ceramic evidence indicates a relationship between Mortlach and Vickers Focus and, by extension, probably with the Scattered Village complex. The ceramics of all of these groups bear strong evidence for an Eastern Woodlands origin by way of the river valley complexes that extended into the eastern Dakotas, such as the Minnesota, Maple, James and Sheyenne rivers, and into southwestern Manitoba by way of the Pembina and Souris river systems.

The case has been presented for an association of Scattered Village ceramics and the ethnicity of its makers with the Hidatsa (Ahler et al. 1991). Similarly, the case for a Hidatsa ethnicity of Vickers Focus people has also been made (Nicholson 1991: 174).

The evidence for an ethnicity of the Mortlach people is much less certain. The major controversy is whether Mortlach is also of Hidatsa origin, or a large footprint left by Assiniboine as they moved westward. Other groups such as Gros Ventre and Atsina have also been proposed. It may be that the Mountain Poets in the uplands of the Manitoba escarpment, referred to by Kelsey (Meyer and Russell 2007a), were part of an advance of the Assiniboine across central Saskatchewan and they may be the makers of Wascana ware, through a synthesis of Selkirk and Lake Midden phase traits. Meyer and Russell (2007b: 73) indicate that the Cree occupied the boreal forest of central Saskatchewan during the winter and the forest parkland fringe in summer. In this forest fringe they came into contact with the Assiniboine. Under these circumstances it is highly probable that there would be an exchange of ideas as well as an opportunity for gene flow between these groups.

Similarly, Kelsey's intended search for the *Naywatame Poets* (Meyer and Russell 2007), in what is now southern Saskatchewan, was based upon early reports of informants who noted that the *Naywatame Poets* (Hidatsa) were present in southeastern Saskatchewan (Russell 1993). This presence may indicate that the Hidatsa were the makers of Lake Midden subphase wares. It is likely that they would have come in contact with the Vickers Focus people, an idea supported by Mokelki (2007).

Alberta

The Old Women's phase emerged in southern Alberta ca. AD 750–800 following Besant and Avonlea (Reeves 1983: 20), and it continued into the Protohistoric period in Alberta (Figure 5.1). These people are believed to have followed a specialized bison-hunting subsistence strategy employing jumps, traps, pounds and a range of small-scale procurement techniques, including surrounds, stalking and ambush at water sources. This is to be expected, given the Besant and Avonlea antecedents that have been proposed. While the tool styles and inventory changed slowly over time, there is nothing to suggest any dramatic influx of people from outside the region, although it is likely that there was gene flow from other adjacent areas. It is a general consensus among archaeologists working in Alberta that the Old Women's phase people were the ancestors of the present Blackfoot bands (Walde 2008: 17).

The One Gun/Cluny phase first appears in southern Alberta ca. AD 1740 with their major site at Cluny on the Siksika Blackfoot Reserve. Oral tradition among the Blackfoot indicates that the One Gun people came from the south and likely stayed in the area for less than a generation before returning to the south. Their ceramics and the "fortified" village at Cluny all indicate connections to the Middle Missouri area. Vessel forms and decorative elements on the vessels resemble those found on Mortlach Aggregate wares and some authors (Syms 1977) have suggested that this is a Mortlach incursion from Saskatchewan. However, the manufacture and decoration of the Cluny vessels is more crudely executed and others (Walde and Meyer 2003: 145–46) see no direct linkage between One Gun and Mortlach. It is noted that those most familiar with the sites deny this direct link to Mortlach aggregate.

Peck and Hudechek-Cuffe (2003: 94) state that the One Gun phase is found in the South Saskatchewan drainage basin in southern Alberta but is absent from the North Saskatchewan drainage to the north and the Milk River drainage to the south.

Summation

During the period centred on 500 BP, the southern area of the CPE was occupied by a succession of groups from the Eastern Woodlands and from the south, with Plains Woodland and Plains Village affiliations. It appears that in southwestern Manitoba these people had Hidatsa affiliations. The same may be true for southern Saskatchewan although a case has been made for an Assiniboine affiliation. North of the Qu'Appelle Valley the ethnic affiliation for the Wascana subphase may be the northern Assiniboine, although Gros Ventre and Atsina have been suggested. In Alberta, the Old Women's phase persisted until the protocontact period. Much later, during the protohistoric period, the One Gun/Cluny phase, which indicates a Middle Missouri influence, arrived from the south into southern Alberta and briefly settled among the resident Blackfoot population. Some of their wares have been found in late Old Women's sites and, as noted above, some authors believe these Old Women's sites represented the ancestors of the historic Blackfoot.

While a strong case has been made for horticultural practice in southwestern Manitoba and the Red River valley, there is, at the present time, no published evidence for horticultural practice in either Saskatchewan or Alberta. Throughout the CPE there is a dominating presence of bison in sites from this time period, with only the Vickers Focus, the Vickers subphase of the Mortlach Aggregate, and the Lockport site displaying good evidence for horticultural production.

References

Ahler, Stanley A., Thomas D. Theissen and Michael K. Trimble. 1991. *People of the Willows: The Prehistory and Early History of the Hidatsa Indians*. Grand Forks: University of North Dakota Press.

Anfinson, Scott F. 1979. *A Handbook of Prehistoric Minnesota Ceramics*. Occasional Publications in Minnesota Anthropology No.5. Fort Snelling Minnesota Archaeology Society.

Belyea, Barbara (ed.). 2000. *A Year Inland: the Journal of a Hudson's Bay Company Winterer*. Waterloo: Wilfrid Laurier University Press.

Boyd, Matthew, Clarence Surette and B.A. Nicholson. 2006. Archaeobotanical Evidence of Prehistoric Maize (Zea mays) Consumption at the Northern Edge of the Great Plains. *Archaeological Journal of Science* 33, no. 8: 1129–40.

Brooks, James F. 1995. Sing Away the Buffalo: Faction and Fission on the Northern Plains. In *Beyond Subsistence: Plains Archaeology and the Postprocessual Critique*, ed. Philip Duke and Michael Wilson, 143–68. Tuscaloosa: University of Alabama Press.

Brumley, John H. and B.J. Dau. 1988. *Historical Resource Investigations within the Forty Mile Coulee Reservoir*. Archaeological Survey of Alberta, Manuscript Series No. 13. Edmonton: Alberta Culture.

Brumley, John H. and C. A. Rushworth. 1983. A Summary and Appraisal of Alberta Radiocarbon Dates. In *Archaeology in Alberta, 1982*, ed. D. Burley, 142–60. Occasional Paper 21, Archaeological Survey of Alberta.

Buchner, A.P. 1986. A Brief Note on the Lockport Radiocarbon Dates. *Manitoba Archaeological Journal* 10, no. 1: 72–73.

Burpee, L.J. 1973. *The Journal of Anthony Hendry 1754–1755*. Toronto: The Champlain Society.

Byrne, William J. 1973. *The Archaeology and Prehistory of Southern Alberta as Reflected by Ceramics*. 3 vols., Mercury Series, Paper No 14. Ottawa: Archaeological Survey, National Museum of Civilisation.

Duke, Philip. 1991. *Points in Time: Structure and Event in a Late Northern Plains Hunting Society*. Niwot: University Press of Colorado.

Epp, Henry T. 1988. Way of the Migrant Herds: Dual Dispersion Strategy Among Bison. *Plains Anthropologist* 33, no. 121: 309–20.

Fagan, Brian. 2000. *The Little Ice Age: How Climate Made History 1300–1850*. New York: Basic Books.

Forbis, Richard. 1961. Review of the Long Creek Site, by Boyd Wettlaufer and W. J. Mayer-Oakes. *Plains Anthropologist* 6, no. 13: 217–18.

———. 1977 *Cluny: An Ancient Fortified Village in Alberta*. Occasional paper No. 4. Calgary: Department of Archaeology, University of Calgary.

Fowler, Loretta and Regina Flannery. 2001. Gros Ventre. In *Handbook of North American Indians*, volume 13: *Plains*, ed. Raymond J. DeMallie, 677–94. Washington, DC: Smithsonian Institution.

Frison, George. 1978. *Hunters of the High Plains*. New York: Academic Press.

Gough, Barry M. (ed.). 1992. *The Journal of Alexander Henry the Younger 1799–1814*. Toronto: The Champlain Society.

Gregg, Michael L. 1994. Horner-Kane Site (32RY77) *Archeological Excavations, Grahams Island State Park, Ramsey County, North Dakota, 1991 Field Season*. Contribution Number 285. Grand Forks: Harriman Research Center, University of North Dakota.

Gibbon, Guy. 1998. Sandy Lake. In *Archaeology of Prehistoric Native America: An Encyclopedia*. New York: Garland Publishing, Inc.

Gruhn, Ruth. 1969. *Preliminary Report on the Muhlbach Site: A Besant Bison Trap in Central Alberta*. Contributions to Anthropology 7. National Museums of Canada Bulletin 232, Paper 4: 128–56.

Haberman, T.W. 1993. The Randall Phase Component at the Dirt Lodge Village Site, Spink County, South Dakota: Late Woodland/Early Plains Village Transitions on the Northeastern Plains. In *Prehistory and Human Ecology of the Western Prairies and Northern Plains*, ed. Joseph A. Tiffany. Memoir 27, *Plains Anthropologist* 38, no. 145: 75–116.

Hamilton, Scott and B.A. Nicholson. 1999. Ecological "Islands" and Vickers Focus Adaptive Transitions in the Pre-contact Plains of Southwestern Manitoba. *Plains Anthropologist* 44, no. 167: 5–26.

———. 2007. Proto-contact Mortlach Use of European Metal at the Twin Fawns Site, Southern Manitoba: Selective Integration of Foreign Technology. *Canadian Journal of Archaeology* Special Volume 31, no. 3: 137–62.

Hamilton, Scott, James Graham and B.A. Nicholson. 2007. Archaeological Site Distribution and Content: Modeling Precontact Blackduck Land Use in the Northeastern Plains. Canadian Journal of Archaeology Special Volume 31, no. 3: 93–136.

Hanson, J.R. 1984. Bison Ecology in the Northern Plains and a Reconstruction of Bison Patterns for the North Dakota Region. *Plains Anthropologist* 29, no. 104: 115–30.

Hems, David. 1997. Features at the Lockport Site (EaLf-1). *Manitoba Archaeological Journal* 7, no. 2: 2–6.

James, Edwin. 1956. *The Indian Captivity of John Tanner*. Minneapolis: Ross & Haines Inc.

Kehoe, Thomas F. and Alice B. Kehoe. 1968. Saskatchewan. In *The Northwestern Plains: A Symposium*, ed. Warren W. Caldwell, 21–35. Billings: Center for Indian Studies, Rocky Mountain College.

Kooyman, Brian P. 2000. *Understanding Stone Tools and Archaeological Sites*. Calgary: University of Calgary Press.

Krause, Richard A. 1998. A History of Great Plains Prehistory. In *Archaeology on the Great Plains*, ed. Raymond A. Wood, 48–86. Lawrence: University of Kansas Press.

Lamb, W.K. 1957. *Sixteen Years in the Indian Country—Journal of Daniel Williams Harmon 1800–1816*. Toronto: MacMillan of Canada.

Landals, Alison. 2004. Horse Heaven: Change in Precontact to Contact Period Land Use in Southern Alberta. In *Archaeology on the Edge: New Perspectives from the Northern Plains*, ed. Brian Kooyman and Jane Kelly, 231–62, edited by Brian Kooyman and Jane Kelly. Calgary: University of Calgary Press.

Malainey, Mary E. 1991. Relationships of Saskatchewan Plains Pottery Assemblages: Circa A.D. 1300 to Contact. MA thesis, University of Saskatchewan.

Malainey, Mary E. and Barbara Sherriff. 1996. Adjusting our Perceptions: Historical and Archaeological Evidence of Winter on the Plains of Western Canada. *Plains Anthropologist* 41, no. 158: 333–58.

Mann, M.E., R.S. Bradley and M.K. Hughes. 1998. Global-Scale Temperature Patterns and Climate Forcing Over the Past Six Centuries. *Nature* 392, no. 23: 779–87.

———. 1999 Northern Hemisphere Temperatures During the Past Millennium: Inferences, Uncertainties and Limitations. *Geophysical Research Letters* 26: 759–62.

Mandelbaum, D.G. 1940. *The Plains Cree*. Anthropological Papers of the American Museum of Natural History, Volume 37, Part 2.

McCullough, Edward J.1982. *Prehistoric Cultural Dynamics of the Lac La Biche Region*. Archaeological Survey of Alberta Occasional Publication No.18. Edmonton

Meyer, David. 1987. The Old Women's Phase on the Saskatchewan Plains: Some Ideas. In *Archaeology in Alberta 1987*, ed. Martin Magne. Occasional Paper No. 32, Archaeological Survey of Alberta, Edmonton.

Meyer, David and Henry T. Epp.1990. North-South Interaction in the Late Prehistory of Central Saskatchewan. *Plains Anthropologist* 35, no. 132: 321–42.

Meyer, David and Dale Russell. 2007a. Through the Woods Whare Thare Ware Now Track Ways. In *Building a Contextual Milieu: Interdisciplinary Modeling and Theoretical Perspectives from the SCAPE Project*, eds. B.A. Nicholson and Dion Wiseman, 163–97. *Canadian Journal of Archaeology* 31, no. 3 (Supplement).

———. 2007b. Aboriginal Peoples from the Ice Age to 1870. In *Saskatchewan: Geographic Perspectives*, eds. Bernard D. Thraves, Marilyn L. Lewry, Janis Dale and Hansgeorg Schlichtman, 63–80. Regina: Canadian Plains Research Center.

Millar, J.F.V. 1981a. The Oxbow Complex in Time and Space—Introduction. *Canadian Journal of Archaeology* 5: 83–88.

———. 1981b. The Oxbow Complex: 1980 Perspectives. Canadian *Journal of Archaeology* 5: 155–60.

Michlovic, Michael G. 2008. The Shea Phase of the Northeastern Plains Village Culture. *North Dakota Archaeology* 8: 35–52.

Mokelki, Lorie L. 2001. Middle Woodland Settlement Patterns in Southern Manitoba and Southeastern Saskatchewan: Besant, Avonlea and Laurel. Manuscript in senior author's files.

———. 2007. Vickers Focus and Mortlach—Examining Cultural Connections in the *Makotchi-Ded Dontipi* Locale. MA thesis, University of Saskatchewan.

Morgan, R. Grace. 1979. An Ecological Study of the Northern Plains as Seen Through the Garratt Site. Occasional papers in Anthropology No. 1. Regina: Department of Anthropology, University of Regina.

Mulloy, William. *1942. The Hagen Site: A Prehistoric Village on the Lower Yellowstone*. The University of Montana, Publications in the Social Sciences No. 1.

Nicholson, B.A. 1987. Human Ecology and Prehistory of the Forest-Grassland Transition Zone of Western Manitoba. PhD dissertation, Simon Fraser University.

———. 1991. Modeling a Horticultural Focus in South-Central Manitoba During the Late Prehistoric Period—The Vickers Focus. *Mid-continental Journal of Archaeology* 16, no. 2: 163–88.

———. 1994. Interactive Dynamics of Intrusive Horticultural Groups Coalescing in South-Central Manitoba During the Late Prehistoric Period—the Vickers Focus. *North American Archaeologist* 15, no. 2: 103–27.

———. 1996. Plains Woodland Influx and the Blackduck Exodus in South-Western Manitoba During the Late Precontact Period. *Manitoba Archaeological Journal* 6, no. 1: 69–85.

Nicholson, B.A. and Scott Hamilton. 1997. Preliminary Report on Middle Precontact

Occupations at the Vera Site in the Makotchi-Ded Dontipi Locale in Southwestern Manitoba. *Manitoba Archaeological Journal* 7, no. 2: 37–49.

———. 2001. Cultural Continuity and Changing Subsistence Strategies During the Late Precontact Period in Southwestern Manitoba. *Canadian Journal of Archaeology* 25: 53–73.

Nicholson, B.A., Scott Hamilton, Matt Boyd and Sylvia Nicholson. 2008. A Late Plains Woodland Adaptive Strategy in the Northern Parklands: The Vickers Focus Forager-Horticulturists. *Journal of the North Dakota Archaeological Association* 8: 19–34.

Nicholson, B.A., Scott Hamilton, Garry Running IV and Sylvia Nicholson. 2006a. Two Cultures—One Environment: Vickers Focus Adaptations Contrasted with Blackduck Adaptations in the Tiger Hills. *Plains Anthropologist* 51, no. 199: 335–53.

Nicholson, B.A., Sylvia Nicholson, Scott Hamilton and Garry Running IV. 2002. Vickers Focus Environmental Choices and Site Location in the Parklands of Southwestern Manitoba. *Géographie physique et Quaternaire* 56, nos. 2–3: 315–24.

Nicholson, B.A., Dion Wiseman, Scott Hamilton and Sylvia Nicholson. 2006b. Climatic Challenges and Changes: A Little Ice-Age Response to Adversity—The Vickers Focus Forager-Horticulturists Move On. *Plains Anthropologist* 51, no. 199: 325–34.

Oetelaar, Gerald A. 2004. Stone Circles, Social Organization and Special Places: Forbis Skepticism Revisited. In *Archaeology on the Edge: New Perspectives from the Northern Plains*, ed. Brian Kooyman and Jane Kelly, 126–56. Calgary: University of Calgary Press.

Peck, Trevor R. and Caroline R. Hudecek-Cuffe. 2003. Archaeology on the Alberta Plains: The Last Two Thousand Years. In *Archaeology in Alberta: The View from the New Millennium*, ed. Jack W. Brink and John F. Dormaar, 72–103. Medicine Hat: The Archaeological Society of Alberta.

Peck, Trevor R. and J. W. Ives. 2001. Late Side-notched Projectile Points on the Northwestern Plains. *Plains Anthropologist* 46, no. 176: 163–93.

Playford, Tomasin and B.A. Nicholson. 2006. Vickers Focus Subsistence: Continuity Through the Seasons. *Plains Anthropologist* 51, no. 199: 399–424.

Russell, Dale. 1993. The Puzzle of Henry Kelsey and His Journey to the West. In *Three Hundred Prairie Years*, ed. H. Epp, 74–88. Regina: Canadian Plains Research Center.

Scribe, Brian. 2001–03. Transcribed interviews with Elders on First Nations reserves in southwestern Manitoba, southeastern Saskatchewan and North Dakota. Documents in confidential files of B.A. Nicholson, SCAPE Project Director.

Surette, Clarence. 2005. Archaeobotanical Evidence of Maize in Southern Manitoba, A.D. 1000–1500. Honour's thesis, Lakehead University.

Syms, E.L. 1977. Cultural Ecology and Ecological Dynamics of the Ceramic Period in Southwestern Manitoba. *Plains Anthropologist* 22, no. 76, Part 2, Memoir 12.

Taylor, Jill. 1994. An Analysis of the Ceramics Recovered During 1992 and 1993 at the Precontact Duthie Site (DiMe-16). Specialist thesis, Brandon University.

Taylor-Hollings, Jill. 1999. The Northwestern Extent of Sandy Lake Ware: A Canadian Perspective. MA thesis, University of Saskatchewan.

Vickers, Roderick. 1986. *Alberta Plains Prehistory: A Review*. Edmonton: Archaeological Survey of Alberta, Occasional Paper No. 27.

Vickers, Roderick and Trevor R. Peck. 2004. Islands in a Sea of Grass: The Significance of Wood in Winter Campsite Selection on the Northwestern Plains. In *Archaeology on the Edge: New Perspectives from the Northern Plains*, ed. Brian Kooyman and Jane Kelly, 95–124. Calgary: University of Calgary Press.

Walde, Dale. 1994. The Mortlach Phase. PhD dissertation, University of Calgary.

———. 2004. Mortlach and One-Gun—Phase to Phase. In *Archaeology on the Edge: New Perspectives on the Northern Plains*, ed. Brian Kooyman and Jane Kelly, 39–52. Calgary: University of Calgary Press.

———. 2008. The 2008 Archaeological Field Season at Blackfoot Crossing Historical Park. Annual Summary Report #1, Department of Archaeology, University of Calgary.

Walde, Dale and David Meyer. 2003. Pre-contact Pottery in Alberta: An Overview. In *Archaeology in Alberta: A View from the New Millennium*. Medicine Hat: Archaeological Society of Alberta.

Walde, Dale, David Meyer and Wendy Unfreed. 1995. The Late Period on the Canadian and Adjacent Plains. *Revista de Arqueologia Americana* 9: 8–66.

Wettlaufer, Boyd. 1960. *The Long Creek Site*. Regina: Saskatchewan Department of Natural Resources.

Will, George F. and George E. Hyde. 1917. *Corn Among the Indians of the Upper Missouri*. Lincoln: University of Nebraska Press.

Wilson, Gilbert Livingstone. 1977 (1917). *Agriculture of the Hidatsa Indians: An Indian Interpretation*. Reprints in Anthropology Volume 5. Lincoln, NB: J &L Reprint Company.

Wood, W. Raymond. 2000. Ethnogenesis on the Great Plains. *The Review of Archaeology* 21, no. 1: 41–44.

Zarillo, Sonia and Brian P. Kooyman. 2006. Evidence for Berry and Maize Processing on the Canadian Plains from Starch Grain Analysis. *American Antiquity* 71, no. 3: 473–99.

Index

A

Agate Basin complex, 20, 21–24, 41–42
Albanese, J., 59
Alberta complex, 27–30
Allen/Frederick complex, 35
Amundson, L. J. "Butch," 36, 37–38
Anderson, David G., 10–11
Anderson, Dennis, 8
anthropogenic burning, 65, 111, 167–68
Arthurs, David, 134
Arzigian, Constance, 131, 134–35
Ashford site, 36
Assiniboine, 156–57, 158, 173, 174
Atkinson site, 63–64, 69, 71
Atsina, 156, 174
Attrill site, 15
Avery site, 127
Avonlea Horizon: and Besant complex, 107–8; and bison kills, 111; described, 118–24; and Elk Lake Culture, 127–28; and Old Women's phase, 131, 159, 169–70
Awaxawi, 156, 172
awls, 84, 93

B

Bamforth, D., 64, 66, 67, 68
Basally-Thinned Triangular complex, 12–16
base camps, 22, 24
beads, 84, 93
beamers, 84
beans, 103, 161, 166, 172

Bell site, 132
Below Forks site, 63, 67, 70, 71
Berkech site, 32
Besant complex: connected to Old Women's phase, 158–59, 169–70; connected to Sonota, 107, 111, 112, 115, 116; described, 106–13
Bicycle site, 19
bifaces, 22, 37, 38, 39, 92, 93
Birch Hills collection, 8
Birk, Douglas A., 134
bison: and Agate Basin populations, 22; and Avonlea, 120; and Besant complex, 109, 110–11; and Blackduck Horizon, 131, 132, 160; in burial mounds, 116; in Clovis times, 40; and Cody complex, 30, 31–32; and Folsom populations, 18; and Goshen populations, 18; and Hell Gap complex, 26; and Hypsithermal, 57, 64, 65–66; in Lake Lenore upland, 16; and Late Plano, 41; and McKean complex, 88, 89, 90; and Middle Woodland Culture, 105; and Mortlach Aggregate, 167–68, 169, 173; and Old Women's phase, 170–71, 174; and One Gun phase, 159, 171; and Oxbow complex, 84–85; and Pelican Lake complex, 93–95; and Plains Woodland, 103, 138; pounds, 88, 91, 94, 110–11, 168, 169, 170–71; and Sonota complex, 113; at St. Louis site, 38; and

INDEX

Valley complex, 117, 118; and Vickers Focus, 163–65. *see also* mass kill technology
Bison antiquus, 16, 32, 38
Bison bison occidentalis, 65
Blackduck Horizon, 104, 105, 131–33, 136, 153–54, 160
Blackfoot, 169, 170, 172, 174
Blair site, 20
Boarding School Bison Drive, 170
boreal forest, 28, 30
Boss Hill site, 35, 71
bow-and-arrow technology, 99, 106, 119, 121
Boxall site, 28
Boyd, Matthew, 2, 17, 20, 87, 111
Bracken Cairn, 94
Bradshaw site, 163, 165
Brainerd Ware, 123, 124–27
Bromhead, SK, 17
Brooks, James F., 172
Brumley, J. H., 112, 170
Buchner, A. P., 59
Buffalo Bird woman, 163
Buffalo Narrows, SK, 30
burial mounds: functions of, 104; and grave offerings, 116; of Middle Woodland, 104; of Psinomani Culture, 134; of Rainy River Coalescent, 136; of Sonota complex, 111, 115–16; spread of, 102, 139; of Valley complex, 118
burial sites: McKean, 91; Oxbow, 84, 85; Pelican Lake, 94–95; Vickers Focus, 165
burins, 22, 31, 34
burning grassland, 65, 111, 167–68
Burns, James A., 9
Byrne, William J., 130, 159

C

Cactus Flower site, 89
Canadian Prairie Ecozone (CPE), 1–2
canids, 84, 117
Capes, Katherine H., 122
carbon dating: Agate Basin, 21; Alberta complex, 26; Avonlea, 123; and Basally-Thinned points, 12; and Brainerd pottery, 126–27; and Clovis, 11; Cody complex, 31, 32; Lake Plano, 35, 37; Old Women's phase, 169; Oxbow, 82, 85, 87; Vickers Focus, 166
Carlson site, 32
Carter/Kerr-McGee site, 30
Casper site, 25
chalcedony, 17, 28, 108, 113, 115, 120
Charlie Lake Cave, 12
Clovis complex, 10–11, 12, 39–40
Cluny Complex pottery, 171
Cluny site, 106, 159, 171–72
Cody complex, 29, 30–34, 41
Cody knife, 8, 30, 32, 34
cometary explosion, 11
Cooper, Leland R., 131, 134
copper, 84, 93
corn, 161, 163, 164, 166, 172, 173
Cree, 156, 168–69, 174
Crown site, 89
Cumberland Reserve site, 20

D

Daniels, Dave, 164
Dau, B. J., 112, 170
Davis, Leslie B., 119, 121
Dawe, Robert J., 31
deciduous parkland, 26, 30, 35
deer, 18, 22, 121
Denali, 21
diet, 64–66, 70–72, 84–85, 88–91
Dirt Lodge Village site, 166
Dixon, James E., 20–21, 40
drills, 22, 24, 87, 93
Duck Bay complexes, 136–37, 153–54, 160
Duck Bay Ware, 136
Duke, Philip, 93–94, 159, 170, 171
Duncan points, 85–87, 90
Dunn site, 31
Duthie site, 166
Dyck, Ian: and Avonlea, 120; and Besant complex, 109–10, 112; on Hypsithermal diet, 64; and Pelican Lake complex, 91–92, 93, 94, 95;

on point types, 66, 82, 91–92, 114; on Sonota-Besant controversy, 115

E
earthworks, 103
Eastern Woodlands: connection to Besant complex, 109, 112–13; connection to Valley complex, 118; influence on northern and eastern Plains, 99–100, 138–39, 140; and Mortlach Aggregate, 173; move west, 103, 154; spread of pottery, 102–3
Eclipse site, 26
Eden points, 31, 34
elk, 18, 22, 89
Elk Lake Culture, 123, 127–28
endscrapers, 22, 24, 31, 87, 93
Epp, Henry T., 167, 168, 169
European contact, 135, 155–56, 163, 166, 172
Evelyn site, 15

F
Fedje, Daryl, 21
Fennell site, 28
Fenton Ferry site, 5, 19, 22, 23, 42
fire pits, 70
fish, 90, 105, 117, 121, 135, 138
Fisher, J. W., 121
Flannery, Regina, 156
Fletcher site, 27
Flintstone Hill, 7
Folsom complex, 16–18, 41
foraging: in Avonlea, 121; and Blackduck Horizon, 131, 132–33; of Middle Woodland, 104; in Plains Woodland Tradition, 103, 138; and Psinomani Culture, 135; and Valley complex, 117–18; and Vickers Focus, 161
Forbis, Richard G., 27, 58, 59, 70, 169
Fort à la Corne delta, 13, 15–16, 20
Fort Yates Ware, 160
Fowler, Loretta, 156
Frey collection, 8

Frison, George C.: and Besant complex, 110; and Goshen complex, 20; and human habitation during Hypsithermal, 59, 64, 69, 70; and Leigh Cave, 85; and mass bison kills, 110; and Pelican Lake points, 91; and Sonota complex, 117
fuel, importance of, 168–69
funerary objects, 104

G
Galbraith site, 28
Garratt site, 123, 167
Garrick, SK, 28
geoarchaeological landforms, 61–62
geomorphological processes, 57–58, 59–60
George Hey site, 88
Gibbon, Guy, 104–5, 134
Gillam, J. Christopher, 10–11
Goltz, G. E., 125–27
Gompf site, 132
Goshen complex, 18–20
Gowen 2 site, 68
Graham, Russell W., 35
grassland: of Agate Basin times, 22; of Alberta complex, 30; of Cody complex, 30; of Hell Gap complex, 26; of Late Plano complexes, 5, 6, 35, 40–41, 42
Gray Burial site, 84, 85
Green, D'Arcy, 84
Gregg, Michael L., 101–2, 103–4, 109, 115, 118, 135
Greiser, S. T., 66, 71
grinding slabs, 71, 87, 88
Gronlid, SK, 24
Gros Ventre, 156, 167, 174
Gull Lake site, 133

H
Hagen site, 172
Hall, Jonathan B., 16–17, 17n3, 18, 19n4
hammerstones, 71–72
Hanna, Margaret G., 136
Hanna points, 85–87, 90

INDEX

Hanson, Lawrence, 8
Harmon, Daniel W., 168
harpoons, 84
Harris Lake site, 7
Harvey site, 32
Havholm, K. G., 62
Hawken site, 65, 66
Hawkwood site, 35, 82
Head-Smashed-In, 95, 120, 170
hearths: of Central Plains, 68; of Cody complex, 31; Hypsithermal evidence of, 66, 69, 70, 71; of McKean complex, 89; of Pelican Lake complex, 92; at St. Louis site, 37; of Vickers Focus, 161
Hell Gap complex, 24–27
Hell Gap site, 18, 25, 27, 66, 68
Henning, Dale R., 138
Heron-Eden site, 31–32
Hidatsa, 156, 157, 172, 174
Hofman, Jack L., 35
Hohman-Caine, C. A., 125–27
Hokanson site, 132
Holliday, Vance T., 25
Hopewell Culture, 104, 111
Hopewell Interaction Sphere, 109, 115, 116
Horner-Kane site, 156
Horner site, 30
horses, 9, 11, 41, 169
horticulture: of Middle Woodland Culture, 105; and Mortlach Aggregate, 167, 173; and One Gun phase, 159; and Plains Village, 103, 106, 137; in Plains Woodland, 103, 137–38; in prairie provinces, 175; and Valley complex, 118; and Vickers Focus, 161, 163–65, 172; and village life, 137–38, 140
houses, 68–70, 111–12, 137, 138
Hudecek-Cuffe, Caroline R.: and Avonlea sites, 120, 121, 123; and obsidian, 116; and Old Women's phase, 131, 169, 170; and One Gun phase, 175; and summary of perspectives, 106
Hudson-Meng site, 27

Hurt, W. R., 59
Huseas, M., 85
Husted, W. M., 59
Hypsithermal: architectural remains of, 68–70; climatic conditions of, 42; cultural sites, 58–61, 63–64; dates of, 82; effect of, 55, 57; food preparation strategies, 70–72; and Late Plano, 35, 40–41; settlement strategies during, 62–68, 72–73

I
ice sheets, 7
Ives, John W., 11, 12, 130

J
J-Crossing site, 31
Jackson site, 162, 164
James Pass, 12
Jennings, Jesse D., 126
Johnson, Alfred E., 115
Johnson, Ann Mary, 115
Johnson, Elden, 124–25, 131, 134, 135
Jones-Miller site, 25

K
Kain site, 94
Kehoe, Alice B.: and Avonlea, 111, 118, 119, 120, 122; and Besant complex, 106–7; and Old Women's phase, 170
Kelsey, Henry, 158, 174
Kinney, J., 165
Kivett, M. F., 117
Knife River flint, 17, 28, 107
knives, 8, 30, 32, 34, 87
Kooyman, Brian, 72, 92, 171
Krause, Richard A., 155

L
La Roche site, 112
Lake Lenore upland, 15–16
Lake Midden site, 173
lanceolate points, 6, 20, 37, 39, 41
Landals, Alison J., 65, 169

Larence site, 20
Late Plano complexes, 34–39, 40–41
Laurel Culture, 104, 123, 124, 125, 136
Leacross, SK, 26
Lebret site, 121
Leigh Cave site, 85, 88
Leyden, Jeremy J., 32
Lindoe site, 26
Linius, Brian J., 131, 136, 137
Lints, Andrew, 128
Llano Tradition, 9–20
Lockport site, 138, 154
Long Creek site, 82
Lost Terrace site, 121
Lovstrom site, 159, 160
Lowton site, 159, 160–61
Lugenbeal, Edward, 125
Lusk complex, 35

M
MacNeish, R. S., 122, 124
maize, 121, 135, 137, 138, 171
Malainey, Mary E., 156, 166
mammoths, 9, 11, 41
Mandan, 155–56
Mandelbaum, D. G., 168
manos, 71, 87
Maple Leaf site, 70
marginally utilized or retouched lithics (MURLs), 87
mass-kill technology: of Avonlea complex, 120; of Blackduck, 132, 160; of Mortlach Aggregate, 169; of Old Women's phase, 170–71; of Pelican Lake complex, 94–95; and problem of surplus production, 117, 140, 160; social implications of, 110–11, 112–13, 139–40; of Vickers Focus, 165
Mazama ash, 57–58
McConnell, Frank, 8
McCorquodale, Bruce A., 118
McDougall, John, 168
McKean complex, 82, 85–91, 95
McKean Lanceolate points, 87
Melhagen site, 107, 108
Meltzer, D. J., 59

Meskanaw point, 17
Meyer, David: and Avonlea points, 119; and Avonlea pottery, 122–23, 124; and Cree, 174; and ethnic connections, 156; and Mortlach Aggregate, 167, 169; and Nipawin complex, 36; and Old Women's phase, 131; and St. Louis site, 38
Michlovic, M., 105
microblade cores, 21
Middle Missouri: described, 106; and horticulture, 137; influence of, 108, 153, 154, 159; and One Gun phase, 171
Middle Woodland cultures, 104–5
Middle Woodland River House complex, 123
Mill Iron site, 18
milling stones, 71, 87–88
Miniota site, 104, 121, 123
Mokelki, Lorie L., 158, 165, 166, 174
Mona Lisa site, 70–71
moose, 22, 89
Morgan, R. Grace, 121, 124, 127, 167, 169
Morkin site, 159, 170, 171
Morlan, R. E., 64, 66, 85, 91–92, 94, 95
Mortlach, SK, 17
Mortlach Aggregate: boundaries of, 157; described, 165–69, 173–74; ethnic connection, 156; and One Gun, 171, 175; and Vickers Focus, 158, 165, 166–67, 173
Mortlach phase, 95
Mortlach site, 88, 112
Muhlbach site, 108, 171
Mulloy, W. B., 58–59
Mummy Cave complex, 82, 84
MURLs (marginally utilized or retouched lithics), 87

N
Na-ha-stew-in site, 91
Nakota, 157, 158
Napao site, 31
Naywatame Poets, 156, 174
Near Norbert site, 84

INDEX

Neuman, Robert W., 112, 115, 117
Neumann, T. W., 125, 127
Nevland site, 28
Nicholson, B. A., 138
Nipawin complex, 36, 39
Nipawin delta, 19, 27
Nipawin Reservoir Heritage Study, 1981-85, 8
Niska site, 31
Norby site, 66, 71
Norris, David Stewart, 123, 124, 125, 127
Northeastern Plains Village Aggregate, 154–55, 157

O

Oak Lake Island site, 132
obsidian, 115, 116
Odegard site, 32
Oetelaar, G. A., 61–62, 170
Old Women's Buffalo Jump, 94, 95, 169
Old Women's phase: boundaries of, 153, 154, 157; described, 128–31, 169–71, 174; ethnic connection, 156, 158–59
Olinyk, Dave M., 131, 136, 137
One Gun (Blackfoot historian), 171–72
One Gun phase, 158, 159, 171–72, 174–75
ornaments, 93, 116
ovens, 69
Oxbow complex, 82–85, 87
Oxbow Dam site, 82

P

paleosols, 37–38
Parkhill site, 21
Pas Reserve site, 90
Peck, Trevor R.: on Agate Basin complex, 21; on Alberta complex, 27; and Avonlea sites, 120, 121, 123; and critical resources, 168–69; and obsidian, 116; and Old Women's phase, 129–30, 131, 169, 170; and One Gun phase, 175; and summary of perspectives, 106
Pelican Lake complex, 89, 91–95, 106

pemmican, 70–71, 88
pendants, 93, 116
Peterson, Lynelle A., 134, 135
Pettipas, Leo F., 17, 113, 115
Phenix collection, 8
phytoliths, 72, 111, 137, 161, 164, 166, 173
pit houses, 68
Plains Village Tradition, 103, 106, 137
Plains Woodland Tradition, 103–4, 109, 117, 118, 137–38, 139
Plano Tradition, 5–6, 20–39, 40
plants: in Hypsithermal diet, 70, 71–72; in McKean diet, 85, 88, 89; in Oxbow diet, 84; processing remains of, 72, 171; remains of in Hypsithermal sites, 64–65. *see also* horticulture
Pohorecky, Zenon, 8
political organization, 112–13. *see also* social structure
post moulds, 66, 68
pottery: Avonlea, 119, 121–24; Besant, 107, 108–9; Blackduck, 131–32; Brainerd Ware, 123, 124–27; Cluny Complex, 171; Duck Bay Ware, 136; Fort Yates Ware, 160; Knife River Ware, 161; Laural, 125; Middle Woodland, 104, 105; Mississippian vessels, 161; Mortlach Aggregate, 156, 165–66, 167, 173–74; Old Women's phase, 128, 129, 130–31, 158–59, 170; One Gun phase, 159, 174–75; origins of, 99; Plains Woodland, 117, 137; Rainy River Coalescent, 136; Sandy Lake Ware, 105, 132, 134–36, 157; Sonota, 115; spread of, 102–3, 138; Valley complex, 117; Vickers Focus, 158, 165; Wascana Ware, 166, 174
preforms, 13, 22, 37, 38
Preston site, 34
projectile points: Avonlea Horizon, 118–20, 123; Basally-Thinned, 13–14, 40; Besant, 106–7, 108; Blackduck, 132, 133; and changes in population, 66; Clovis, 10, 11;

Duncan, 85–87, 90; Eden, 31, 34; Elk Lake Culture, 127; Folsom, 16–17, 18; Goshen, 19n4; Hanna, 85–87, 90; from Hypsithermal, 61; lanceolate, 6, 20, 37, 39, 41; Late Plano, 39, 40; McKean, 87, 91; Meskanaw, 17; misidentifying, 62; Old Women's phase, 128–29, 170; One Gun, 171; Oxbow, 82, 83, 85; Pelican Lake, 91–92; Psinomani Culture, 134; Scottsbluff, 31, 32, 34; Sonota, 113–14; Vickers Focus, 164, 172
pronghorn antelope, 121
Psinomani Culture, 105, 134–36, 157

Q
Quigg, J. Michael, 123

R
Rainbow site, 118
Rainy River Coalescent, 136–37
Ramsay, Allyson M., 115–16
Randall site, 159, 160
Rask site, 14, 15
Ratner #2 site, 32
red ochre, 85, 94
Redtail site, 89
Reeves, B. O. K.: and Avonlea, 119, 121; and Besant complex, 108–9; on human habitation in Northern Plains, 58, 59, 70; and Old Women's phase, 169–70; and Pelican Lake complex, 91, 95, 106; on Sonota-Besant controversy, 115, 116; on trade, 116; and Valley complex, 117
refugia, 62–63, 65, 67–68
refuse, 67, 69–70, 117–18, 163
religion, 110, 111, 116, 118
reservoir effect, 126
Riou site, 27
Robertson, Elizabeth, 61, 84–85
Rodeo site, 32
Roll, Tom E., 121
Ross Glen Besant site, 112
Rousell, SK, 120
Ruby site, 110, 170
Running, G. L., 62
Russell, Dale, 156, 174

S
Saddle Butte phase, 170
sampling biases, 59
Sandy Lake Ware, 105, 132, 134–36, 157
Sarah site, 94, 169
Saskatchewan Basin pottery, 159, 167
Scandic period, 101–2, 109–10
SCAPE Project, 2
Scattered Village complex, 154, 156
Schneider, Fred, 105, 165
Scoggin site, 88
Scottsbluff points, 31, 32, 34
Selkirk people, 166, 167
Shea site, 105, 135, 137
Sheehan, M. S., 59, 62–63
Shorter site, 17
Shuddematt site, 166
Sibbald Creek site, 12
side-scrapers, 87, 92
Sinnock site, 35
Sioux, 135
Site DjNf-8, 31
Site DjOn-8, 68
Site FfNf-1, 32
Site FgNe-3, 32
Site FhNe-54, 28
Smith, Thomas, 11
Smith site, 8, 15
Smytaniuk #1 site, 32
Smytaniuk #2 site, 13, 32
social structure, 111, 117, 139, 161–63, 164–65
Sonota complex, 107, 111, 112, 113–17
split-pebbles, bipolar, 84
spruce parkland, 18, 22, 26, 41, 42
St. Louis site, 36–39, 63, 64
Stafford, Thomas W., 10
Stampede site: artifacts at, 67, 68, 70, 71; location, 64; points from, 62; profile of, 60, 68
Stanford, Dennis, 20, 30
Stankowski site, 24

INDEX

Stelzer site, 112
stone boiling, 69, 70, 71
stone circles, 66, 68, 170
storage pits, 69, 72, 103, 117, 137, 138
Stott site, 132
Syms, E. L., 115, 116, 117, 126–27, 173

T

Tailrace Bay site, 90
Tanner, John, 163
Taylor-Hollings, Jill, 134, 135, 157
Thundercloud site, 89
tipi rings, 58, 112
tobacco, 167, 173
trade networks, 84, 93, 108, 109, 116, 171
Trawin site, 28
Tschetter site, 133
Tunaxa Tradition, 121
Tuscany site, 35
Twin Fawns site, 166
Twin Pines site, 12
Type site, 170

U

unifaces, 31, 87, 92, 93
United Church site, 127

V

Valley complex, 117–18
Vera site, 85, 87, 88, 91, 94, 162, 164–65
Vérendrye, Sieur de la, 156–57
Vermillion Lakes site, 12, 21
Vickers, Chris, 122
Vickers, J. Roderick: and Avonlea pottery, 124; and Besant complex, 106, 108, 110; and critical resources, 168–69; and obsidian, 116; and Old Women's Buffalo Jump, 169; and Old Women's phase, 170
Vickers Focus: dates for, 166; described, 159–65, 172–73; and Mortlach Aggregate, 158, 165, 166–67, 173; movement of, 158; and Scattered Village complex, 154, 156; settlement of, 88
Vigrass, Victor, 8

Vigrass #1 site, 15
Vigrass #2 site, 28, 34
volcanic explosion, 161

W

Wahkpa Chu'gn site, 170
Walde, Dale Allen: and Avonlea, 119, 121, 122–23, 124; on Avonlea-Elk Lake mix, 128; on Besant-Avonlea mix, 107–8; and Besant pottery, 108; and bison pounds, 110–11, 112, 120; and Blackduck, 105, 131; and Cluny site, 172; and influence of mass kill technology, 140; and Laurel, 104; and Mortlach Aggregate, 166, 171; on Sonota-Besant controversy, 116
Walker, E. G., 62
Walter Felt site, 94
Wascana Ware, 166, 174
water sources, 62–63, 64
Waters, Michael R., 10
Watt, Sandra F., 91
Webster, S. M., 85, 87, 88, 89, 90
Wedel, W. R., 59
wells, 69
Wettlaufer, B. N., 112
White Earth Creek site, 172
Wilson, Michael C., 9, 65, 112
Wilson site, 8, 15
Windrow site, 36
winter settlement, 168–69
Wood, W. Raymond, 102, 155
Wright, H. E., 84

Y

Yansa, Catherine H., 12, 18, 30
Younger Dryas episode, 11, 16

Z

Zarrillo, Sonia, 72, 171
Zurburg, S. C., 66

Contributors

ALWYNNE BEAUDOIN is Head Curator, Earth Sciences, and Curator, Quaternary Environments, Royal Alberta Museum, Edmonton. She holds a BSc (Leeds University) and MSc and PhD degrees in physical geography from the University of Western Ontario. Using plant remains, she investigates postglacial landscapes, especially in relation to Alberta's human history.

LESLIE (BUTCH) AMUNDSON grew up on a farm near Naicam Saskatchewan. He studied archaeology and geology at the University of Saskatchewan (BA Hons. 1983, MA 1986). From 1986 to 1992, he was owner/operator of Millennium Consulting Ltd. Since 1992 he has been Senior Archaeologist with Stantec Consulting Ltd. in Saskatoon.

SCOTT HAMILTON, originally from Manitoba, Hamilton, earned degrees from Brandon University, University of Alberta and Simon Fraser University. He specializes in fur trade archaeology and ethnohistory, and the pre-contact archaeology of the northern Plains and Subarctic. He is a professor of Anthropology at Lakehead University.

DAVID MEYER is a professor at the University of Saskatchewan, with a concentration on the archaeology of the Canadian plains and the adjacent boreal forest. In particular, he has studied the pottery of this region. Meyer has a long term interest is hunter/gatherer ethnology, especially relating to boreal forest peoples.

BEV NICHOLSON earned a BA from Brandon University and MA and PhD degrees from Simon Fraser University. He specializes in pre-contact Plains and Parkland archaeology, ceramics, zoo-archaeology and archaeological method and theory. He is a professor of archaeology at Brandon University. He has an interest in late pre-contact horticultural practice in the region.

DAVE NORRIS earned degrees at Lakehead University and the University of Saskatchewan. His interests include pre-contact pottery from the Canadian Plains, spatial and site analysis and faunal studies. Currently he is employed at Western Heritage as a project archaeologist.

CONTRIBUTORS

GERRY OETELAAR is a Professor in the Department of Archaeology at the University of Calgary whose research interests center on the perception, organization and use of space at the level of the household, community and region, and the evolution of the natural and cultural landscapes on the northern Plains.

JILL TAYLOR-HOLLINGS is currently an archaeology PhD candidate at the University of Alberta, with previous degrees from Brandon University and University of Saskatchewan. Also, she is a part-time consultant and sessional instructor at Lakehead University. She specializes in northern plains and boreal forest archaeology, pottery studies, and working with First Nations.

SEAN WEBSTER is a senior archaeologist and manager for Golder Associates Ltd. in Calgary, Alberta. He has 13 years of experience working as an archaeological consultant and has participated in studies ranging from Canada's Arctic islands to the rain forests of Panama. He obtained his PhD from the University of Saskatchewan.